What others are saying . . .

“Your message is clear and direct – refreshing in an era of pop psychology.”

Honorable Michael D. Bradbury, DA, Ventura County, California
USA

"Invaluable to anyone seeking to gain control of his or her life — to live from conscious choice rather than unconscious programming. The case studies are both intriguing and relevant. The ideas and methods in this insightful book have dramatically increased my self-awareness and empathy with other people."

Mary Elizabeth Ogle, Homemaker
Canada

"Various therapies trace adult trauma to events which occurred in childhood or earlier. In the case histories included here, Christina sheds light on life patterns which result from such trauma. I am thrilled to know that this fascinating and practical book will help to acquaint many more people with these important concepts."

Jon-Richard Turner, Co-Director of the Institute for Whole-Self Discovery & Development and Past President of the International Society for Prenatal and Perinatal Psychology & Medicine (ISPPPM)
Holland and USA

"Besides offering a profound understanding of the causes of personality and life patterning, this book offers keys to unlock and transform them. I recommend it to everyone interested in understanding the dynamics operating in their own lives."

John-Raphael Staude, Ph.D.
Germany and USA

“Because of this work, I’ve got my life back!”

Pennie Quaile, RN and Homeopath
England

Also by Christina Thomas-Fraser (Christina Thomas)

Secrets: A Practical Guide to Undreamed-of Possibilities

In Tune With The Soul

To Deed
Love Christina

Change Your Patterns, Change Your Life

A Practical Guide

by

Christina Thomas-Fraser

Chela Publications

For information on Lectures and Trainings
by Christina Thomas-Fraser, please contact the publisher.

Change Your Patterns, Change Your Life
A Practical Guide

Published by:

Chela Publications
991-C Lomas Santa Fe Drive, Suite 470
Solana Beach, CA 92075
Tel: (760) 632-2670 • Fax: (760) 632-2551

First Printing
Printed in the United States of America

Library of Congress Cataloging in Publication Data
Publisher's Cataloging-in-Publication
(Provided by Quality Books, Inc.)
Thomas-Fraser, Christina
Change Your Patterns, Change Your Life: A Practical Guide – 1st ed.
P.cm.
Includes bibliographical references and index

1. Behavior modification
2. Behavior modification – Case studies
3. Change (Psychology) I. Title.
BF637.B4T46 1997 158
QBI97-40622

ISBN#0-9622119-8-2
$13.95 Softcover

1 2 3 4 5 6 7 8 9 0

To Cam

Acknowledgments

I am grateful for the help, support and encouragement of many people during the writing of this book, especially:

The late David B. Cheek, MD, for kind and generous support of me and this book and for the material which he so gladly contributed. Thank you, Dr. Cheek, for blazing a trail.

William R. Emerson, Ph.D., Jon-Richard and Troya Turner, John-Raphael Staude, Ph.D., and Barbara Findeisen for the case studies you have contributed.

Brian and Barbara Tracy, for your generous support in countless ways.

Swami Suddhananda: Dear friend and brilliant editor, thank you for your work on this book. You are a shining light in my life.

Nan Jobson, for your consistent, loving support, professional expertise, and honest feedback

Pat Kaufman, for your friendship, editing, and honest feedback.

Pennie Quaile, for your loyal friendship, indomitable humor, and indefatigable effort and support of me and this work.

Julie, who enables me to know many things I might not otherwise understand.

Cam, for your enthusiasm, love and support of me and this book and in so many other meaningful ways.

To my clients and workshop participants: Thank you for trusting me and for the courage to undertake the inner work necessary to change your own patterns. Being of service to you is one of life's greatest gifts to me.

Most of all, I am grateful to the Divine Presence which inspires and guides this work.

Change Your Patterns, Change Your Life

A Practical Guide

Contents

A Letter To My Readers		12
Section I	**Is There a Pattern in Your Life?**	15
Chapter 1	Why Is This Happening To Me Again?	16
Chapter 2	Where Do Patterns Come From?	26
Section II	**Many People – Many Patterns**	36
Chapter 3	Sofia: Promiscuity	37
Chapter 4	Rachel: Emotional Triangles	40
Chapter 5	Dan: Abandonment and Running Away	43
Chapter 6	Elizabeth: Ambush and Victimization	48
Chapter 7	Dean: Rejection, Shame, and Unworthiness	58
Chapter 8	Philip: Addiction and Disconnection	69
Chapter 9	Melanie: Self-esteem Issues	76
Chapter 10	Anna: Caretaking	82
Chapter 11	Debbie: Confidence, High Self-Esteem	85
Chapter 12	Donald: Paranoia	90
Chapter 13	Troya: Eating Disorders, Suicide Issues	92
Chapter 14	Rolf: Running Away	97
Chapter 15	Karl: Panic Attacks	100
Chapter 16	Judith: Loneliness	103
Chapter 17	Jan: Addiction, Scandal, and Shame	110
Chapter 18	Joe: Fear of Intimacy, Time Cycle Pattern	113
Chapter 19	Mary: Fear and Panic	116
Chapter 20	Deborah Abandonment, Time Cycle Pattern	122
Section III	**Change Your Patterns**	126
Chapter 21	Do Your Patterns Contain a Hidden Message?	127
Chapter 22	How To Recognize Your Patterns: The Seven Steps	130

Chapter 23	How to Change Your Patterns	142
Chapter 24	Reinforce the Changes in Your Life	152
Chapter 25	Putting It All To Work	160
Chapter 26	The Unexpected Gift	162
Section IV	**The List of Patterns**	164
	How to Use The List of Patterns	165

The List 168

Abandonment	169
Abundance	170
Abuse	171
Accidents / Physical Ailments	172
Addiction / Addictive Behavior	173
Alcohol Abuse / Drug Abuse	174
Ambition (lack of)	175
Ambush	176
Anger	177
Anxiety	178
Ashamed	179
Authority Issues	180
Belonging (lack of)	181
Betrayal	182
Blocked (feeling)	183
Boundary Issues	184
Caretaking	185
Cold Personality	186
Commitment (fear of)	187
Compulsive Behavior	188
Confidence. High self-esteem	189
Control (strong / obsessive need for)	190
Controlled	191
Dependence	192
Depression	193
Disconnected, Disoriented	194
Dishonesty	195
Dominated	196
Drama	197
Duplicity	198
Eating Disorders	199
Emergency	200
Emotional Triangles	201

Empathy (lack of) 202
Failure 203
Fear 204
"Flat" Personality 205
Giving Up, Quitting 206
Grief 207
Guilt 208
Helplessness 209
Hopelessness 210
Humiliation 211
Illness 212
Incompletion 213
Indecision 214
Infidelity 215
Injury, Injuries 216
Insecurity 217
Integrity Issues 218
Intensity 219
Intimacy (fear of) 220
Isolated (feeling) 221
Late (habitually) 222
Loneliness 223
Manipulated 224
Manipulative 225
Meaninglessness 226
Misfit 227
Misunderstood 228
Money Issues 229
Obsessive Behavior 230
Overwhelmed 231
Panic, Panic Attacks 232
Paranoia 233
Perfectionism 234
Phobias 235
Physical Injuries 236
Possessiveness (of others) 237
Pressure 238
Procrastination 239
Promiscuity 240
Punctuality (compulsive) 241

Purposelessness	242
Rebellion	243
Rejection	244
Rescue Issues	245
Running Away	246
Scandal	247
Self-Centeredness, Selfishness	248
Self-Consciousness	249
Self-Esteem Issues	250
Self-Hatred	251
Self-Pity	252
Self-Sabotage	253
Sexual Abuse	254
Shame	255
Shyness	256
Smoking	257
Stress / Distress	258
Strong Need to "Do It Myself"	259
Struggle	260
Stuck (a feeling of being)	261
Substance Abuse (see Alcohol / Drug Abuse")	
Suicidal Thoughts / Tendencies	262
Superiority (an air of)	263
Time Cycle Patterns	264
Timidity	265
Trapped (feeling)	266
Triangles	267
Trust Issues	268
Unclean (feeling)	269
Unemployment (chronic)	270
Unfinished Business	271
Unloved	272
Unworthiness	273
Urgency (compulsive)	275
Victim	276
Violence	277
Withdrawal / Withdrawn	278
Worry	279

Bibliography 280
Recommended Reading 280
Index 281
Self-Discovery Quiz 284

A Letter to My Readers

Some years ago, I began to recognize patterns in my life – patterns which hampered loving expressions of trust in intimate relationships and generally limited my life and aliveness. I frequently felt frustrated and distressed. To compound my dismay, I sadly observed that I had never personally known anyone who was able to make momentous, lasting changes and subsequently live a new and different kind of life – as I so very much longed to do. Perhaps it was not possible to achieve freedom from these unwelcome patterns, I thought. Perhaps the most I could do was try to make the best of the distressing situations in my life. Although I thought this might be the case, somehow I could not stop searching for ways to heal and resolve recurring patterns with the hope that my life would change.

I am happy to report that I did find ways to recognize and change the undesirable patterns in my life, with corresponding improvements in the troubled areas. Additionally, I discovered that I have an innate ability to recognize patterns in the lives of *other* people, also.

Much of my work involves helping individuals recognize their patterns and undertake the healing work which will result in their own liberating changes. I have come to think of this as the greatest service I can offer, and feel immensely grateful when I hear that, as a result of the work we have done together, a person's life has changed in a beneficial and lasting way.

Over the past fifteen years, I have focused more and more on this element of the human condition; this book was born from that work.

I have presented a number of my own case studies here. Other examples and research results are generously provided by the late David B. Cheek, MD, Jon-Richard and Troya Turner, Co-Directors of the Institute for Whole-Self Discovery, William R. Emerson, Ph.D., Barbara Findeisen, Licensed Marriage, Family, and Child Counselor (MFCC), John-Raphael Staude, Ph.D., and other dedicated professionals whose clients and patients have reported similar phenomena.

In February 1996, when I first spoke with Dr. Cheek during the writing of this book, he asked, "How did you happen to become interested in this work, Christina?"

"I spontaneously re-experienced my own conception," I replied. "While I cannot prove this, of course, I *knew* that it was true *and that experience changed my life,* releasing previously-held anger and resentment toward my father. After that experience, although there was no discussion about this with my dad, our relationship – strained for many years – became much more relaxed and loving."

"You don't have to prove it to me," Dr. Cheek responded. "I've heard similar reports from my patients enough times to convince me that humans are fully conscious even before their conceptions."

Like Doctors Cheek, Emerson, and others, I have discovered in my work with many people that, indeed, there are ways – safe, practical, effective ways – to uncover and change the patterns in our lives, as you will discover when you read the case histories reported here.

This book examines challenging patterns in the lives of many different people. Those who undertake their own personal work and experience the concomitant liberation frequently exclaim, "I did not know that it was possible to become so free. Everyone would benefit from this work!"

How true! If we only knew that we do not have to live with the burdens we carry, we would be eager to find the freedom and happiness awaiting us once old patterns are healed and life's natural color is restored.

When healing occurs, individuals often say, "I feel as though I have been sleepwalking all these years, like I now have eyes that can see for the first time in my life!"

Yes, we need new eyes. My hope is that this book will bring a greater awareness of this groundbreaking work, discovering that it is possible to be healed of the limiting patterns in our lives.

Christina Thomas-Fraser
Encinitas, California
September 1997

Section I

Is There a Pattern in Your Life?

Chapter 1

Why Is This Happening To Me Again?

Are your relationships affected by the patterns in your life? Have you noticed that a situation experienced earlier in life is later repeated in a similar way with yet another person? For example, did your first sweetheart fall madly in love with you, then suddenly cool, leaving you feeling wounded and alone? Have you experienced a similar pattern with another loved one in a subsequent relationship?

While relationships are a common place for life patterns, these recurrences – whether welcome or unwelcome – show up in many other areas as well.

For example, have you ever had an experience where everything you attempted worked out just beautifully? Maybe it was a time when you successfully completed an exam, played a great game of tennis, or experienced your heartfelt communications happily received by a loved one. Can you also remember a time when you felt somewhat like a failure? Maybe it was a time when you failed to complete a work project, bogeyed almost every hole in a round of golf, or felt rejected by your mate. In this book, you will discover specific ways for uncovering the source of the unwelcome patterns in your life, and learn practical, step-by-step ways to change them.

We can better understand these patterns by understanding the way a player piano works. Like a regular piano, a player piano has 88 keys but, when a music roll is in place, it can play only those notes which correspond to holes punched in the roll. That music roll is the pattern for the tune we hear. Although the player piano, itself, has the capacity to play *any* song, its repertoire is restricted as long as the music roll is in place. In much the same way, although we human beings have the innate capacity to make beautiful music – to live lives of almost limitless accomplishment and expression – all too often we are limited by our patterns.

While some patterns produce exhilarating, uplifting melodies, many others confine us to a monotonous range which results in our living only a muted echo of the brilliant, transcendent resonance of which we are capable. These patterns show up in all areas of life, constricting our relationships, dulling our spontaneity, impairing our productivity, limiting our finances, and squelching our creativity. Because most of us have experienced our patterns since birth or early childhood, however, we often fail to realize that our lives could be different.

Observing recurring patterns in the lives of others can sometimes help us become aware of our own patterns. As examples, let us briefly examine the stories of three different people.

She Longs for a Happy Marriage

Sarah was devastated when David left her for another woman. She felt happier when she met Larry, but he abandoned her also, and soon married someone else. This painful theme has reoccurred so often that Sarah has never experienced a lasting, happy relationship. She is beginning to despair of finding the relationship she desires.

The Same Leg Injured Repeatedly

Nine-year-old Mark was hit by a car while riding his bike and lay in a hospital, his shattered left leg in traction. Ten years later, he was carried from a battlefield in Vietnam, his left leg mangled by a land mine. Now 45, Mark is recovering from a ski accident, the same leg fractured again.

Like Riding on a Roller Coaster

Jim's life has been marked by dramatic highs and lows. He was a bright, active 10-year-old when he was run over by a team of horses and hospitalized for almost a year. At 17, when he was in prep school, president of his class, and getting top grades, he developed hepatitis and had to drop out for a year. When he was 30 years old, Jim headed up a prominent money-management company, then was suddenly dismissed when the company was sold. When he was 46 and a self-made multi-millionaire, a bank suddenly called on an old note Jim had guaranteed and he was forced to file for bankruptcy.

In the life of each of these individuals, it is obvious that a pattern exists which seems to repeat again and again. Each of them might ask, "Why is this happening to me again?"

Have you noticed a recurring pattern in your life? Perhaps it manifests in your relationships, your health, your finances, or in another area. Have you ever wondered what causes these difficult patterns? What can explain them? What can be done about them? Is there a way to identify a pattern in your life and then change it so that you enjoy a happier experience next time? These are the questions we will address in this book as we investigate repetitive and puzzling patterns in the lives of numerous people. The case studies included here provide surprising, sometimes astonishing and, most importantly, encouraging answers to these questions.

To benefit from these groundbreaking discoveries, we are sometimes required to put aside certain beliefs and look with new eyes at evidence which points to previously unsuspected origins of the patterns in our lives.

"A few hundred years ago," Marcel Proust stated, "before the invention of the microscope, almost no one believed in bacteria and viruses, so humanity remained powerless before these unseen invaders. Those who did believe in their existence were labeled 'crackpots.' But invisible is not the same as 'imaginary'," he reminds us. "The real voyage of discovery consists not in seeking new landscapes but in having new eyes."

These wise words apply as much to our patterns and their underlying causes as to physical diseases and the underlying presence of bacteria and viruses.

For a long time we have accepted the widespread belief, for instance, that a child's mind and awareness could be compared to a slate which is blank until parents and culture begin to write their potent messages on it. The information in this book provides startling evidence that this is not true, that we human beings are very conscious, not only as early as the first trimester of gestation, but startlingly, even prior to conception. Furthermore, there is clear evidence that early traumatic experiences, whether they occur in childhood or before birth, create powerful imprints which can result in negative patterns later in life. Emotion-filled events which we experience at an early age usually leave their mark on us, setting up psychological and emotional patterns which weave into our adult personalities, corroborating the old axiom that "as the twig is bent, so the tree will grow."

Occasionally we hear of glowing exceptions to this vicious cycle – the mistreated child who, *because* of his early misfortune, grows up and dedicates his life to championing the cause of abused children, for example – but the unconscious *repetition* of painful patterns is far more common.

As a general rule, we tend to treat ourselves and others the way we were treated as children. If, in early childhood, we felt loved and valued, experiencing acceptance and safety in an optimistic, healthy, loving family, we normally grow to see the world that way and stride confidently into life. If, on the other hand, we were born to parents who did not truly love or value us and to whom life was an overly stressful experience, there is a good chance that their fearful, inhibiting attitudes were inculcated into our character long before we could become consciously aware of them. Usually, therefore, if we are valued in infancy, we develop an intrinsic sense of worth that is echoed back to us in positive experiences. If we are not valued in infancy, we tend not to value ourselves, often lashing out angrily when we perceive that someone else sees the humiliating deficit of which we are so painfully aware. Early thoughts, beliefs, and conclusions, whether pleasant or painful, become woven into the very fabric of our personality, predisposing us to pleasant or painful interpretations of the world around us. They function like filters through which we view the world. That view is thus colored or discolored accordingly. We see the world not as it is but as we are.

The Causes For the Worldwide Epidemic of Abuse Patterns

All over our world, the news is filled with accounts of the abuse of one human by another. In addition to the violence and abuse between strangers, competing gangs, or other groups in our society, these violent patterns appear in the places which, above all, should be safe: the home, the school, and the church. Cases of violence among family members are abundant in the news: men and women abusing each other, parents abusing their children, and adult children abusing their parents. Add to this horror the abuse perpetrated upon children by teachers, day-care workers, the clergy, and other authority figures.

These traumatic experiences do not heal themselves, nor are they healed by forgetting an abusive event or by the passage of time. Such patterns warn of a deep pathology which must be dealt with in practical, effective, and healing ways, individually and collectively, if we are to survive and flourish. Like chopping down an ugly weed while neglecting it's virulent root system, these patterns of abuse, left unhealed, will bloom again, leading to still more abuse.

It is now well known, for instance, that 90% of abusive parents were abused themselves as children. The Child & Family Center of the Menninger Society in Topeka, Kansas, is a sophisticated laboratory for research and application of knowledge, offering clarity in our efforts to understand delinquency, drug abuse, violence, incest, and child abuse.

"Without intervention," the Menninger Society states in a 1996 publication, "abused children will become tomorrow's problem. We have found at Menninger that many adults with eating disorders, addictions, and serious psychological problems were abused as children. Furthermore, it has been documented that four out of five convicts were abused as children."

Clearly, experiences in childhood lay much of the foundation for adult life, setting into motion patterns which recur again and again. This premise has become somewhat generally accepted during the latter part of the 20th Century. The late David B. Cheek, MD, of Santa Barbara, California, a Diplomate of the American Board of Obstetrics and Gynecology, underscored this connection between early, stressful experiences and patterns which recur in adult life. In an article originally published by Human Sciences Press, Dr. Cheek stated that "in humans, an experience associated with injury or great emotional stress can occur at any time in life. It and the emotional and physiological responses to the original stimulus will last without fading and can harmfully influence the individual throughout a lifetime." [1]

---

[1] 1986, Human Sciences Press, p.97

If the connection between childhood experiences and later adult behavior is still questioned by some, the hypothesis that pre-birth experiences can influence a person's life understandably leaves many feeling skeptical. But can we afford to ignore the growing body of credible evidence that such primordial experiences do significantly affect life?[1]

Dr. Cheek began recording, as far back as the 1960s, his remarkable observations of the early and vitally conscious life of the unborn. Continuing in the above-referenced article, he further states:

> My purpose in presenting this report is to suggest strongly that infants are keenly perceptive long before birth. They are very sensitive to the thoughts and feelings of people around them, as well as those of the mother.
>
> Imprinted impressions, right or misinterpreted, may affect a lifetime of behavior. We must, therefore, rid ourselves of the belief that the central nervous system of infants is incapable of sensing and remembering during prenatal and perinatal[2] existence.
>
> We may be in a position to learn about guilt feelings, harmful identifications and feelings of rejection that have been unrecognized in the past because we have not known how to reveal them and to expose them to reassessment in the light of mature understanding.[3]

---

[1]See the accounts of this phenomenon reported by David B. Cheek, MD, William R. Emerson, Ph.D., John-Raphael Staude, Ph.D., and others which are included in this book. In addition, the reader is referred to "The Psychic Life of the Unborn Child" by Thomas Verny, MD.

[2]Perinatal means "around birth."

[3]Ibid, p. 109

Dr. Cheek clearly points out the fact that an event occurring *before* birth may be more potent in its later effect than an event occurring in childhood. Although neither an infant nor a fetus has the conscious ability to understand language, it absorbs with great precision the entire experience, complete with feelings and subtle distinctions which he or she will be able to understand and express in words, once verbal ability is acquired.

Another pioneer in the field of very early trauma and its effect on a person's later life is William R. Emerson, Ph.D., a Petaluma, California, psychologist. Dr. Emerson's work, begun in the 1970s, deals primarily with those traumas occurring in connection with abortion, prematurity, birth, adoption, and abuse. In an article published in Indepth News, Dr. Emerson stated the following:

> Physical, sexual, psychological, and substance abuse are on the rise, and commonly surface during treatment. Unwanted and unplanned pregnancies, thoughts of abortion and abortion planning, medical interventions during pregnancy, and family crises are all sources of trauma that frequently show up in the treatment room. But of all traumas, birth trauma is probably the most important. In eastern psychiatry, birth is seen as a vital experience because it is said to crystallize one's karma or destiny. In western prenatal and perinatal psychology, birth trauma is frequently found to be a major factor in a variety of symptomatic patterns, and at a lesser level is often related to dysfunctional feelings and behavior.
>
> The specific influences that birth has can be understood in terms of birth complications, or in terms of the type of birth such as vaginal, cesarean, forceps-assisted, etc. For example, babies born by cesarean section are more likely to have rescue fantasies, to stop tasks in

the middle, to require help and to have boundary issues (i.e., an inability to keep strong influences out, to keep people out of their space, to say 'no' and mean it, etc.)

Anesthetized babies are more likely [in later life] to have self-esteem problems, to be 'out of touch' with their bodies, and to have difficulty with self-initiated direction.

Forceps (or suction) babies tend to see the world as an intrusive and painful place, expect to be controlled and/or manipulated, often feel stuck in life, get headaches when 'under pressure,' and have issues with authority.

Vaginal births with episiotomies often feel guilty for trying hard (because they unconsciously feel that they 'tore mommy with their pushing'). Vaginal births with long labor often feel like life is overwhelming, and need to push away to protect themselves from pressure, or from physical closeness (physical closeness activates memories of the closeness and confinement of birth).

Birth, in fact, provides a basic tincture for life. The verb 'tincture,' according to Webster's Dictionary, is to imbue something with a substance which is foreign to it, and a tincture is defined as an active principle of a substance. Birth provides a basic tincture or template for life. However, this tincture is foreign to our nature, to our substance as humans. As such, the tincture needs to be prevented from entering our systems, or extracted after its infusion.[1]

---

[1]Indepth News, January-February 1992 issue, pp 1 and 7, available from Indepth, The Institute for Developmental Education and Psychotherapy.

In short, early, emotionally-charged experiences, whether before, during, or after birth, unnaturally color a person's life. Until such time as this tinting can be drained away, and the emotional intensity defused, that person is predisposed to create the reoccurrence of unwanted patterns. To attempt to change an undesirable pattern without digging down to remove the real root cause is like taking medication to reduce a fever while ignoring an infection. Both invite further difficulty. Yet so often, when confronted with a recurring pattern, we simply want to remove the symptoms and disregard the underlying causes.

What is the answer? Is there a safe, effective way to clear away our buried pain and disharmony? What process can accomplish this? How long does it take? Once this is done, do life patterns really change?

This book answers these urgent questions. Indeed, if there were no way to heal the underlying disturbances, this subject of patterns might be interesting, but of little practical value. It is precisely because healing *can* be accomplished – and accomplished much more quickly and easily than most people might imagine – that this inquiry is so vitally important. Our lives *can* be cleared of inner turmoil; life's natural color *can* be restored. We *can* cease living reactively and become proactive. We *can* decide what we want to have and how we want to be. We *can* learn to change old patterns and create welcome new experiences in our lives.

In the next chapter, we shall examine how our patterns originated and learn how to understand the information hidden in them.

Chapter 2

Where Do Patterns Come From?

"A new idea is first condemned as ridiculous and then dismissed as trivial, until finally, it becomes what everybody knows."
William James

An eagle's egg fell into a barnyard, landing in a chicken coop. A mother hen dutifully sat on the egg and soon the baby eaglet hatched out. All around were chickens – so he thought he, too, was a chicken. A few months later a fox raided the chicken coop and the young eagle sat on the ground and was killed. He thought he was a chicken and had learned to behave like a chicken. Now, if that eaglet had spread his mighty wings, he could have soared over the highest mountain, let alone fly out of the chicken coop. So we see that it was not what he was but what he *thought* he was which led to his annihilation.

A similar condition occurs with humans. We already have the latent power to create our lives in any way we choose – to be creators of circumstances instead of creatures of circumstances. Yet, rather than soaring like eagles, most of us peck along on the ground, not realizing we have a different choice.

Within each of us resides an infinite well of power. When we become aware of the thoughts, feelings, and beliefs we absorbed in childhood, at birth, or even before birth, we take the first step toward glimpsing our true identity.

Sri Ramana Maharshi, a great spiritual master of South India, taught that one should constantly ask himself, "Who am I?" Indeed this is a worthy inquiry for, like the young eagle, we mistake ourselves for limited beings, when in fact we are essentially limitless. If this is true, however, how is it that we have lost touch with this innate power? For this answer, let us look first to the primordial epoch of life.

During the early stages of formation, we human beings function like super-sensitive psychic receptors, picking up every nuance of thought and feeling from those around us, especially our parents. By the time we are capable of objective observation, we are so loaded – so *programmed* – with this acquired psychic material, that we often are incapable of knowing what we really think and feel. As a result, we usually either conform to the mores of our family and culture, or we rebel against them. We often adopt beliefs without questioning whether or not we *really* believe. Most often, we conform in order to win acceptance and love, for our very survival often depends on them. In this process, we gradually lose touch with the most important resource of all: the connection with our own inner knowledge. Because we are out of touch with our core, we feel afraid, powerless, and alone in a world we do not understand.

During mating season, the musk ox emits a wondrous, haunting scent. Madly seeking the source of the intoxicating odor, it sometimes plunges headlong over the side of a mountain to its death, never realizing that the irresistible smell emanates from inside its own body. Is it possible that like the musk ox, the love and power and peace we seek also lie hidden deep within? If so, how do we peel away the layers which camouflage this magnificent true Self? If the natural birthright of a human being is joy, happiness, health, and limitless power, how is it that so many human beings are unfulfilled, unhappy, unhealthy, and relatively powerless? What specifically makes up our burdens and limitations? Is there a way to unload these without shirking the responsibilities of life?

We attempt to make sense of the deepest questions of human nature by thinking, yet how can the mind – which is the source of thinking – yield information about events which occurred before it existed? If we are to gain access to the superordinate level of self-knowledge which knows how to decipher the patterns in our lives, we must find a different way than simply thinking about it.

For decades we have measured intelligence by evaluating what is known by the conscious mind, and although the conscious mind is a priceless tool, it fails to take into account a much vaster intelligence possessed by all of us, regardless of IQ. We human beings know far more than we are consciously aware of knowing, far more than our conscious minds can comprehend, as the following examples illustrate. For this reason, the patterns in our lives usually fail to make sense to our conscious minds.

Is She Missing Her Biological Father?

Karina was adopted when she was 11 days old, and never knew her biological parents. Although an attractive and intelligent young woman in her late twenties, she had failed to connect with a male in a meaningful relationship. In a discussion about this aspect of her life, which seemed most disappointing to her, I asked if she thought the difficulty might involve her missing father.

"But my dad was always there," she objected, referring to her adoptive father.

"How about your biological father?" I inquired.

"Oh! I never knew him, or my biological mother, for that matter," she retorted. "How could *they* have any effect on me?"

This attitude is not unusual. How often we assume that we are affected only by those people and events of which we consciously have been aware. But as is shown in case after case, we are inextricably linked to our biological parents, not only in the cells of our physical body, but in our mentality and often in our emotional and psychological makeup as well, quite regardless of the fact that we may never have met them.

The Man Who Wasn't There

Another woman, Helena, was born in Eastern Europe at the beginning of the Second World War. Her father, a professional soldier, had been stationed on the Russian front during most of her gestation and her birth, and had seen his little daughter only a few times when at home on military leave. He was later killed, though the family did not learn of his death right away.

"I don't remember him at all," Helena said, "though I was aware of his existence. He was the man who wasn't there."

Her mother later re-married and her stepfather, a responsible, loving man, adopted her and raised her as though she were his own child, creating a quiet, stable home.

The family immigrated to the United States and Helena grew up, got married, and had three children. Very early in the marriage, however, her husband withdrew from both her and the children. He resisted all of their attempts to draw him into communication and relationship. Finally, she gave up hope and resigned herself to the situation, feeling very alone throughout the years when the children were growing up.

Helena was in her late forties when she participated in an Intensive workshop which I conducted. As we looked more deeply into her life patterns, she stated that she felt like she was shadowboxing with a ghost. Just as her biological father had always been physically absent, she found herself once again dealing with "a man who wasn't there." Although her husband was physically present, he was emotionally absent, and this absence left her feeling bereft and disconnected from him, just as she had felt as a small child.

Helena eagerly undertook her own inner work, willing to confront fears and anxieties of which she had never consciously been aware. During this time, many frightening memories surfaced. Though painful, this catharsis ultimately released her to live a freer, more authentic life. Although she tried to save the marriage, her husband remained adamant in his refusal to dialogue or interact, denying that a problem existed, and she finally left him. Today, several years later, the old pattern has been cleared and she is engaged in a happy, mutually-supportive relationship for the first time in her life.

Why Did She Feel Guilty For Looking Pretty?

In still another case, Paula, a nurse in her mid-thirties, found that she often felt guilty and afraid when she wore pretty clothes, although she loved being a woman and wearing feminine things. After she began doing inner work, she spontaneously recalled an event which she believes is the root of her feelings. As children, she and her brother, 18 months older, were inseparable and she idolized him, following him around and wanting to please him. One day while they were playing, he said to her, "I don't like girls."

"Right then and there," she says, "I think I decided, in order to please Mark, not to look like a girl." After this memory – and all its attendant emotions – surfaced, she was able to "re-negotiate" this decision within herself. Now she wears, without guilt, the pretty, feminine things she so enjoys.

She Had All the Right Stuff - *Almost*

Claire was a strikingly attractive and highly successful young woman. The walls of her elegant apartment were lined with citations of her achievements, both academic and professional. At first glance, one might think she had it all together.

Claire had enrolled in the Women's Air Corps when she graduated from high school at the age of 18. Whereas other young women found the regimen tedious and boring, Claire liked the order and structure of military life. At night she took college courses. Later, she re-enlisted for another tour of duty and completed a degree in aeronautical engineering. In addition, she qualified for her pilot's license.

After she completed her second tour in the service, Claire was hired by a commercial airline and earned her captain's wings in a remarkably short time. She was an excellent pilot – cool, calculating, and seemingly imperturbable under pressure. But although the other pilots respected her professionally, they avoided her socially.

Men who did venture past Claire's icy exterior were usually quite surprised to discover that sexually she was torrid, aggressive, and wildly uncontrolled – the direct opposite of her usual steely reserve. When a man exhibited a sustained interest in her, however, seeking to deepen their relationship, Claire would either pick a fight or leave on a trip. This reaction occurred regardless of whether the man was arrogant and conflictive, or warm, gentle, and understanding. What could explain her bizarre behavior? When we examine her childhood, we gain a better understanding of her deep fear of intimacy.

Claire's early family life had been very chaotic. Both parents were alcoholics, though they sometimes took turns going "on the wagon." More often, though, they got drunk together, while Claire, being afraid of them, hid out in her room. She needn't have worried, for they were hardly aware of her existence.

Claire left home as soon as she could by enlisting in the Air Force. For the first time in her life, she felt safe. In this new environment, she knew what to expect and what was expected of her. While busily pursuing her military career and simultaneously completing her engineering degree, Claire never recognized how deeply lonely she was. Instead, while focusing on her achievements and enjoying the financial rewards of her profession, she congratulated herself on her success.

With all her accomplishments, however, Claire was completely alone emotionally. There was not one person – no relative, friend or lover – with whom she experienced any trust or real closeness. While her adult life appeared, superficially, to be very different from her childhood, her utter loneliness was *exactly the same.* Tragically, Claire did not undertake the inner work which eventually could have helped her connect with her own inner reservoir, opening her up to an experience of intimacy with her own feelings, with other people, and with life. Instead, she rented a small plane one afternoon, went for a solo flight, and drove the aircraft into the ground. It was officially ruled an accident. People who were acquainted with Claire, however, suspected that she had committed suicide.

Regardless of how busy or accomplished we are, and regardless of how surrounded we are by people, until we are connected to our own inner core, we will feel alone, empty, and lacking in the meaning which makes life worth living. Like the musk ox, some of us plunge headlong over a cliff when all along we held our own missing key to the secret of life.

This inner core is the source of a wisdom which transcends ordinary intelligence, defying all explanations which would appeal to the logical mind. A remarkable illustration of the accuracy of unconscious knowing is that of George Wilson.

He Had Always *Felt* Different

George was tall and blond, while his father was short and had dark brown hair. But more important than looking different, George realized that he had always *felt* different. He was haunted by a recurring nightmare: Sitting at a dinner table surrounded by strangers, they would all glare at him and say, "You're the one!" He had no idea who they were nor of what they were accusing him. One thing was clear, however: he felt like he did not belong.

By the time he reached his mid-twenties, George was addicted to both alcohol and drugs. One day, feeling deeply troubled, he pressed his mother for answers to his disturbing questions about his background. In response, she finally admitted that his conception was the result of artificial insemination by an unknown sperm donor. Although this revelation initially quieted many life-long doubts and helped him in his struggle against substance abuse, George found that it also raised many additional, unsettling questions: "Who was the sperm donor? What was he like? What did he look like? What did he do for a living? Was he right-handed or left-handed? What was the health history of his family? Is it possible that I inherited my alcoholism from him?" This absorption became almost an obsession.

"I felt bewildered," George said, "like I was stuck in some kind of genetic Twilight Zone."

George's doubts and questions festered for several years. Unable to escape his nagging preoccupation with his origins, he tracked down his mother's old physician, who was dying of cancer. Following the doctor's death, George broke into his office and found the file of his donor father, who was a college student at the time of the sperm donation. George was eventually able to locate the man, who was by then a professor at a university. He drove to his house unannounced, and rang the doorbell. When a refined-looking tall, blond man opened the door, George's heart was pounding and he was nearly speechless.

Unable to utter the thoughts and feelings he had long dreamed of sharing, he finally managed to speak the name of his mother's deceased doctor. The two men exchanged a long, knowing look, then shook hands and George left. Although brief, this meeting with his biological father was enough to help George quit drinking.[1]

George's story reminds us that a deep part of us always knows more about our beginnings than does our conscious mind. When we gain access to this expanded knowing, we often become aware of the origins of our patterns and usually recognize how they have been playing out.[2]

Are you interested in uncovering the patterns which operate in your own life? Do you experience, as so many others do, that it often is easier to be aware of behavior in others than in yourself? In the following section, I have included case histories which deal in depth with many different patterns. As you read them, pay careful attention to those which feel familiar or which stimulate some recognition, even though it may be uncomfortable. You may find that you identify with certain stories, or begin to experience hunches about your own patterns or those of friends and loved ones. Remember that these recurring patterns do not happen at random, devoid of meaning. Rather, when we begin to observe them and break down their symbolism, we take the first step toward releasing and clearing them. This leads us to re-connect with our innermost sense of self and its peaceful, limitless power.

---

[1]In addition to finding his biological father, the illegal trespass into the doctor's office yielded an unexpected bonanza for George, for he was able to locate six of his donor siblings as well. One was the daughter of nearby neighbors, and another was a tall, blond girl he'd had a crush on in high school. One wonders what would have happened if, unaware of their kinship, George and his half-sister had married and produced a child. Because the genes of their offspring would be too closely inbred for sound mental and physical health, marriage between such close relatives is prohibited by law. Perhaps this example, alone, provides sufficient reason to question the secrecy which often still surrounds adoption and sperm or ovum donations.

[2]Information and instruction for accessing the unconscious is included in Section III.

ANIMAL CRACKERS®
By Rog Bollen
YOU'RE PULLING MY LEG!
NO...
I'M SERIOUS!
NO WAY!
ROG BOLLEN
REALLY! IT'S SOMETHING THAT I'VE ALWAYS BEEN ABLE TO DO!
... IT WAS VERY WARM AND PEACEFUL, SEE ...
... AND I FELT LIKE I WAS FLOATING, SEE... AND...
GO ON! NOBODY CAN REMEMBER BACK BEFORE HATCHING!
8-28

Section II

Many People – Many Patterns

Through the experiences of the individual people in the following stories, the recognition of patterns operating in their lives, and discovery of the origins of those patterns, we may come to understand a great deal more about ourselves and the way we function.

These individual case studies derive from my work and research, and that of several other professionals. Although our approach and techniques may differ, our ultimate aim is the same: To assist the individual to tap into that part of himself or herself which knows about the traumatic event(s) which set into motion a pattern which now recurs in his or her life. Further, it is the work of each of us in our own way to support that individual in experiencing underlying suppressed emotions – the lethal, unconscious storage which has burdened that person ever since the unfortunate event. Once these repressed emotions are fully experienced, he or she will feel more free. While the memory of the old event will remain, the intense emotional charge will have been drained away. As a result, that person's life will improve. Thereafter, rather than being an unwilling participant in events which had a life of their own, the newly liberated person, now more free of unconscious compulsion, can direct his or her own life through choice for the first time.

The case studies in Chapters 11 through 15 are from the work of other professionals, re-stated here with their permission. All the others are taken from my own work and research.

Chapter 3

Sofia: Promiscuity

Sofia has had numerous relationships, including three failed marriages. Currently single again, she relates that, as much as it is her heart's desire to be in a warm, close, loving, stable marriage, she now recognizes that her own behavior has made this an unrealizable goal so far. For in every one of her relationships, there has always eventually been another man.

"Regardless of how much in love I was in the beginning," Sofia says, "and how much I enjoyed my lifestyle (her husbands were upper-class Europeans), soon I would engage in a secret, clandestine affair. In addition, although I presented myself as the most feminine of women, I actually *competed* with my husbands and lovers, never content to just enjoy our similarities and diversities, but always intent on getting the best of them. I would sarcastically deride any failure on their part while taking offense at any perceived criticism of me." Sofia's driving ambition led her to lofty social status as the beautiful wife, first of an industrialist and, later, a diplomat, and also to professional achievement in a position with a large multi-national corporation.

Queried about her background, Sofia revealed that she was the third child born to her family in Warsaw a few years after the end of World War II. The eldest was a girl and the second was a boy. Having longed for a son, the boy's birth gave cause for mother and father to celebrate. He died at four years old, however, and the family never recovered from their grief. Most Poles had suffered the loss of loved ones during the long and ravaging German occupation, but with the death of their little son, the sense of loss in Sofia's family became much more personalized. Her parents were struggling to survive – like most others in the war-torn city – and both father and mother reacted to the extreme stress in their lives with anger and manipulative behavior, lashing out indiscriminately at times. Grieved, embittered, and frightened, they wanted another little boy to replace their lost child. It was into this painful chaos that Sofia was born.

She states that both father and mother were deeply disappointed that she was not a boy. Furthermore, as she grew, she was often the target of their rage: both of them called her despicable names – names like "whore" and "slut" – and her father regularly unleashed his fury onto her with a strap. At these times, her mother either looked on without intervening or listened from the next room. Pretty, young Sofia felt helpless, angry, and betrayed.

In addition, her father carried on sexual affairs with many women and there were whispered rumors that he had fathered another child with someone. Since their mother had to work outside the home, a series of nannies was hired to watch the children and Sofia heard that he got one of them pregnant, too.

Listening to this horrific story, I began to understand the complexity of Sofia's confused life and relationships. Competing with the men in her life was a way of "trying to be a (good) boy" – an attempt to gain the acceptance and approval of her parents. At the same time she has always desired, naturally, to experience and express her own femininity. Sofia said that she always feels at odds with herself because of this inner conflict.

"I never feel completely 'real'," she confides. "I am always afraid that I will be exposed and people will see what a phony I am."

The usual vent for her frustration was to seek out yet another man to become her next lover – blindly following the example her father had set throughout her childhood. Unconsciously attempting to be the boy her father so wanted, Sofia emulated the only model she had of masculinity, characterized by the discordant qualities of anger, duplicity, and promiscuity.

"What chance do I have," Sofia asked, "of becoming the sincere, strong woman of character I long to be? I know what power is, but I am just beginning to learn how quiet and peaceful true strength can be."

"True power is not force," I responded. "Like *real* strength, it comes from a quiet and peaceful place deep within." I felt compassion for the painful struggle that had characterized Sophia's checkered life. At the same time, I had much admiration for her strength, which brought her to the place where she was genuinely ready to become honest and sincerely begin her healing process.

Often the beginning of wisdom is clarity about one's present reality. Sofia is on the right track, for she is beginning to see her patterns more clearly now. At the end of a two-week Intensive workshop, she stated that she has now consciously chosen to make integrity the touchstone of her life, although she knows she has not yet *fully* grasped what integrity is. She also realizes that her patterns were not instilled overnight and they will not be changed overnight. She is willing to proceed carefully to make corrections in her own character and behavior before engaging in another relationship.

Chapter 4

Rachel: Emotional Triangles

Some people experience patterns which end relationships. Others find themselves unable to *form* any meaningful relationship, notwithstanding physical beauty, buoyant personality, high intelligence, love of life, and wide-ranging interests.

Rachel is a strikingly attractive woman in her late thirties. Well educated, she works for a public relations firm where she meets many eligible men. She has lots of friends, both male and female, but has never had a relationship with an available man which could be considered special, let alone one which could lead to marriage. Rachel says that over the years her closest male friends have been married and usually a good bit older than she. She insists that these friendships are not sexual ones and that in each case the man's wife has known of their friendship.

A number of times, Rachel says, she has been an invited house guest in the home of one of her male friends and his wife. Although Rachel professes to be on friendly terms with her friend's wife, she privately criticizes her, finding faults which would seem to indicate that Rachel feels the woman is "not good enough" for her husband. Instead, Rachel points out, the warmth and close bond *she* shares with him provides the supportive nurturing for which he truly longs.

Describing one relationship, Rachel becomes starry-eyed and soft-spoken.

"Steven and I are very close," she says, "so close I cannot describe it. We went for a walk recently and sat on the grass in the sunshine looking out over the mountains. Amidst all that natural beauty, the love and contentment we felt were transcendent."

As she neared forty years old, longing for a husband and children but still living alone, Rachel began to feel the deep loneliness in her life. With therapeutic support, she began to see the reality of her relationships, stripped of the illusions in which she had enveloped them.

"How can such a pretty, friendly, caring woman wind up so alone?" we might ask. As is so often the case, her early childhood provides the answer.

By the time she was three years old, Rachel had become her daddy's little girl. When he came home from work at the end of the day, she would fly into his arms. He would spend hours reading to her, holding her, carrying her around, and listening to her child-talk. Rachel speaks of this as the most perfect childhood she could imagine. When asked about her mother, Rachel described her as a person who was cold to everyone, including both husband and children – a woman who (in Rachel's view) was not good enough to be her father's mate. In Rachel, however, her father found a warm, spontaneous, carefree, and happy companion. Rachel had fallen in love with her daddy, as many three-old-girls do, and thought she was better at filling his need for aliveness and warmth than his wife.

As natural as it is for a small girl to be in love with her father, it is unhealthy not to mature beyond this phase as she grows up, so that she can relate to her peers. Rachel's pattern, however, was too deeply ingrained to move naturally into a healthy adult relationship, and she had recreated her childhood pattern of emotional triangles over and over again. During the "glowing moments" with her married friend, she would feel unimaginably happy because the relationship recreated for her the joy of the little three-year-old with Daddy.

Over the course of our 2-week Intensive, Rachel became aware that this pattern of emotional triangles would lead her to a life without a husband of her own and the children she so dearly wanted. As she allowed herself to experience her feelings about this whole dynamic, her perspective began to change. She is now becoming much less interested in spending her time with a man who is unavailable and hopes eventually to marry and have her own family.

Chapter 5

Dan: Abandonment and Running Away

A few years ago, I unexpectedly stumbled onto a pattern in the lives of my two dear friends, Dan and Janet Sorenson. A tense drama suddenly began one Sunday afternoon when my phone rang. I answered it on the third ring. Janet's voice was slow and measured, "Christina, we can't find Dan. Please pray."

"What do you mean, you can't *find* him? Isn't he in Belgium?" I asked.

"He's *supposed* to be in Belgium but he doesn't answer the phone at the apartment and he hasn't shown up at his office for three days. No one has heard from him since last Wednesday."

My stomach tightened a little and my mind began to race. "Of course, I'll pray, but what else...? Have you called the police?"

"Yes, but they don't want to get involved, especially since no one *there* has made a request. I called the manager of the apartment complex but he says they have a rule against going into a person's apartment unless there's a very good reason. He rang the doorbell repeatedly and also knocked on the apartment door, but there is no answer. He's convinced no one is there."

Reluctantly, I asked the next question. "Janet, please forgive me for asking this, but is it possible that Dan has a girlfriend?" They had been married for almost 30 years. I could imagine other men who might be involved in an extramarital affair, but somehow I would have been shocked to learn that Dan might be seeing another woman. I was even shocked when I heard myself ask Janet this question.

She seemed neither offended nor surprised, though, and replied without hesitation, "I wonder about that myself, but I really don't know. I haven't noticed anything unusual."

"What about the business?" I asked. "He just got everything rolling with this new stock offering, didn't he?" Two years earlier Dan had sold his share of the company he had run for many years, taking early retirement and almost a million dollars in severance pay. Too young to be put out to pasture, it turned out, he soon felt bored and restless and itchy to get back to work. When he found a new business opportunity, he had invested their entire life savings. I thought back to his comments earlier in the year when I was visiting them in Virginia. He had shared some thoughts about the new venture with Janet and me.

"This company has the potential to make really big money," Dan had said. "We're either going to be very rich or broke."

I asked Janet to keep me informed. "Let me know if there is anything I can do," I said, and hung up. I had a sinking feeling, wondering if Dan's business had collapsed. I was afraid he might have committed suicide – and I knew Janet was worried about the same thing.

The next two days went by with no word from Dan; Janet was becoming frantic with worry. I encouraged her to fly to Brussels to search for him personally. She wanted to wait, though, hoping he would call.

On Tuesday, I was waiting with her at their house when, in a matter-of-fact tone, she dropped a bombshell: "Dan disappeared once before when we lived in Detroit."

"Dan has done this *before?* I asked, incredulous.

"Yes," Janet replied quite matter-of-factly, "when the children were still teenagers. We didn't know where he was for more than a week. Later I found out that something had gone wrong with the business.

He had checked into a motel and hid, afraid that if he couldn't support his family, he didn't deserve to have one."

"Janet," I replied almost in disbelief at what I was hearing, "this is *very* important information. I didn't know Dan had ever done this before."

I thought about these two incidents, pondering the apparent pattern. I wondered where he could be, whether he was dead or simply hiding out again.

I asked Janet, "Have you notified Dan's folks?"

"Not yet. I don't want to alarm them," she said. "Maybe Dan will call. Besides, what could they do anyway? His disappearance in Detroit was almost more than they could take, and they're really getting on in years now. They were getting older by the time they *adopted* Dan. I'm afraid *this* could kill them!"

"Dan is adopted?" I asked, shocked again. "I didn't know that."

"Oh! Yes. His birth mother was only about fifteen – a young, unmarried girl who couldn't keep her baby. Dan's parents got him when he was eight days old."

Suddenly, I saw the pattern clearly. Clinical research points to the fact that stress which occurs around the time of birth often makes a very powerful impact on the rest of the child's life. Although there are therapeutic methods which often bring about healing and subsequent changes in the person's life, as shown in the case histories in this book, it is necessary, first, to *recognize* that a pattern exists. In this case, immediately after Dan was born, he was separated from his mother – *from his family.* Years later, when he felt overwhelmed with stress, he repeated the pattern, *getting lost from his family again.* He had been abandoned by his family as a baby; as an adult he unconsciously repeated the pattern by abandoning his own family. I felt more hopeful that he would be found alive this time, too.

The next day, in response to Janet's long-distance pleas, the Brussels police agreed to go to the apartment. After yelling through the door and pounding repeatedly, they were preparing to enter with the manager's key when the door quietly opened. Dan stood in the doorway, eyes down, unshaven, looking disheveled. He had been isolating himself, afraid to answer the phone, suffering from severe depression.

We soon learned what had happened. Dan discovered too late that the new company was worthless. He had risked all of his and Janet's money – and had lost it. At best he had grounds for a lawsuit, but with two different countries involved, he feared he would never recoup his losses. His hopes for a lucrative investment came crashing down. With this devastating realization, he felt overwhelmed, became deeply despondent, and hid out, getting "lost from his family." The pattern had been repeated once again.

Janet flew to Brussels to help Dan close up the apartment. After they returned to the United States, they came to see me for a BodhiSoul© Breathwork session. During this session, Dan opened up a little and began to discuss his childhood. I shared with him my sense of the pattern in his life which began when, as a tiny newborn, he had felt lost after being separated from his birth mother. He talked about his feelings, verbalized unanswered questions about his long-lost mother, and wept at times. A left-brained, no-nonsense businessman, Dan initially found it hard to believe there was any correlation between this early stage of infancy and his behavior as an adult, but he was fascinated to hear about the growing body of evidence to the contrary, which shows that the early stages of womb life and the time just before, during, and after birth are a most important time of life in terms of setting up patterns which show up later on.

Over the next few months, he returned for additional sessions. Through the breathwork, he experienced more and more of the unconscious pain buried deep in his psyche, at times feeling afraid, helpless, and overwhelmingly sad over the loss of his birth mother. He was understandably quite surprised that, by simply breathing, he could contact and dislodge these powerful, stored-up energies. Once he had consciously experienced his old feelings, he began feeling much lighter and freer.

Later Dan accepted a position with another company, which he saw as a great opportunity. Even though he and Janet had to start over again, Dan has done well and the old pattern has not recurred. Now when he begins to feel overwhelmed with business pressures, instead of keeping them to himself as in times past, he talks about his fears with Janet. This openness helps him feel connected to her – just as he wanted so desperately to feel connected with his birth mother long ago – and diffuses the tendency for anxiety to build. With their new and deepened level of communication, their relationship is closer than it ever has been.

Chapter 6

Elizabeth: Ambush and Victimization

Although most events fall into an identifiable pattern, others defy all explanation, seeming to be purely accidental. Elizabeth felt this way about two shocking experiences which presaged a terrible downturn in her life.

A successful account executive with an advertising agency in Chicago, Elizabeth lived alone in a lovely East Lake Shore Drive apartment, only a few blocks from the glittering Magnificent Mile. On weekends, she sometimes strolled along the lakefront, either alone or with a friend. The expanse of water and wind was recharging to her and she felt lucky to have such a pleasant lifestyle. But it was not to last.

About six months after she moved into her new apartment, she experienced the most traumatic event of her life. Sometime after falling asleep one night, she was startled awake, a hand pressed roughly over her mouth. She could hardly breathe and was utterly terrified. The intruder held a knife against her throat, and whispered guttural commands for her to remain silent.

"If you scream, I'll kill you," the intruder said. He brutally raped her.

The attacker fled, leaving Elizabeth feeling paralyzed with fear. The police later determined that he had gained entry by picking the lock on her door.

This horrifying episode might be viewed as a random occurrence, except that Elizabeth was the victim of another shocking attack eighteen months later while vacationing in Hawaii. After dinner, she was walking back to her hotel when a man leaped out of a darkened area next to some bushes and grabbed her from behind. As he was dragging her to the ground, two people came out of a building across the dimly-lit lawn. Her assailant abruptly dropped her and fled.

Now doubly traumatized and afraid to venture outside her hotel room alone, Elizabeth cut short her trip and returned to Illinois, badly shaken. Once at home she hoped she would regain her self-confidence, but recurring nightmares of being attacked disturbed her sleep so regularly that she felt fatigued most of the time. In the twenty months following the first assault, her life had begun disintegrating. Whereas she had once been a self-assured, strong, creative woman, she now felt unsure, frightened, and self-absorbed. She found it difficult to concentrate on work and her productivity sharply declined. Desperate for help, she made an appointment with a therapist.

The therapist was a caring, friendly woman who listened thoughtfully as Elizabeth related her recent, disturbing experiences. Being able to openly talk about her fears and feeling truly heard, Elizabeth grew calmer and began to feel a little more grounded. Her stress was significantly lessened by the empathic interchange that occurred between her and her therapist week after week, although she was well aware that she still had not regained her former optimism. She would experience days on end when her world seemed brighter, then she would feel suddenly pulled back down with the memory of the attacks. Trying to live each day fully, she would still find herself lost in periods of grief and rage.

Any number of events could trigger a relapse. Riding along the street in a taxi, for instance, and glimpsing a scuffle on the corner between two teenage boys, Elizabeth felt the muscles of her back tense with fear and anger. Or stepping into an elevator when Hawaiian music was playing would presage another descent into grief, for instead of the pleasure she once experienced on hearing these beautiful chords, she would recall the second assault. Clearly, although Elizabeth was coping better than immediately after the traumatic events, she was far from being healed. She began to despair that she would ever get her life back.

It was at this time that I appeared on a radio show focusing on my first book, "Secrets" and the tremendous healing that can result from connected breathing. Elizabeth heard this interview and attended a workshop I conducted the following weekend.

"During the first, introductory hour," Elizabeth says, "I began to feel more hopeful about truly resolving my unhappy situation. For whatever reason, I felt I could trust Christina. She promised that the breathing session, later that day, would allow a safe opportunity to bring up any unconscious conflicts we were ready to deal with. It made no sense to my rational mind, but at the same time I felt hopeful that it would help."

I explained to the group that at the time of a traumatic event, a person is seldom able to fully feel the overwhelming emotions which arise, pointing out that this is true when the event occurs in adulthood and even more so when one is traumatized as a child.

"Real healing does not result from intellectual discussion alone," I said, "but comes about only as a result of a complete and full experiencing of suppressed feelings."

Elizabeth listened intently, having also observed that discussing things helped for a while but did not bring lasting relief from her distress.

A man in the front row of the workshop raised his hand.

"Assuming we all have suppressed feelings," he asked, "how does one go about 'fully experiencing' them, as you say? It seems to me that I have felt old feelings over and over again. I don't understand why experiencing them would release anything anyway."

"This is a very understandable question," I replied. "All this will make more sense to you in a few hours after we have completed the breathing session. Briefly, however, I want to point out that one of the great lacks in the world today is that there are very few places where it is safe to experience your true feelings. Usually, we have to conform to some outer code which requires us to repress our deepest emotions. Perhaps only certain emotions were allowed in your family," I told them. "For many people, there was not even one person in the family with whom they felt safe when they were little. A child needs to be heard and to have his feelings validated. If his feelings are judged, he will feel judged. When he feels judged, he will feel unaccepted and will often be unable to express himself."

I scanned the faces of the people, checking to see if I was communicating with them. They were attentive, seeming eager to hear more.

"Imagine, for instance, that you are feeling nauseated, perhaps having eaten contaminated food," I continued.

A pretty young woman in a red blouse wrinkled her nose at the unpleasant thought.

"At such times, if you are like me, you probably become quiet, hoping to reduce the sickness," I said. "If a friend arrives and suggests going out to dinner, you might cover your mouth, shake your head and attempt to avoid even the thought of food, right?" I asked. "Or perhaps a loved one wants to discuss plans for the weekend. You might wave them away, unable to interact in the discussion."

They were listening, probably remembering times when they had experienced nausea.

"It is common to go to great efforts to keep the nausea from getting worse, isn't it?" I asked. "But as long as you are preoccupied with retaining such toxic material, you are not able to participate in other activities, are you? Even pursuits which you normally would enjoy hold no appeal when you are feeling ill. It is all you can do to keep from vomiting, isn't that right?"

Heads were nodding here and there as they identified with this unpleasant but familiar scenario.

"Then all of a sudden, there comes a moment when you can wait no longer and you run for the bathroom and begin to vomit. And for thirty or forty seconds, chaos prevails as the contents of your stomach erupt into the toilet. Then, feeling clammy and weakened, you wash your face and get back to bed. Usually within five or ten minutes, you will begin feeling better, having emptied your stomach of this sickening material. Soon you will feel more vigorous, able to participate fully in activities once again."

I surveyed the people in the audience again, as I continued to make the next important point.

"All of us understand physical nausea and the value of vomiting, don't we?" I asked.

A few hands raised spontaneously.

"But we seem to have no model for the same kind of release at the emotional level," I said. "For instance, where can you go to empty emotions that are making you sick? There are few truly safe places. There are very few people who understand that this is just as essential and healing as is the emptying of physical toxins."

The group was watching and listening intently.

"And so, when you are loaded with some emotional contaminant, you spend lots of time and energy attempting to keep it down, just as you may attempt to avoid vomiting. In both instances, you are unable to participate fully in life. At such times, it's as though you have excess baggage in both hands. When you finally are able to set the baggage down, your hands will be free to create and work and participate in the real experience of living."

The expressions on their faces reflected relief and hope, but also doubt.

"This is the primary purpose of the breathing session which is coming up. This will finally be a safe place and time for you to let go of emotional conflicts that have kept you stuck or sick. It will finally be safe for you to release them."

Elizabeth asked, "If I experience overpowering emotions that are suppressed, how will I know what to do?" She looked puzzled and seemed very anxious to make headway.

"Fortunately, your subconscious knows what to do," I replied, glad she asked the question. "If you tap into an old traumatic event which is frightening, for instance, you will feel afraid. In this way you will be bringing up a toxic emotion which has been stored, and empty it once and for all. Even though this may seem scary or chaotic while it is happening – just like vomiting – you will find that, afterwards, you will soon feel lighter and healthier."

Elizabeth said, "I hope you're right about this. It sounds almost too good to be true. I've been struggling with a really heavy situation for more than two years. To think that I might be able to be rid of this today seems like a dream."

"I understand," I responded, not yet knowing her or the ordeal she had endured. "And the real proof of what I am saying is the freedom that you, yourself, will experience. You won't have to take my word for it; you will know."

I added a further caution before I explained the breathing process itself.

"Please be aware that you may breathe for 45 minutes or so and experience nothing more than a feeling of relaxation. It is possible that you will be aware of no 'clearing' or 'emptying' whatsoever. But at the same time, there is no possible negative side effect. At the very least, you will feel good later. At best, you may have the most magnificent experience of your lifetime."

We agreed to take a break and reconvene in 20 minutes to prepare for the breathing session.

After the recess, I gave the group instructions for the breathwork, discussing what to expect and how to breathe. Elizabeth, covered by a blanket, rested her head on a small, blue silk pillow she had brought with her.

The blanketed participants lay on the floor, separated from each other by a comfortable space. The room was dimly lit. Each person began to breathe, some more strongly and forcefully than others. After a while, a woman sobbed a little, and another wept softly. A young man in a plaid shirt clenched his fists and breathed through a grimace.

Elizabeth had been breathing rhythmically and strongly when, all of a sudden, she raised her arms as though defending herself, screaming at the same time and scrambling as though to escape some terrible assault. I went quickly to her, to provide support, to help her fully experience the conflict she had tapped into, and to make sure that her flailing did not disturb other people.

"Good! Good! Let this come up!" I said to her, sitting close enough to be sure she could hear me, but making sure I did not actually touch her. I had no idea what awful event she might be re-living.

"It's safe to let all of this come up now," I repeated.

As horrid as the experience might appear to an onlooker, I knew from having observed many other people that she was undergoing a very healing catharsis — a complete and full experiencing of feelings which had probably been suppressed for a very long time. I also knew that as traumatic as this might seem, it would lead to true healing and that Elizabeth would feel much better after her experience.

She seemed gripped in the throes of a wild interaction that lasted for several minutes, then suddenly dropped her arms as though drained. She wept, uttering sounds of almost unbearable anguish. I inwardly saw an image of a small, bewildered, and terrified child who felt heartbreaking sadness and confusion. After a few minutes, her sobbing ceased; she whimpered and then fell silent. As the rest of the group experienced their own individual processes, I kept an eye on her. She seemed to have gone to sleep.

One by one the breathers completed their session, as soft music played, gently filling the room. I then told them quietly that they could tiptoe out of the room for a break.

Later, as several people shared their experiences, Elizabeth listened attentively but said nothing. Her tear-streaked face look relaxed though pensive. After we concluded our program for the day, Elizabeth approached me at the front of the room.

"I just want to thank you," she said, taking my hand in both of hers. "I can't say much right now … maybe tomorrow. But I'm so thankful I came. Thank you, Christina."

I knew that she had experienced a major event, and looked forward to learning more about it when she felt ready to talk.

The next day, during a time when participants were sharing their experiences from the day before, asking questions and looking forward to another breathing session, Elizabeth raised her hand and walked to the front of the room. Wearing a gray wool jacket and slacks, she looked relaxed and quietly elegant.

"I want to share my experience of yesterday," she began. "While I don't understand how this is possible, I remembered something that I somehow know has been at the root of many traumatic experiences in my life, including two terrifying experiences in recent years when I was physically attacked."

You could have heard a pin drop.

"Yesterday, during the breathing session," Elizabeth continued, "I experienced an event which happened when I was about 6 years old. My mother had saved up a complaint about my behavior until my father came home. 'I'm going to tell your father,' she had told me threateningly. I never looked forward to seeing my father; I was afraid of him and didn't want him near me. But when he came home, she often would recite my transgressions to him — sometimes even embellishing them — and insist that he punish me."

"That night I was upstairs in my room, and all of a sudden he was there, in back of me. He grabbed me from behind and began lashing at me with his belt, stinging my legs and arms and buttocks. It felt like a tornado had hit, swirling me wildly and destructively. He seemed like a crazy man. I was screaming and trying to pull away from his grip on my arm. He then leered at me and said, 'You better think twice before you do that again!' I didn't even know what I had done! He then stepped toward me again, and put his hand on my leg. I hated the sickening look in his eyes. He leaned forward to kiss me, reeking of beer, but I tore away and ran into the bathroom, locking the door behind me."

Elizabeth was trembling as she repeated this story. She looked down most of the time and tears rolled down her face. She was visibly shaken, but she also seemed strong and determined.

"I waited a long time before I came out of the bathroom. He was gone by then. Later, I guess I just forgot the experience," she said, sounding resigned and a little helpless. "I never told my mother or anyone. After that I stayed away from him even more than before."

I was surprised that Elizabeth had decided to share this ugly incident with the group, but she seemed to want to get through her whole story while she still had the courage.

"The shock and surprise were worse than his blows," she continued, adding "As I grew up, I always knew I didn't trust my father, but I had no idea why. I didn't know it was possible to completely forget something like this."

Thinking about the dynamic in her family, I realized that Elizabeth's pain was three-fold. First, she felt terrified by her father's sudden attack and inebriated sexual groping and, second, she felt guilty in response to his subtle, devious insinuation that she had caused the problem. The combination of these two emotions was so overwhelming that the young girl could not have felt them at the time. They, of course, made no sense at all. Third, because her mother was emotionally unavailable to her and, worse, she was also part of the abuse, Elizabeth felt completely alone in her pain and confusion. Having no safe person to turn to, she buried all her fear, anger and grief inside. Thus buried, it became like an unseen boiling repository, waiting to erupt.

"I feel sure," Elizabeth concluded, "that this experience with my father set me up to be victimized again."

She then stood and turned to me for a warm hug before she returned to her seat. It seemed to me that the whole group took her into their hearts as she finished her painful story.

"Carl Jung observed that '...when an inner event is not made conscious, it happens outside'," I said to Elizabeth and the group.

"My hope for you, Elizabeth, is that this trauma has now been made completely conscious so that you will be freed of its power to attract further trauma to you. You will know if this is the case by observing the events in your life. Should it happen that you do experience additional trauma, please do not become discouraged. Remember, instead, that this just means more healing is needed."

Elizabeth and I have stayed in touch in the years since that workshop and I am happy to report that, so far, she continues to feel free of the terror and rage which burdened her for so long. She also reports that the pattern of ambush has not recurred.

Chapter 7

Dean: Rejection, Shame, and Unworthiness

Sometimes *many* different patterns swirl chaotically in a person's life, intertwining in a complex and confusing fashion. Such was the experience of Dean, a client whom I saw for a series of ten BodhiSoul© Breathwork sessions. Shame, guilt, fear of the dark, rejection, abandonment, ambush, abuse, and unworthiness, to name a few, had all been his recurring experiences.

At the time of our first meeting, Dean was 60 years old. He had been diagnosed with cancer of the liver two months earlier. The tumor was inoperable, his doctors said, and Dean declined the recommended chemotherapy and radiation, choosing instead to try to heal himself through more natural means, and to embrace to the fullest whatever time he had left. The expectation of his physician was that Dean had about four more months to live.

I kept a detailed record of Dean's ten sessions, recording his comments in shorthand, along with noting my own intuitive impressions. In addition, Dean kept his own journal, and after the tenth appointment, I wrote down additional details as he read his notes to me session by session. Because of this, I have a very accurate account of his amazing confrontation with the fear and guilt which had plagued him for a lifetime, and the concomitant catharsis and liberating transformation which brought him a much deeper sense of peace and self-acceptance. Perhaps the clearest way to tell Dean's story — a traumatic and painful one — is to describe those sessions here.

February 15th - Session #1

"I have felt ashamed all my life," Dean told me that first day, "and I've always worried about what other people thought. At times I have felt so self-conscious about my shirt or my trousers that I have gone back home and changed, afraid that people would criticize my clothing. Eight years ago I developed very severe asthma and retired. Since then I have been less uncomfortable because I have not been required to mingle with many people, but the shame and self-consciousness has not gone away."

I glanced around at his spacious living room. A beautiful oriental rug, tastefully placed on the smooth hardwood floor, accented the main seating area. A huge tapestry wing chair and ottoman stood near a graceful antique armoire, which blended comfortably with contemporary pieces and held historical, architectural, and literary volumes. A wall of windows overlooked an expansive deck and a lazy river curling through the valley below. In the distance, layers of blue-tinged mountains waited for the sunset. I reflected that I had seldom seen a more charming home. Dean had exquisite taste, and apparently had been very successful. Furthermore, even during our initial meeting, he referred to his interest in a wide variety of topics, and he seemed warm, open, and eager to learn. How few people are so accomplished, I thought. Yet throughout his life he had felt such shame and self-doubt that he had never been able to accept himself. Well aware that such debilitating emotions do not stem from the rational, conscious mind, I suspected that the origins of Dean's pattern of shame and self-loathing lay in his childhood — or even earlier.

"I was an illegitimate child," Dean confided in response to my questions about his early family. "My mother was 14 years old and unmarried. This was back in 1935, so it was a big scandal."

As he spoke, Dean occasionally glanced at me, but usually averted his eyes.

"When I was born, the physician who delivered me wanted to place me for adoption with one of his friends in New York. But Emily, my mother, decided she wanted to keep me. She did not claim me as her son, though. Instead, there was a pretense that Big Mama and Big Daddy (Emily's mother and father) were my parents, and that Emily was my big sister. This was ridiculous, of course, because almost everyone in Raleigh knew. I was consciously aware that Emily was my mother by the time I was about six, but went along with the pretense because I didn't know what else to do."

I began to see a clearer picture of Dean's painful past and to feel deep empathy for the plight of a little boy who felt completely alone emotionally. I had witnessed wonderful results with many other breathwork clients, and hoped that Dean would find release and comfort, too. I thoroughly explained the process, and it was time to begin the breathwork portion of the session.

Dean lay on a wool throw, placed over the carpeting, with a small pillow under his head. He was covered by a cotton blanket. As he breathed, he seemed to become more energized and tears rolled out of his closed eyes and down his temples. His fists clenched, his body occasionally tensed, and he clutched the blanket under his chin, as though trying to get warm. After about 45 minutes, his breathing relaxed and he rested. When he opened his eyes, they were aglow.

"I'm here!" Dean declared, with a tone of wonder. "I was back in the womb feeling anger, hate, rejection, fear, confusion and cold," he said all in one breath. "I could feel all the chaos that was going on with my mother and the people around her. I knew that this lifetime was going to be difficult and that Emily and others thought it would be better if I were not born, but I made a conscious choice to come into this body and a conscious choice to stay." Dean continued reporting his remarkable experience. "Then I was born. When I took my first breath, I felt such freedom!"

"A lot of questions got answered," he continued. "It started off in a dark room. It felt like I was in the womb. I felt like I was swimming. I was scared to death. I had a fear of being alone in the dark for many years. This became a source of ridicule by others, teasing me because I was 'scared of the dark.'"

"Marvin, my cousin, a year and a half older than I, would sneak off and leave me and when I became upset because I was alone, he would jump out and scare me. Or, when we would play hide and seek, I'd go hide and all the kids would run off somewhere else and abandon me in my hiding place. At other times, we would go to the graveyard and Marvin would sneak away and hide behind a tree or a tombstone and jump out and frighten me. He seemed to enjoy tormenting me. This was very unnerving to me and I felt very fragile. Even now when I walk into a dark room, if something startles me, it brings up all those old feelings again."

Dean continued describing his experience during the breathwork. "When I first began the breathing, I had pain in my stomach and the pain is gone now. It feels like many layers of insulation have left me. In addition to feelings of abandonment, it is as though many feelings of rejection, hurt, ridicule and humiliation have been lifted off."

"How are you feeling now?" I asked.

"Great," he replied. "I feel lighter and more free than before."

I suggested that he just lie still and rest for a while.

"I'll find my own way out, Dean," I told him as I left a little while later.

"Okay," he said, "but let's make another appointment. I want to do this again."

That done, I tiptoed out of the room. As I drove away, I knew he had tapped into and experienced emotions that had been suppressed for a long time. By experiencing such emotions, the underlying causes are healed. I expected this releasing would continue in the next sessions.

February 23rd - Session #2

After the breathwork, Dean reported reliving the following events in his inner experience during the session:

"I got caught playing 'doctor' with a little girl in the neighborhood and felt very ashamed. Then, when I was five years old, I used to go with some other boys from the neighborhood to Raymond's workshop which was behind his garage. (Raymond was a man who lived a few blocks away.) He would build things out of wood and we would watch him. One day I was down there alone and he got hold of me and molested me. He told me he would kill me if I told anyone. Then he let me go and I left and was walking home. I felt so scared and alone. I knew I had to go home; I didn't want to but I didn't know where else to go. I remember hanging around a street corner, feeling lost, and it was getting darker and I knew I had to go home. Of course, I never told anyone — I had no one to tell, no one to talk to about *anything.* Raymond went on molesting me for about a year."

February 27th - Session #3

During the third session, Dean experienced a lot of anger and hatred, primarily directed toward four significant males in his life. The first was Robert, his biological father, whom he never met. The second was Raymond. The third was Jack, an older homosexual with whom Dean lived when he first left home as a young adult.

"I did not want to be with Jack," Dean stated, "but was dependent on him for a place to live. I had no place else to go. I felt very diminished by this relationship and felt used and somewhat abused by Jack. After about a year, I joined the Army to escape."

"So you tolerated this situation for about a year," I observed, "the same amount of time during which you were molested by Raymond."

Dean gasped slightly when he recognized the similar time frames for the two situations, one as a child and the other as an adult, which had engendered identical, painful feelings in him.

"I felt humiliated, frightened, lost, alone, used, worthless, and angry in both situations," he said. "I don't even know why I stayed with Jack for that long. Looking back, I realize that I could have joined the Army at any time, but it didn't occur to me to take action sooner."

"It would not be surprising," I replied, "if you were unconsciously 'programmed' for tolerating this unhappy situation for a one-year time period. The year with Raymond may have set up a one-year cycle, without your being consciously aware of it, of course. I have observed the repetition of similar time cycles many times. But please continue," I said to Dean. "You mentioned earlier that you felt enraged at *four* males."

"When I enlisted in the Amy," Dean went on, "I felt so relieved to get away from Jack, but I found myself in yet another humiliating situation when a colonel approached me wanting sexual favors. He promised special privileges if I complied with his wishes or a tough time in the Army if I refused. I felt trapped again."

"How long did that last?" I asked.

Dean seemed pensive for a moment, then looked up at me and smiled slightly.

"A year," he replied, nodding his head a little and smiling slightly. "I was transferred to another base then and never saw him again."

At the end of this third session, Dean seemed relaxed and very relieved.

"It feels like there's more of me inside now, Christina. I wish I could have experienced this healing 20 years ago."

"I understand," I replied. "As suppressions* are brought up and experienced, more of you *is* available," I told him.

Dean was eager for the next session, and made an appointment for three days later.

March 1st - Session #4

After about forty minutes of easy breathwork, Dean looked almost radiant as he opened his eyes.

"This time I experienced so much energy, and lots of colors. It was like a fantastic voyage!" he exclaimed. "I feel like I can hardly contain it all. At one point, I felt a pain in the area of my heart, then that left me. Then I felt, and still feel, energy pouring out, throbbing out of my body, especially out of my fingertips. I feel waves of light and energy. It feels like I am whole and at home in this body for the first time in my life," he said.

He looked more peaceful than I'd ever seen him.

"During this session," he added, "I felt anger, hurt, and pain, especially pain in my liver. But now I feel so whole. I have felt ashamed all of my life but I no longer feel ashamed of anything."

Dean had to re-enter the hospital for some further tests, so his next appointment occurred more than two weeks later.

*Suppressions: emotions and thoughts which have been held back and kept out of the conscious mind.

March 17th - Session #5

At the end of the breathwork portion of the fifth session, which seemed a little more of a struggle than usual for Dean, he reported the following remarkable experience:

"When I first began the breathing, I was in a place of light, and it was just before I was conceived. I did not want to come into a physical body. Then I was conceived, and once in, I did not want to stay because I immediately saw the chromosomal structure – that it was a male body, and I wanted to have a female experience this time."

"Then what happened?" I asked.

"A wise presence convinced me to stay," Dean said. His reply was so natural that I wondered if he was aware of the enormity of the transcendent experience. Then he added, "This was without coercion, however. I could have left then if I had insisted. Instead, I accepted and chose to come in and stay."

March 19th - Session #6

During the sixth session, his cathartic healing continued. Dean felt more of the shame and humiliation which had plagued him throughout his life, venting these toxic emotions little by little.

"I was playing with Tommy, a boy who lived in my neighborhood. We were playing 'doctor' down in his basement and his father came down and caught us. It was really traumatic. His father called me 'that nasty boy,' and sent me out the door. Instead of going home, though, I went to Billy Jordan's house. After a while, Big Daddy* found out where I was and came to get me. As we walked along the sidewalk toward home, Big Daddy kept hitting me on the legs with a switch. People were sitting on their front porches laughing at me. I felt so humiliated."

---

*Dean's grandfather who posed as his father.

March 24th - Session #7

Re-reading my notes of Dean's breathwork sessions, I am reminded that such experiences in breathwork sessions are often not chronologically sequential. The seventh session took Dean back to another major event which occurred while he was in the womb.

"It was at seven months' gestation," Dean said. "I experienced an angry argument between my mother and her parents. They were angry with her because she was pregnant, and were blaming her and yelling at her. She felt utterly desperate, and not wanting the baby, began squeezing her big belly and beating on her belly with her fists, screaming at the unborn child inside, 'Why are you here?'"

Dean continued, "I just thought, 'I'm here and I'm gonna' stay.'"

At the end of our time together that day, Dean said, "Emily* has been wanting to get closer and for years I have been pushing her away, but as a result of these breathing sessions the past few weeks, my feelings for her have really changed. I think I'm going to call her."

March 27th - Session 8

This session dealt primarily with Dean's strong will to live. As he breathed, he re-experienced the time when he had whooping cough.

"It seems like I was looking for a way to die. I was almost ready to die," Dean said, "and I nearly did. I was turning blue when my aunt saved me. I feel that, once again, I chose to live."

March 29th - Session 9

"During this session, my lungs felt hot," Dean told me after the breathwork was complete. "I relived two different occasions when I almost died as a result of fire. The first was when I was seven years old and our Christmas tree caught on fire. My bedroom was filled with

---

*Dean's biological mother.

smoke. I jumped up and ran into the living room, grabbed the tree and dragged it through the kitchen into the yard. The second time was when I was in my twenties. I lived in a garage apartment. The day before Thanksgiving, I put a roast into the oven to cook slowly overnight. I had no thermostat, however, and fell asleep. I dreamed that I was suffocating, then awoke to a smoke-filled room. I jumped up and ran outside just as the fire engine arrived."

March 30th - Session 10

"I felt tremendous empathy for Emily," Dean said when his breathwork was complete. "All my life I have been mad at her and Robert for conceiving me the way they did, and for the fact that I never had a 'real' family. But now I wonder if I really need to ask them to forgive *me* because I think I *chose* them as my parents and *chose* to be born this way. Maybe I had as much to do with creating this as they did. Anyway, I feel such complete forgiveness for them. Rather I would say that now there is nothing to forgive."

The Healing of Painful Patterns

In this story, we see how many patterns are seeded from conception, gestation, birth and early childhood. These patterns weave like vivid threads through Dean's life almost to the end. Thankfully, as a result of the inner work he so courageously undertook, he also began experiencing a deep sense of peace, authenticity, genuine self-acceptance, and unconditional love. The fact that these came at the very end of his life make them no less precious.

Dean died in November, a year after the malignancy in his liver was diagnosed. He had again tolerated tremendous pain for a one-year period.

I am personally sorry that he died; I wish he could have lived longer to enjoy his new-found wholeness. But my sorrow is muted by the enormous gratitude I feel for the healing he experienced. The last time I saw him, he said, "Of course, I would like to live a long time; my life is very pleasant now, but I am also ready to go when it is my time."

Dean's traumatic and painful story reminds me that there is no pattern which cannot be healed, no hurt which cannot be soothed, no heart which is not inherently full of love. The challenge is to empty the hurt so the love can surge up to the surface.

Chapter 8

Philip: Addiction and Disconnection

Philip arrived for a two-week workshop alone, but he soon had several new acquaintances among the other participants. One pretty, blonde young woman, Melanie, seemed particularly attracted to him. Philip was tall and handsome, with light brown hour and soft blue eyes. There was an almost "dreamy" quality about him.

As a Colorado social worker, Philip interacted with people most of the time: children in foster care, unwed mothers on welfare, youngsters lacking a home life and struggling to find their way – all very needy people.

"My week is pretty busy," he said, as he sat in the chair in front of the class, signaling that he wanted to talk. "I meet a lot of folks," he continued, "but I never feel really connected. That's why I came to this workshop – to see if I can feel more like I'm part of life somehow. I'm 32 years old and still living like I'm just out of college."

He seemed disappointed with his life and anxious to make changes.

"When am I going to grow up? " he asked, taking an audible breath and shaking his head in self-disapproval.

Philip described his childhood as 'pretty good.'

"My dad was a salesman," he said, "and traveled a lot, but my mom stayed home with us."

Philip said he had an older sister and a younger one.

"And, although we were not rich, we always had everything we needed," he added. "My dad provided pretty well."

"Did you feel connected to your folks, Philip?" I asked him?

"I've never felt connected to anyone," he replied. "I'm not sure I even know what it means to be connected. I wouldn't describe what I feel as 'fatigue,' but I sorta' feel like I'm dragging myself through life. I would like to experience the enthusiasm that some people seem to feel. Maybe it's not possible to find what I'm looking for, but somehow I haven't been able to quit looking."

"Tell us about your teenage years, Philip," I said.

"I didn't have to work too hard to get decent grades in school," he replied, "and I didn't really give any thought to what I would do with my life. I would hang out at a friend's house or maybe have some kids over. We would go to the show or go skating or skiing sometimes."

"What was really fun for you, Philip?" I asked. "What was your favorite thing to do?"

"When I was 13, I was at this kid's house. His parents were gone and he asked me if I wanted to smoke a joint. I had never tried anything like that, but he said that no one would know – that he did it a lot. So I tried it. That was my first experience with drugs."

"What was that like for you, Philip?" I noted that he had mentioned this experience when asked about his favorite activity.

"Great!" he replied, tossing his head back for a moment and grinning. "That was the first time in my life that I ever remember feeling 'normal.' It doesn't make much sense, I guess, but after I smoked that joint, it felt like an anesthetic that helped me sorta' wake up."

"That is a pretty unusual combination of feelings, isn't it?" I asked. "And did you smoke marijuana again after that first time, Philip?" I asked.

"All the time. From then on, I smoked pot and did some other drugs, too. It was like I could function better that way."

"Do you still do a lot of drugs?" I asked, truly concerned now, for one of the requirements of the Intensive is that a participant must be drug-free, including abstaining from all alcohol throughout the two weeks.

"Mostly just marijuana, now," Philip said. "I hit the drugs pretty heavily for a while during high school — I went a little crazy at first — but later I would just smoke on weekends, so I managed to graduate and go on to college."

"How do you think you're going to feel being here with no drugs, Philip?" I asked him.

"I don't know. I hope it's possible to somehow break through so I'll just feel better generally. If I felt connected to someone or to something, I hope I'd no longer need pot."

This seemed sincere and I respected his candor. Melanie nodded as she listened to him, her eyes glistening.

"Tell us about your life now, Philip," I said.

"I share an apartment with a buddy, but he's gone a lot so it's really almost like having the place to myself."

"Do you have a girl?" I asked.

Melanie's eyes widened as I asked this question, and she straightened herself slightly, looking upward as though viewing a picture in the air, her lips apart.

"I date several girls now, but I'm not in love with anyone. I was engaged for a while but she said she wanted somebody with more ambition," he responded with a slight shrug.

"Do *you* want more ambition, Philip?" I asked.

"Yes," he replied, "but the biggest lack in my life is emotional, not financial. I want to feel connected and happy. Having more money without that doesn't interest me much."

"So you feel disconnected," I acknowledged, "and are you lonely, too?"

Melanie was all ears.

"I guess you could call it loneliness, but I don't feel lonely for anybody I've actually ever known. It's almost as though I feel lonely for 'me,'" he said, pausing, "but that doesn't make any sense, does it?" he asked.

"It makes a lot of sense to me, Philip," I told him. "I think most people are lonely for themselves. When we connect with ourselves, then it's possible to connect with another person, really for the first time."

For all his expressed lack of connection, I observed that Philip seemed to be more comfortable with opening himself up in front of a group than are many people. I wondered if it was this vulnerability, even more than his appearance, which was so attractive to the females in the group.

Pursuing an intuitive hunch, I then asked him, "Philip, tell us about your birth. Were your folks happy to have a second baby?"

"Yes, I think so. My sister was three years old. My mother said they wanted another child and they were glad I was a boy."

"Were you breast fed?" I asked. (This is a very important part of a new baby's bondedness and connection to mother.)

"No," he replied. "My mother said we were all bottle-fed.

"Were you born in a hospital?" I asked.

"Yes," Philip replied, "the same hospital where my sister was born."

"Was your mother awake during your birth?" I asked, anticipating that Philip would have this information since we had suggested people try to obtain the answers to these questions as part of their preparation for the workshop.

"No," he said. "They knocked her out before my birth. She said that when she woke up, they had already taken me to the nursery."

"Was your father at the hospital?"

"Yes. He saw me before she did," Philip said.

"Philip," I said somewhat cautiously, "I have an idea about what may be at the source of your disconnection."

He was listening attentively.

"When an expectant mother is drugged during labor and birth," I said, "the baby is also drugged."

Philip nodded, eager to hear more.

"Your experience of being born, of coming to life – of coming alive! – was associated with your experience of being drugged. This may be why you felt, as you said earlier, that being on drugs made you feel more alive, made you feel 'normal,' Do you see?" I asked him.

"It makes sense," he responded, nodding his head.

"In addition, as soon as you were born, you were taken from your mother – she was not awake anyhow – and you spent your first hours either alone in the nursery or with strangers," I said. "Those first hours are the most important hours of a baby's life, for this is the most critical time for bonding."

Philip just listened silently.

"When physical contact between mother and baby does not occur during this crucial time, this connection is often missed."

I watched Philip to be sure he was able to take this in.

"That makes sense, too," he acknowledged.

"So a connection that should have happened with your mother was missed right there at the beginning," I continued, "and, in addition, both of you were drugged."

Philip looked bewildered and sad.

"So am I just out of luck?" he snapped, sarcastically, shrugging his shoulders and opening his hands as though attempting to cover his sadness with flippancy.

"No," I said. "But the baby who endured all those overwhelming feelings of loss at birth is still sad and hurt and alone. This may be why you feel disconnected. Until these feelings are experienced, this aloneness and disconnection will persist. Once you feel these unexperienced hurts, you will feel more connected and whole."

Philip took a breath. "It's hard to imagine," he said. "I've always felt this way."

"Imagine," I told him, "that a heavy, sealed vault is submerged deeply into a pool. It would take up space in the pool, wouldn't it?" I asked.

Philip nodded.

"Now imagine that the vault is brought to the surface," I went on. "When it is opened, it is discovered that it contains a lot of stagnant water. Exposed to the fresh air, however, that water soon evaporates."

Philip and the others in the group were listening intently.

"As soon as the vault is removed, the water in the pool will surge in to fill up the space it previously occupied, right?" I asked.

"Right," Philip agreed.

"So this is similar to what happens when emotions are so overwhelming that we are unable to experience them – to feel them. They automatically store in the subconscious. They take up space inside you," I explained. "The way to bring them up and out is to experience them. Once this blockage is removed, you will feel much lighter. You will feel more connected with yourself. Does this make sense, Philip?" I asked.

He took a long breath and nodded, straightening his shoulders.

"Thank God, you were never able to quit looking for this connection," I told him. "Thank God, some part of you kept driving you toward this wholeness."

"It's hard to believe we're actually talking like this," Philip exclaimed, shaking his head. "This has been on my mind forever, but I've never been able to verbalize this with anyone before." He suddenly lowered his head, squinted his eyes shut and rested the bridge of his nose on his thumb and forefinger. For a moment, I thought he might cry. Instead he regained control, took a deep breath and dropped his hand to his lap.

"In one way or another," I told him, "everybody in this room probably feels the same way. This is the real purpose of this workshop – to bring up these isolated parts: the fear or anger or separation. At the end, you will feel more whole."

During the remaining days of the Intensive, Philip fluctuated between active participation and passive withdrawal. With each breathwork session, though, it seemed to me that his spirit was taking up residence in his body more and more fully. During breathing sessions, he sometimes tended to fall asleep. This commonly occurs when a person is releasing some of the anesthetic which was given to his or her mother just prior to *birth*. As the drugs were purged from Philip's consciousness, he looked increasingly enthusiastic and alive.

In addition to the work we undertook at the Intensive, I urged Philip to get into treatment for the drug addiction. He called me a few months later and said that he had completed the primary drug treatment and was attending regular meetings with a support group. He also said that he felt much less alone and more connected than ever before.

Chapter 9

Melanie: Self-Esteem Issues

When Philip originally shared his story with the group, Melanie had seemed especially attentive. When he walked back to his seat, she moved to the chair next to him, leaned toward him and placed her hand on his back. Her bold gesture did not take me completely by surprise, for she had seemed intent on connecting with him since the workshop began and showed strong feelings while he was in front of the room.

"Melanie," I said to her, "just let Philip be for now, please."

"I'm sorry." she began, "He looks like he's hurting and I just want to comfort him."

"Well, for now, I don't want anyone to comfort him," I told her. "It's important that he be allowed to feel these uncomfortable feelings; it's the only way he will free himself. And it's better for you to just focus on you for now."

She dropped her head, embarrassed.

"There'll be plenty of time to exchange ideas with each other later, Melanie," I reassured her. "What's going on with you, though?" I asked. "You've been close to tears for the last little while."

Melanie seemed relieved to have her agitation addressed so openly. She looked down and sighed deeply. Her chin began to tremble and her lip quivered. She then buried her face in her open palms and began sobbing.

I waited silently, allowing the time and space for her to experience her anguish.

"Breathe," I whispered to the class, "breathe with her." I took a deep breath, too.

After a few moments, Melanie stopped crying and removed her hands, staring sadly into her lap.

"Melanie," I called to her softly, "do you want to come up and talk about whatever's going on with you?"

Without looking up, she sobbed again. Then, recovering, she replied, "Sure, I mean, what do I have to lose?

Melanie stood up, moved forward, and sat in the chair next to mine, facing the class. She dropped her hands into her lap with obvious nervousness.

"It's okay, Melanie," I told her. "There's no need to be afraid. It's safe here."

She raised her head and looked into my eyes, as though checking to see if she could trust my words.

"All we're going to do is just talk about whatever is bothering you," I assured her, "just as Philip and the others have done."

She took a breath, then sighed and relaxed a little.

"And you can just be yourself," I added.

Again she began to cry.

"What's going on, Melanie?" I asked, putting my arm around her. "What are you feeling?"

Dressed in khaki pants and a bright red T-shirt, she seemed more like a lost little girl than the sexy-looking, sophisticated young woman she sometimes appeared to be.

"Oh! I don't know where to start, Christina," she said, her voice cracking a bit. "I'm so grateful to have your help and at the same time, I'm really nervous being up here in front of the group."

"That's understandable," I said. "Most people feel that way at first."

"But the thing I'm most afraid of is putting on an act while I'm here and not actually getting anything accomplished."

"Is that what you do, Melanie?" I asked.

"Oh! Yeah! All the time," she retorted, as though disgusted with herself. "I'm afraid to let anyone really see me. I'm good at fooling people."

"Why do you put on an act, Melanie?" I asked. "Why are you afraid to let people really see you?"

"'Cause if people really see who I am, they'll want nothing to do with me," she replied.

"What are you afraid they will see?" I asked.

"That I'm a phony and a slut," she shot back.

"Why do you say you're a slut, Melanie?" I asked.

"Because I've slept with a lot of guys," she replied.

"And how do you feel about that, Melanie?"

"I hate myself! I hate myself," she said, her voice rising.

"So why do you do it?" I asked.

"I don't even know," she said, adding, "I really don't sleep around anymore, what with AIDS 'n' all. "But in the past it was because I wanted affection or approval, or sometimes because I needed their help in some way. And I always wind up with nothing." There was a sarcasm in her voice that seemed only a thin cover-up for anguish. "By the time I really realized what I was doing, it seemed like I didn't matter anymore, so why not?" she asked.

"When did you begin to 'not matter,' Melanie?"

"When I was 14 years old, I guess. I met a guy – he was a few years older – and he said he loved me and wanted to marry me. I would have done almost anything to get out of the house and away from my mother and I thought I loved him. He said there was no reason to wait until we got married, so I slept with him. After that night, I never saw him again. He completely dropped me; I couldn't even get him to answer my phone calls. He'd been lying to me all the time – and I was such a silly kid, I fell for it all."

She was breathing faster and her eyes looked fiery.

"You're pretty angry, aren't you, Melanie?" I asked.

"Well, wouldn't you be?" she screamed, her eyes blazing and her face now flushed. She doubled her fists and pounded her thighs, almost springing out of the chair as she shrieked,

"Yeoooooww! Of course, I'm angry!"

She was panting now and her nostrils flared as rage boiled up inside her.

"That son-of-a-bitch lied to me – used me!" she screamed.

"Good, Melanie," I encouraged her. "That's good. Go for it. Let all that rage come up. It's safe for it to come up now."

She was up on her feet, clenching her fists in the air. We shoved a thick cushion in front of her on the floor.

"Beat on this, Melanie," I said, motioning toward the cushion. "Scream it out."

Melanie dropped down onto her haunches and with both fists, pounded and screamed until she was limp with exhaustion. The others were watching. A few people seemed frightened by her outburst; others sat quietly, breathing deeply.

Finally, spent, Melanie collapsed onto the cushion and sobbed out her anguish. I was sure that there was still more work to do, but Melanie had dealt with a big chunk already, and needed rest right now. There would be time to complete her process later. I was thankful that we had almost two more weeks to work together.

I stayed with Melanie while the group left the room for a break. She was tired and limp, but she already seemed more authentic. I didn't know if she recognized yet that she had allowed a whole room full of people to see a very real side of her, and instead of rejecting and abandoning her, as she had feared, they had loved and supported her. Wherever her process would take her after this, she had made a very good start.

During Melanie's next session a few days later, she shared that her birth and early childhood had been painful experiences of feeling worthless. She was the third of four children – all unplanned. From an early age, her mother drank too much, spending much of her time in bed while Melanie's father was at work. The two parents often engaged in loud brawling arguments when he came home. Melanie felt terrified much of the time, as did her sisters. When Melanie was five years old, her parents separated and her father moved to New Orleans, almost a thousand miles away. He seldom saw his daughters, and they felt less and less valued. Melanie's painful pattern was already becoming apparent.

During one breathwork session, Melanie regressed to the time when she was six months in utero. Her father had come home from work to find his pregnant wife asleep. Their two toddlers – unsupervised – were playing with the sewing basket, and needles were scattered about the linoleum. He became alarmed and confronted his wife about her negligence. An argument ensued and she picked up a pair of of scissors and threw them at him. They narrowly missed him. He swore at her.

"I wish none of these children had ever been born," he said.

"So do I!" she retorted.

And Melanie, the tiny fetus in the womb, knew that she was unwanted and unwelcome. From that moment she felt worthless, and that sense of worthlessness listened for an echo of corroboration from the outer world. The painful self-judgment was validated again and again as she grew up with an addicted mother and without her father. At 14, when she met her first lover, she hungrily listened to the words of endearment he spoke – words she had longed to hear all her life. Predictably, they soon led to her feeling even more worthless than ever.

In breathwork sessions throughout the next two weeks, Melanie experienced more and more of the anger, sadness, and self-loathing which had been suppressed since before her birth. As she emptied this seething mass of pain, she felt increasingly lighter and clearer.

At the end of the Intensive, during a private meeting with Melanie, I suggested that she continue the inner work she had so courageously begun.

"It is unreasonable to expect that patterns which have been in place for years will be completely released in such a short time," I told her.

Today, she has begun a new of life with greatly increased self-esteem.

Chapter 10

Anna: Caretaking

Frequently, a pattern is set in motion as a result of a single, traumatic event like the one suffered by Elizabeth. Sometimes, however, it seems to take root not as a result of any one episode, but develops out of an atmosphere of hurt, subtle abuse, neglect, or other harmful causes. Though less shocking, perhaps, such a pervasive, malignant environment in a person's early life may be just as insidious as a sudden shock.

Anna is a brilliant and talented artist. Some people think of her as impractical and a bit eccentric. When I met her, I was struck with how ethereal she seemed, almost as though she were a citizen of some gossamer world. Yet I listened to her story and learned that, in spite of her delicate appearance, she was a very strong person indeed. She had been married twice and, though each man seemed strong and self-confident when they met, Anna usually wound up taking care of him, usually with no one to care for her in return. This pattern had been consistent, though it had played out differently from one relationship to another. Her first husband was dependent upon her for care because he frequently felt ill. The second time, she married a man from Eastern Europe whose cultural background required a wife to be more of a servant than a friend and peer.

"As much as he seemed like a cosmopolitan citizen of the world, with liberal views," she said, "after we were married, we went to live in Hungary, his homeland. As soon as we arrived there, he expected me to wait on him and take care of his personal needs, including his laundry and all the cooking. I would have been willing to serve him a lot, but we were dependent on income from my work. Clearly, I could not manage everything." Becoming very tired and finally realizing that none of her needs were being met, she eventually left this marriage also.

Anna is a very centered person and has been pursuing a spiritual path for many years. She states that she came to understand what was behind this caretaking pattern during a deep meditation about a year after the end of her second marriage.

"I was the youngest child in the family," Anna said. "My oldest brother has been schizophrenic for as long as I can remember and my next older brother was always irresponsible. My mother seemed scattered, leaning on me, and my father, a biologist, was at work all the time. If our family was to hold together, it was up to me, it seemed." Anna continued, "I have no idea how or why I felt stable enough to provide the strength in my family, but that certainly seemed to be my role. My mom is dead now, but I still fill this same role with my dad and my two brothers."

As I completed the interview with Anna, reflecting on all she had shared about herself, as well as what I had personally observed, I learned that she was just completing the construction of her own house in the woods, to function as both her art studio and her home. Of the many descriptions of Anna, I thought, "impractical" is the one which fits the least.

During her initial breathwork session, Anna felt a variety of emotions, including sadness, anger, and grief, most of which stemmed from her lonely childhood. In addition, she experienced some anger about her failed marriages and the fact that she had been treated unfairly. During this and a number of subsequent sessions, Anna was very eager for clarity about her own patterns and for assistance in clearing them. Vigilant in her own self-observation, she was one of the most honest persons I have ever met.

After our initial sessions, I stayed in touch with Anna. A few months later, she told me that she had met another man, Jack, in whom she was, personally, very interested – and she wanted to talk out her thoughts and feelings regarding him and the possibility of another serious relationship. She made another appointment.

Although this man seemed quite different from others with whom she had been involved, she wanted to proceed cautiously to avoid making another mistake. As I listened to her description of Jack and their fledgling relationship, I saw indications that Anna would again wind up taking care of him, even though he was not consciously seeking a caretaker. I asked questions to help Anna become clearer and shared the warning signs which concerned me.

Although she was not defensive about the traits I pointed out about Jack, Anna nonetheless felt sad when she realized that it was not in her best interest to pursue the relationship with Jack. She made a conscious decision to remain friends with him, but to end their romantic relationship. Both Anna and I felt sure that this choice would allow her to continue with her own inner work so that, when she did enter into another relationship, it could be a healthy, mutually-supportive one. In the meantime, although she is lonely at times, Anna is busy with her inner work, her artwork, and the completion of her home.

The next case study comes from the work and research of the late David B. Cheek, M.D. For better understanding in reading this account, it is helpful to know that in addition to his OB-GYN specialization, Dr. Cheek also used clinical hypnotherapy as a way to help patients access the subconscious mind. Prior to inducing hypnosis, he would set up a system of finger signals which would allow the person to respond to his questions while still in hypnotic trance.

Chapter 11

Debbie: Confidence, High Self-Esteem

Dr. Cheek discovered, quite accidentally, that experiences occurring in utero, long before the advent of conscious memory, can set the stage for later events in a person's life. Although much of his work dealt with attempting to help patients find healing for painful patterns of disease and inhibition resulting from traumatic early experiences, he also found that positive early occurrences can contribute to glowing health and high self-confidence.

A Memory from The Womb

Dr. Cheek was conducting a therapeutic interview with an anxiety-ridden woman. Accompanying her to his office that day was her 13-year-old daughter, Debbie, whom Dr. Cheek had delivered. Because she appeared to be a caring, intelligent, outgoing youngster, Dr. Cheek asked Debbie to sit in during the session.

"I felt it might bolster the self respect of the mother to point out what a success she had been as a mother," Dr. Cheek confides. "I was working with the mother when I noticed that the young girl was also in an altered state. Hoping to diminish the woman's feelings of unworthiness as a mother and wife, I began also to question Debbie, as the mother sat waiting passively." (Finger signals were set up with the daughter indicating "yes," "no," and "I don't want to answer that" responses.)

"Feeling that it might be helpful to the woman if this bright and popular girl – she was the president of her high school class and a straight "A" student – could enlighten her mother about the good job she had done in raising her," Dr. Cheek continues. "I asked the girl, 'Debbie, does your subconscious mind know what has allowed you to grow up to be such a delightful young lady?'"

"Her 'yes' finger lifted in an intermittent way," Dr. Cheek states. "I knew she was in a deep state. I asked her, 'Is there any one single event that started you off in this way?' Again, her 'yes' finger lifted,'" he said.

"Debbie, please go back to the start of that event," Dr. Cheek requested. "When you are there, your 'yes' finger will lift. When it has ended, your 'no' finger will lift."

He studied the girl's face as he spoke these instructions to her. Her mother sat passively, her eyes closed.

"Don't try to remember anything, Debbie," he said. "Just wait until a thought comes to your conscious mind as you go over that period."

Dr. Cheek was intrigued when Debbie began to smile after this review.

"It's when I know I'm supposed to be a girl," she said, almost beaming.

"Please go to that moment, Debbie, and look around in your subconscious mind," Dr. Cheek instructed her. "See where you are. If there are people there, see them. When you know it well enough to talk about it, your 'yes' finger will lift. As it lifts, please tell me what is going on."

"After ten seconds, Debbie's 'yes' finger lifted," Dr. Cheek reports, "and she moved her head from side to side as though looking at external objects."

"I'm inside," she said.

"What do you see?" asked Dr. Cheek.

"Mother is sitting on a couch," Debbie responded. "She's knitting something. Then Daddy comes in and is asking why she is knitting something for a girl."

"From the unpleasant tone of voice used when the word 'girl,' was repeated," Dr. Cheek said, "I could tell that her father apparently had wanted a boy."

"But," Debbie continued, "mother is saying, "It's a girl! I know it's a girl. It has to be a girl!"

Dr. Cheek could tell from the lilt of her voice that the mother was very happy to be having a little girl.

"See what your mother is wearing," Dr. Check directed. "When you can see this, your 'yes' finger will lift."

"She has on a green plaid dress," Debbie said. "I can't see any other color; I think it is dark."

Dr. Cheek confesses that he was amazed by Debbie's response, since he had never experienced this before.

"At this point in the session," he reports, "I looked at her mother, sitting across from me in my office. She was totally alert now, with her eyes open, looking surprised. Fortunately she did not comment until later."

Dr. Cheek said that he later asked the mother, "What do you think about that?"

"I had a green and black plaid dress on," she replied, "and I can remember when that was. I had just begun feeling the baby kicking."

"Fetal movements are usually noticed by the mother soon after 18 weeks of gestation," Dr. Cheek confirms.

"It was in April," Debbie's mother continues. "I gave that dress away right after Debbie was born.[1] I would have been almost five months along. That's incredible!"

Dr. Cheek commented that this 1961 experience was his first glimpse into the possibility that a fetus could have clairvoyant knowledge.

"Of course," he observed, "there is always a chance that the mother may have been mistaken in her memory and that the daughter could have seen this or a similar dress at a later time. It is also possible that her hypnotized mother, across the room, was recalling the event and projecting her recollection of the dress telepathically to her daughter. The facts as described, however, were enough to open my mind to this interesting form of fetal awareness of it's mother's world."

Dr. Cheek added that his motivation to keep searching prenatal impressions stemmed from having patients teach him that traumatic experiences prior to the dawning of conscious memory may, indeed, set the stage for subsequent experiences.

"I was learning," Dr. Cheek said, "about some of the reasons why we doctors fail to help patients who are suffering from feelings of rejection, guilt, negative identifications, and passive acceptance of bad luck and disease."

Debbie's experience of her mother's happiness at the feeling that she would have a baby girl left Debbie with very positive, unconscious

---

[1]This precludes the daughter having seen the dress later, as an older child.

feelings. Her confidence and self-esteem were, evidently, very pronounced, as is reflected in her academic success and popularity among the other students.

In other instances, however, intrauterine experiences are painful and frightening, resulting in severe physical, emotional and psychological problems, as is evident in the next four case studies.

Another psychologist who helps people recognize and resolve life patterns is William R. Emerson, Ph.D., of Petaluma, California.

Dr. Emerson, whose work includes a variety of techniques, including breathwork, explains that sometimes difficult patterns are resolved only when the prenatal or perinatal epoch is addressed. Birth forms the foundation for interpreting life experience. When it is traumatic, powerful residual emotions linger in the physical body as well as in the subconscious, giving rise to fear, anxiety, sadness, and other feelings which may seem unfounded. In other cases, it is not birth which traumatized the child, but an event which occurred around the time of conception or later during the nine months of womb life.

When a person experiences emotions which have been suppressed since the traumatizing event which engendered them, very powerful changes take place. These changes are not only subjective, making a vast internal difference to that person, but they are also objectively observable in his or her behavior as well.

Furthermore, Dr. Emerson says that significant life patterns do not resolve themselves until the traumatic prenatal and birth events are re-patterned through conscious experience – an observation I also have made repeatedly.

"When traumatic events are brought into awareness and are catharted, they cease affecting the behavior of the person," Emerson states.

He discusses two ways to experience such a prior traumatic event:

(a) repeatedly and consciously, or

(b) when the process is experienced once, but deeply and intensely.

Both kinds of experience lead to resolution and healthier functioning.

The next case, contributed by Dr. Emerson, is an excellent example of changes brought about by the emotional catharsis which is a part of any successful therapy.

Chapter 12

Donald: Paranoia

Donald, whose condition was very resistant to treatment, had been diagnosed as a "schizoid personality with strong delusional and paranoid tendencies," according to Dr. Emerson. The primary delusional aspect was his paranoia, which was chronic and unchanging.

In his work as a detective, Donald seemed obsessed with following and being followed. In addition, he had minor brushes with drug usage, and was seen by co-workers as a bit overzealous in cases involving drugs.

With Dr. Emerson's help, Donald was regressed to the time before his birth, and experienced himself as being "pursued by those on the outside, invaded by toxic substances, and poisoned by the dark ones." Following this experience, his paranoia was quickly eradicated.

Dr. Emerson then was able to locate records of Donald's actual birth and was amazed to discover that it had been a traumatic cesarean one. Dr. Emerson explains that this was the origin of Donald's feeling that he was being "pursued by those on the outside." Further, Donald's mother had attempted suicide – using drugs – in the last trimester of her pregnancy, giving rise to Donald's fear of "being invaded by toxic substances, and poisoned by the dark ones." These themes were played out in his life patterns.

After his experience of these painful prenatal emotions and the therapy with Dr. Emerson, Donald felt free of his obsessive focus and began to express an interest in other aspects of detective work. His peers also reported that he seemed more normal.

Jon-Richard Turner is a past Vice President of the International Society for Prenatal and Perinatal Psychology and Medicine. He and his wife, Troya Turner-Groot, a former Head Psychiatric and Social Nurse, are Co-Directors of the Institute for Whole-Self Discovery & Development in Amsterdam, Holland, and Santa Fe, New Mexico. They have presented their work in more than 25 different countries.

They have generously shared the following case, which is the fascinating and encouraging story of Troya's own triumphant battle with anorexia, bulimia, and cancer. Troya's healing from cancer occurred more than 19 years ago.

Chapter 13

Troya: Eating Disorders, Illness, and Suicide Issues

Just as a traumatic experience can show up in a pattern which later becomes an emotional or psychological handicap, it also can lead to patterns which result in physical diseases, sometimes very serious ones.

She Was Slowly Committing Suicide

Troya suffered from anorexia nervosa and bulimia for more than ten years. Because she was a psychiatric nurse, she was familiar with the treatments usually prescribed for these serious diseases. Feeling that these treatments would not be effective in her case, she sought another remedy.

"I had begun reading a book about meditation," Troya said, "and had just arrived at a chapter dealing with the use of imagination during meditation. I got the inspiration to imagine in meditation how my life had started, expecting to see myself as this little baby whom I knew from pictures. I anticipated that I would then go on to one year old, two years old, and so on, to find out where something went wrong, attempting to answer the question, 'Why am I ill?' When I closed my eyes, I saw, instead, an image of my mother, who was pregnant with me, in her doctor's office. She was overjoyed that the surgery which she had undergone to correct her tipped uterus had been successful and that she finally was pregnant, but the doctor was much more cautious than she. I 'heard' him telling my mother, "...because of this problem with your tipped uterus, I am afraid that this first baby could be born dead!' Aware of my mother's unbridled elation, he, apparently, was attempting to prepare her for this unfortunate probability. His ominous prediction dashed my mother's joy, a pattern which has been a familiar one for me, too."

Troya goes on describing her unusual experience. "Because I was in an altered state in meditation, I understood that the doctor's morose forecast was the cause of my being anorexic and bulimic – which are both passive forms of suicide. Subsequently, I was able to heal myself because I had discovered and experienced the root cause of my behavior and my illness."

Although it was very early in gestation, the tiny baby which was forming in the womb had felt or telepathically received or sensed in another way the belief of the doctor that she would be born dead, translating this morbid expectation into an unconscious life decision which concluded, "I am supposed to die." Such a decision would later function as a directive for how to live – or die.

As Troya was adjusting to a more normal life after the anorexia and bulimia, she discovered that she had malignant melanoma, one of the most virulent forms of cancer. Although she did undergo surgery for removal of the tumor at the base of her spine, she refused chemotherapy.

"If you take chemotherapy," her doctor had told her, "there is a good chance that you can live as long as six months."

Troya had a different perspective, however.

"As a nurse, I knew the state of chemotherapy at that time (1977) would not give me any life I could call really living," she states.

At dawn the next day, she called a taxi and furtively left the hospital without checking out.

"I was determined that I would spend any remaining time enjoying myself as best I could," Troya said, adding, "I began treatment and the study of homeopathy, and, through meditation, began to explore within myself why it was that in the midst of surviving the anorexia and bulimia, I should be staring death in the face once again.

"One day I realized that going back to my birth had given me the clue to begin healing the eating disorders," Troya continues, "so I decided to look back to that same time to try to heal the cancer also. Suddenly I was confronted with a very clear picture of what appeared to be a different historical period, a flashback to a time before my mother's pregnancy. It was like watching a movie in which I was also playing a part. The most amazing thing was that this flashback gave me the answer to the cause of the melanoma, of which I also later healed myself."

In 1984 – seven years after her miraculous healing – Troya traveled from her home in Amsterdam to Swanwick, England, for a spiritual psychology conference. One of the lectures she attended was given by Jon-Richard Turner, Director of the Institute for Whole-Self Discovery.

"I was astounded," Troya states, "when I heard him teaching exactly the method which I had used to heal myself of the anorexia, bulimia, and 'terminal' cancer. I then realized that I had known all along that someday I would teach what I had learned about healing. Until that day, I had the excuse that I did not know how, but Jon-Richard had already developed the method, so my excuse was smashed."

Several years later, after they were married, Jon-Richard asked Troya, "Have you ever asked your mother about the prenatal visit with her doctor and his expectation that the baby would be stillborn?"

"No," replied Troya, "I have not."

The next time they visited her parents, Troya questioned her mother and father, describing the bizarre information she had uncovered years earlier in her meditation.

"Did this happen?" she wanted to know.

"My father immediately denied it," chuckles Troya. "He said, 'Oh! No! We had a beautiful pregnancy.' But my mother just looked at me in astonishment and asked, 'How did you find out what the doctor told me? I never told anybody – not even your father!'" Her mother then validated that the scene in the doctor's office had occurred exactly as Troya had "seen" it in her meditation.

"So this was the basis of my believing that there was no place for me in the world," Troya explains.

Messages accepted by the unconscious are powerful maps which lay out the roads we travel – the patterns that are repeated – in our everyday lives. Because the repetitive occurrence of a pattern in life can be so painful, we have a powerful motivator to uncover the underlying cause. When we experience the suppressed emotion at the source of the pattern, the energy fueling those repetitions is exhausted and the pattern is much less likely to recur.

Troya has learned a great deal about herself and about life because of her pre-birth experience and the pattern it set in motion. In fact, this pattern has formed the basis of her life's work. She and Jon-Richard travel all over the world giving lectures and workshops to disseminate this vital information and to assist people in their own healing and transformation.

"The discovery that a baby is a fully conscious being, even in the womb," Troya points out, "re-emphasizes the great importance of everything the mother is doing while the baby is in utero (and the father, also, to a lesser extent). It seems that the baby is aware of everything its mother does, and uses this awareness to form lifelong conclusions."

Because the pre- and perinatal epoch is such a creative time, so often determining the events of a baby's life, Troya feels strongly about the significance of the entire period of gestation. Both she and Jon-Richard express the hope that people everywhere will become aware of these important discoveries and begin to provide the protection and concern for expectant mothers which will result in happier, healthier newborns.

"If women can be aware of what happens during pregnancy," Troya says, "they can be more aware of what the baby is going to deal with in life, and can support the child where it needs support."

Chapter 14

Rolf: Running Away

Another case involving strong patterns originating before birth was reported by John-Raphael Staude, Ph.D., former Professor of Sociology at the University of Pottsdam in Germany. Dr. Staude refers to this person as "the man who could not stop running."

A man in his mid-50s, Rolf was paranoid and deeply depressed, but his major challenge was a sense of uprootedness, of never having a home, even during the time when he had been married and had children. Although he was successful in his career, he suffered from low self esteem and was unable to stay in a close relationship of any kind, always feeling compelled to run away. Rolf exhibited classic puer etærnis (eternal boy) characteristics and was ambivalent and obsessive toward his mother and all the women he had pursued.

Rolf described to Dr. Staude how his mother, an artist from Boston, became pregnant during a passionate affair with a musician. Abortion was illegal at that time and was also condemned by her Roman Catholic religion. In shame and unable to tell her parents, she fled to New York City. This flight apparently encoded into Rolf's makeup the pattern of running away. When the young pregnant woman's shame became unbearable, she prevailed upon an unethical physician to deliver her baby two months early.

She then abandoned Rolf to an incubator for almost two months, then left him with other caretakers and visited him only rarely. When he was two, his mother married and legally adopted Rolf, but continued to delegate his upbringing to others.

When Rolf was 10, she took an extended trip to Europe, leaving him with his stepfather, who repeatedly abused him sexually. This abuse went on until Rolf was 12 and felt strong enough to forbid it. It was not until he was an adolescent that his mother told Rolf the truth about his parentage.

Rolf went on to attempt several gay relationships, but found them unsatisfactory. Pursuing women was equally unfulfilling. Rolf was simply incapable of transcending the innate debilitating patterns in relationship and sexuality experienced by his mother during his gestation. Even though his college studies revealed his brilliance, he was never able to translate his academic excellence into feelings of self-worth. He later married, but never felt intimately connected with his wife or children. When the marriage fell apart, Rolf started running.

He was attracted to Europe just as his mother had been and the flight pattern repeated itself there. A long history of prematurely-terminated therapies (just as his gestation had been prematurely terminated) left him deeply despairing of ever achieving any happiness or of having any roots.

Rolf met Dr. Staude at a workshop in Germany where he developed an interest in exploring his birth more deeply. With Dr. Staude's help, he was able to contact and describe very specific experiences and feelings of his mother during her passionate affair, her devastation on learning she was pregnant, the terror which precipitated her running away, the shame, fear, and scandal of having other people see her pregnant (knowing that she was an unmarried woman), the panic of having this unbearable thing growing in her belly, and the terrible conflict of having the baby prematurely removed from her belly to erase the shame.

Through ongoing therapy with Dr. Staude, Rolf was making significant progress, experiencing emotions he had never felt before. Regardless of these positive advances, however, at exactly seven months into the therapy (the same number of months he had spent in the womb), Rolf suddenly terminated the sessions – just as his own gestation had been terminated – and ran away to Spain.

Two years later, Dr. Staude received a letter from Rolf which included photographs showing Rolf's house and the woman with whom he had been sharing his life in the interim. Rolf confessed that he occasionally still experienced bouts of depression but was no longer running away as before. The key to Rolf's improvement was his discovery that the source of his patterns lay in his mother's emotions and behavior while he was in the womb. He recognized that the nearly overwhelming emotions he had frequently felt were really his mother's reactions to traumatic events in her life, which Rolf had been unconsciously and obsessively living out. With this new awareness, he was beginning to disconnect from her emotional patterns, and his own life was becoming more stable. He reported that he no longer felt like a square peg attempting to fit himself into a round hole.

Rolf's story adds weight to the hypothesis that not only is our physical body the synthesis of the genetic coding of our parents, but that there is also a merging in our psyche of their emotional and mental patterns as well.

Psychotherapist Barbara Findeisen is President of the Star Foundation and Vice President of the Association for Pre- and Perinatal Psychology and Health (APPPAH) in Geyserville, California. She lectures and teaches all over the world, working with individuals and groups. The next story comes from Barbara's work.

Chapter 15

Karl: Panic Attacks

Karl experienced panic on hearing the ordinary noise of dishes clattering and other kitchen sounds. His panic was so extreme that he was unable to go to a restaurant; he could only eat at home with his mother. His discomfort with these symptoms severely limited his life. In his early twenties, Karl wanted to go out on dates, but because dating usually entailed dining, his social life was at a standstill.

When Barbara Findeisen was working in Europe, Karl went to see her, hoping she could help him with his debilitating problem. Barbara questioned Karl about events in his childhood. He told her about a frightening event that occurred in the school cafeteria one day when he was nine years old. Amidst the sounds of dishes clattering and plates and cutlery being placed on stainless steel shelves, someone suddenly slammed a door. Karl experienced an acute panic attack, began screaming, ran out of the building, and hid in the woods.

"I felt certain that there must have been an earlier traumatic event," Barbara states, "so I helped Karl to relax and, using guided imagery, regressed him back to the time when he was in the womb. When he reached the time of five months in utero, Karl suddenly became agitated, frightened, and began screaming. He was clearly terrified of something."

Barbara reassured Karl, and made it safe for him to continue experiencing the terror. After some time, the intense panic exhausted itself and he became quiet. Later Karl described the experience which had so horrified him.

> My mother – five months pregnant with me – was standing at the kitchen sink, doing dishes. My father was outside the kitchen window and he had a shotgun in his hand. A cat had given birth to a litter of kittens and my father was shooting the kittens. One last kitten remained alive, partially hidden behind the others. My father bent forward to move the kitten so he could shoot it, too, but he leaned onto the gun and shot himself instead. He died right there. My mother became hysterical and ran out into the yard to see his bleeding, dying body slumped over on the ground.

After he re-experienced the grisly episode, Karl began to feel lighter than before – and more free of the old phobia. The regression allowed him to contact and empty the overwhelming, toxic emotions which had been poisoning his life since that traumatic moment four months before his birth.

Karl continued to improve. The therapy session occurred almost 20 years ago and Barbara states that Karl, now in his forties, is happily married and functioning normally in everyday life.

As Barbara related the above story to me, I remembered the time a few years earlier when I was working with a client, Dana, in a private session. Dana told me that, on a few occasions, she has had panic attacks. She said she once experienced an episode of panic while she was an inpatient in a mental health hospital.

"I was sitting down outside the nurses' station," she said, "when all of a sudden I had a panic attack. A nurse recognized what was happening and, standing over me, using a loud, commanding tone of voice, she kept saying to me, 'Go back to your room! Go back to your room!' Dana continued, explaining, "She was just trying to get me out of it."

I felt strongly that she would have been better served had the nurse known how to assist her to move *into* the panic, experiencing the underlying emotions and, thereby, exhausting them.

"Once you are able to feel the terror buried underneath," I told Dana, "these panic attacks will cease."

The remaining case studies are taken from my own work and research.

Chapter 16

Judith: Loneliness

"I want most of all to be able to love deeply," Judith wrote in her application for our two-week Intensive. "I want to marry, have a family and discover a purpose to which I can joyfully give my life."

A pretty, dark-haired young woman in her mid-30s, Judith has boundless energy and great artistic talent. A professor of theater at a large university, she was a Metropolitan Opera finalist a few years ago. She is friendly and eager to uncover and heal the patterns which have sabotaged her fondest dream so far – the joy of a happy family.

In order to have some time to think, Judith drove across the country alone to attend the workshop, held in Virginia that fall. She arrived feeling excited and full of anticipation. I observed her as she interacted with others; she was usually animated and jovial but, at times, a haze muted her eyes, like a cloud passing in front of the moon. I sensed that, deep down, she was very sad.

The puzzling contrast between her enthusiasm on one hand and her melancholy on the other played alternately in her personality. During our group songs and dances, for instance, Judith usually engaged wholeheartedly, seeming more like the song leader or choreographer than one of the group, but I watched as the life seemed to drain out of her at other, quieter times and wondered what thoughts had suddenly darkened her mind. Most of all I hoped to help her find herself and looked forward to the moment when she would feel ready to look into the causes underlying her complexity.

The opportunity presented itself early one morning after a day of silence. Judith raised her hand.

"Yes, Judith," I said.

"I would like to come up front and talk about some things that are bothering me," she said quietly but with precise diction.

"Good," I responded. "Come on up."

She stood, wearing a long denim skirt and red T-shirt, walked toward me, and sat down next to me.

She inhaled deeply, seeming apprehensive.

"Where do we start?" she asked, with feigned brightness.

"Why don't you talk about how you're feeling," I said.

"You...you mean right now?" she asked hesitantly.

"Ummhuh," I nodded.

Her eyes darted a look up at mine, as though checking to see if she was safe, then she looked down at her hands and sighed heavily.

"Sad," she said. "I feel really sad. But I'm also scared and excited and I feel almost too much energy in my body to sit still," she blurted out.

"What are you afraid of, Judith?" I asked her.

She thought for a few moments, then replied, "I'm afraid if I don't do it right, I'll lose my chance to work on this. I'm afraid I'll be too much of a bother and you won't want to help me anymore."

"What does 'doing it right' mean?" I asked.

She looked puzzled and her eyes shifted about as though looking for an answer. Finally, she looked back at me and said, "I don't know."

"Is that how it was when you were little, Judith?" I asked. "You had to 'get it right' but you never knew what 'getting it right' meant?"

She seemed relieved to have someone help her verbalize her feelings.

"Yes," she said slowly. "That's how it was." She glanced down again and I wondered if she were remembering an old painful scene.

"So, Judith," I said, "you don't have to get anything right here. Just be as honest as you can about how you feel. You can do that, can't you?" I asked.

"Yes," she answered, as a quick grin moved across her face.

"What's that about?" I asked.

"It's hard to believe," she said, "that you really want to know how I feel — that you want to take the time to hear about me."

"Well, it's true," I told her, adding, "You didn't get much attention when you were little, did you?"

"That's for sure," she said.

"Tell us about your early home life, Judith."

"Will it be all right if I get my notebook?" she asked.

"Of course," I replied.

She quickly moved to her seat, grabbed her notebook and came back to the chair beside me, arranging her skirt as she sat down. Red toenails and tan bare feet showed below a graceful hem.

"I was the third of five children, all close together – too close together," she said. "My mother never had any extra time, trying to take care of all of us."

"What is your earliest memory?" I asked.

She pondered for a few moments, then answered, "Lying in my crib and the room is almost dark, crying and crying, and no one comes."

Her deep sadness was almost palpable as she spoke these words.

"Then the door opened and he stuck his head in and yelled, then slammed the door again," she said, now sniffling a little.

"Who was he?" I asked.

"My father, I think."

"What else do you remember?"

"Mama and the five of us huddled in a room," she said. "She must have locked the door, 'cause he was outside, pounding and screaming at her to let him in — that he was gonna' kill us. I was so scared. We were all whimpering. I think Mama must have been scared, too. In a loud whisper, she just told us to hush and he'd go away."

"Then what, Judith?" I asked.

"I guess he went away. I don't remember any more about that either."

"Do you have any other memories of your father, Judith?" I asked her.

"No."

"Is he still alive?"

"Oh! No. He went off to prison when I was two," Judith replied. "Mama said later that he died in the prison mental hospital, that he was manic depressive."

"So after he went away, you all just lived with your Mama?"

"Yes."

"What was that like, Judith?" I asked.

"Pretty lonely. She had to work, and would be so tired when she came home. I wanted so much to be with her, but she never had much time."

"And you felt like a bother?" I asked.

She quickly looked up at me, as though wondering how I knew.

"Yes," she nodded. "I always felt like a bother. When I would get a few minutes with her, I always tried to be on my best behavior so she would approve of me. I thought maybe then she wouldn't leave so soon. But it never worked. She always left and got busy with something else."

"Do you think she knew how you felt, Judith?"

"No," she replied.

"And that's why it surprises you that we want to know how you feel?"

"I guess so. Yes." she replied.

"Judith," I told her, "the emotional deprivations you endured as a child were immense. No amount of rational thinking or discussion can heal these deep wounds."

"So is there *anything* I can do?" she asked, seeming suddenly smaller and even more frightened.

"Yes, and it's not necessarily easy to do."

"Oh! But I'll do *anything* to get better," she assured me.

"I believe that, Judith," I said. "You need to experience many emotions which have been suppressed for years, and the fear which you will feel will probably seem very scary to you. We can support you in the process, but it will take the greatest courage to confront this inner pain and allow it to surface; moving up through your consciousness would be another way to describe it. 'Allowing' rather than 'doing' is a more accurate way to think of the process. You can't make it happen – it will occur in its own time – yet it takes tremendous strength to remain open and vulnerable to the onslaught. This allowing is harder than "doing" sometimes.

She was listening intently, but I knew she didn't fully comprehend. None of us can comprehend this process until we have experienced it and realize it is safe to allow old suppressions to move through us and exhaust themselves.

"So what I want to ask of you, Judith," I said, "is this: during the next few days, whenever you feel afraid or sad or lonely, let yourself feel that feeling and make sure you are not holding your breath. Whether it occurs during a breathing session, while you are seated here in the classroom, when we are standing in a circle singing, while you're eating lunch, when you're brushing your teeth, or when you're getting ready for bed – whenever it is, allow your feelings to surface. It will seem uncomfortable and perhaps frightening, but you will get through it and some of this painful inner emotional charge will dissipate. You then will begin to feel much freer."

"So are we through for now?" she asked tentatively.

"Yes, we have to let this energy move in its own rhythm," I replied. "Sometimes this way of working can seem like it will take forever, but it's really much more efficient and thorough than any direct approach. You'll see," I told her.

"Can I have a hug?" she asked, childlike.

I stood and pulled her up beside me, embracing her tightly, kissing her hair, and feeling the need of a tiny girl to receive her mother's love. After a few moments, she drew away and gazed at me with tear-filled eyes.

"Thank you," she said, and walked quietly back to her place.

I observed her at odd moments over the course of the next few days as the Intensive proceeded, seeing her struggle with emotions which seemed to rise and fall of their own accord, feeling the deep sadness which seemed to envelop her.

During a breathwork session one Wednesday morning, she experienced powerful, chaotic emotions, alternately weeping grievously, then screaming angrily, pounding her fists on the carpet and occasionally kicking her feet as she lay on the floor under a blanket. She would then begin sobbing again, like a small child. I stayed close enough to encourage her, making sure she did not touch others nearby as she flailed about. As the emotional siege subsided, she was drenched in perspiration, her arms flopped lifelessly at her sides. Occasionally she whimpered, like a frightened puppy. I murmured softly, reassuring her that she was safe and not alone. Suddenly feeling chilled, she pulled the blanket up under her chin, burrowed under the covers and fell asleep. A well-earned rest, I knew.

This experience was the first of several such cathartic releases Judith experienced during the two weeks we had together. Toward the end of the Intensive, I suggested to her that she consider beginning regular psychotherapy to help her continue her healing and to build new, healthier structures into the shaky underpinnings of her life.

At this writing, more than three years later, I am happy to report that Judith continues with her therapy and is growing more and more whole. She telephones to discuss things with me from time to time, and has matured and found a strength which is much greater than any she has experienced before. When I think about her now, I see Judith's physical beauty and artistic talent — which have always been her glowing attributes — but I also recognize that she is becoming a strong, grownup, sincere woman who is engaging in life with increasing integrity. Having learned to respond lovingly to herself and her feelings, she has become much more alive in a deeply authentic way. I have little doubt that a happy, loving relationship awaits her.

Chapter 17

Jan: Addiction, Scandal, and Shame

Jan lives in Atlanta. Although she now is a psychotherapist with a thriving private practice, for many years she searched in vain for a sense of well-being, regularly abusing alcohol and a variety of other drugs.

"I never felt like I belonged anywhere," Jan says. I felt like my life was an accident, like I somehow was not supposed to be here. That made no sense but it didn't change the way I felt. It didn't seem like I fit in anywhere," she continues. I was never comfortable, but I felt less uncomfortable when I drank or did drugs.

"After I went through treatment for drug and alcohol addiction, I realized that the reason I felt less uncomfortable when I drank or did drugs was because I felt less period. The substances numbed my body, my senses, and my feelings."

Jan and I first met quite by accident (if there is any such thing!) at a bookstore in her area. I was busy with a booksigning when she approached me, gazed directly into my eyes and asked, "Who *are* you?"

I introduced myself and we chatted for a few moments.

"I came in looking for a book," she said, "but now I can't remember the name of it." She hesitated for a moment, then added sincerely, "I think maybe I came in here, though, because I was supposed to meet *you.*"

I have experienced unusual first encounters before, and accepted this meeting as a happy synchronicity. Jan left the bookstore with a copy of "Secrets"* in her hand, then returned half an hour later to ask about the workshop I was conducting the following weekend. Jan changed her schedule and came to the workshop.

"That weekend changed my life," Jan now says, "for since that time, several years ago, my whole life has been renewed."

A few months later, Jan attended a two-week Intensive and, together, we were able to identify the pattern which had caused so much pain and discomfort in her life.

Jan's mother and father were 45 and 50 years old, respectively, when they discovered that another child was on the way. They already had two sons, nearly grown, and did not want another child. The pregnancy was considered an "accident." Even by today's liberal standards, the mid-40s are late for bearing children, but in 1953, it was almost unheard of. Her mother was from a small southern town and had been raised in a prim and proper manner; to be involved in a situation which she deemed inappropriate in any way was humiliating to her. She felt embarrassed and ashamed that she was pregnant. To make matters worse, Jan's father, a successful insurance salesman, was teased mercilessly by co-workers and colleagues about the impending birth. Both of the expectant parents felt mortified to be the brunt of so much laughter and ridicule.

---

*My first book

When Jan was born, her parents fell in love with their baby girl, but the life of a human being begins long before its birth, and the messages Jan received throughout her gestation left her with feelings of rejection, scandal, shame, and disconnection, which she later tried desperately to escape through alcohol and drugs.

As discussed earlier, Dr. David B. Cheek conducted extensive research into intrauterine awareness. In papers published in the Pre- and Perinatal Psychology Journal,* he clearly states that an unborn child "... is alarmed by maternal distress. The fetus registers the mother's feelings as signs of rejection, even abandonment. The damage of such interpretation will not fade and can be greatly augmented by later traumas." His report concludes: "It is important in therapy to bring this repressed information into conscious awareness."

When the repressed material surfaced during the Intensive, Jan consciously felt the sadness, shame, hurt, and anger which had marked her time in the womb. Once these emotions were fully experienced, she began to feel centered and peacefully happy – *for the first time in her life.*

Her own life has been resurrected. She is now engaged in a happy, peaceful, personal relationship and she utilizes her transformational experience in her busy psychotherapeutic practice, watching for patterns which show up in her clients' lives as a way to better serve them.

---

*Winter 1992 issue.

Chapter 18

Joe: Fear of Intimacy and Time Cycle Pattern

Relating closely, vulnerably, and trustingly with another human being – relating *intimately* – is an experience most people long for, yet one which is somewhat rare. Whether with a lover, our spouse, our parents, our children, or our closest friend, we often feel more comfortable if we hold back a little. Selflessly loving another is a state about which we all seem to dream, but "looking out for number one" is also a very popular idea. This dilemma of reaching out for another yet holding ourselves back is very common, for countless thousands of people are afraid of intimacy.

This pattern may be experienced in many different forms. One way is for an individual to approach intimacy with yearning and eager anticipation only to reject it at the last moment. Of course, we usually do not *consciously realize* that we are rejecting intimacy – we have become angry or critical for reasons which seem *justified* to our conscious minds – but if we are honest in our self-contemplation, we may recognize this behavior in our own lives.

Fear of intimacy is illustrated in the following case study of a man named Joe.

Joe's wife, Brenda, began to notice this puzzling pattern after she and Joe had been married for about a year.

"No matter how well Joe and I were getting along," she said, "he would blow up about something every four or five days. At first, I thought I was somehow causing his angry outbursts, and began to be more introspective. In spite of all my efforts, however, the upsets continued. I began to feel desperate and wondered if our marriage would survive."

"Whenever I tried to talk to Joe about the blowups," she said, "he became agitated, usually blamed me, and refused to talk. My attempts to discuss the blowups only created more blowups."

Brenda began to keep track of this pattern on a calendar.

"When I finally mentioned to Joe that I was observing an almost predictable cycle to his pattern, he thought I was crazy. He was convinced that he always became conflictive only because of something I did or failed to do."

One day, however, a letter arrived from Joe's mother, spontaneously mentioning some of the details surrounding Joe's birth and infancy. This in itself was puzzling, since he had not requested this information.

"Joe read the letter first," said Brenda, "and seeing nothing noteworthy, passed it on to me. I was awestruck when I read it, for I could see the origin of the painful pattern which had been sabotaging our marriage. Joe was the fourth child and the only son. His parents and the whole family were elated to have a little boy. His mother lovingly breast fed her precious infant, watching over him with great devotion. But when Joe was five days old, she developed phlebitis and was hospitalized, leaving the baby for several months to be fed from a bottle and cared for by a hired nursemaid.

"When I read about Joe's early experiences as a newborn, I suddenly understood the deep loss he had suffered. Losing his mother was the greatest pain he could have endured. Now, as an adult, an infantile and unconscious part of Joe was afraid that another such trauma was imminent – *every five days!*"

The pattern had begun soon after Joe and Brenda had married, mirroring the initial painful experience soon after his birth. We can understand the behavior and motivation of the grown-up man by understanding what really happened to the newborn:

> As a tiny infant, Joe was nurtured at his mother's breast, fulfilling his most fundamental need. Suddenly, at five days old, the source of nurturing disappeared – the greatest loss a baby can suffer – and he was frightened and enraged. Now, upon entering an intimate, adult relationship, which is necessarily characterized by vulnerability, that old need for nurturing re-surfaces and, along with it, the irrational fear that it will again be taken away. The rage of the five-day-old infant surges up and is directed in a desperate lashing out at the nurturer – in this case, his wife, Brenda.

Since Joe and Brenda have become aware of this pattern and its cause, they are better able to manage when it appears. Joe has found a qualified therapist for help in dealing with these issues and also has learned to breathe and feel the overpowering emotions as they arise, observing his own thoughts and feelings, and overcoming his tendency to rage at Brenda.

"I have discovered," Joe now says, "that underneath the anger, I am terrified that I might lose Brenda – and I don't know what I would do if that happened. When I remember to ask myself what I am experiencing, I usually can breathe and allow myself to feel the fear. It passes pretty quickly and I soon feel safer. I then don't want to yell at anybody, especially Brenda."

Chapter 19

Mary: Fear and Panic

Mike and Mary had been married for more than fifteen years when Mike was sent to Australia for a month-long business trip. Mary, as usual, stayed behind in England. Although she never liked being separated from him, travel had always been a part of his job and she had managed somehow, keeping busy with the children and tending to housework. This was the longest separation ever required, however, and the first time he had gone so far away.

"Soon after his departure," Mary says, "I began to have debilitating headaches and felt so afraid I could not even leave the house."

Mary's anxiety quickly turned into panic.

"I felt frozen, fearful of everything, and became almost completely incapacitated," Mary stated.

As soon as possible, Mike returned home.

"I was quite shocked at Mary's condition," he said. "It felt to me as though she had withdrawn very far inside herself."

To Mary, the world apparently seemed much too unsafe to re-enter. Mike felt confused and overwhelmed, but spent as much time with her as his job would allow, holding her, reassuring her, and hoping her symptoms would soon subside. Her depression and agoraphobia, however, seemed to become worse.

"Over the next two years," Mary said, "I received some help and healing through my spiritual faith. This calmed my anxiety somewhat, allowing me to function, but the real underlying fear has never left me."

Twelve years later, Mary and Mike applied to attend our Intensive two-week workshop, the purpose of which is to identify and clear troublesome patterns. Mary was hopeful that she would be able to face and resolve this old terror. Midway through the Intensive, she felt that she was ready to work on her patterns of fear and panic. At the same time, however, she faced a new dilemma.

"I want to work on this," Mary said, "but I feel afraid of exposing my fear in front of the group. At the same time, I am even more afraid that I will *fail* to do it and wind up going home just as stuck as when I came."

As I reviewed the required written materials which Mary had submitted before the Intensive, it seemed clear to me that she felt overwhelmed about her plight.

"This fear has dominated my life," she had written. "Getting rid of it is my Number One goal from this Intensive. The thought of leaving home and traveling all the way to America also scares me, but I am determined to rid myself of this terrible fear."

Aware of her shyness, I had her sit on the floor next to me at the front of the room as we began her work.

"Go back to the beginning of this problem, Mary," I asked her softly.

Immediately, Mary's eyes closed and her head sagged forward. I realized that, although we had begun the process only thirty seconds before, Mary was already in an altered state of consciousness. This was an amazing experience for me in that I had never seen a person enter such a state so rapidly and with almost no preparation. I wondered if Mary had felt so frightened that she had "retreated" to the safety of the subconscious, perhaps as a kind of defense.

"Where are you, Mary?" I asked.

She replied so softly that I could not hear what she said.

"A little louder, Mary. Where?" I asked again.

"I'm out in the road in front of our house," she said in a voice that sounded more like a three-year-old girl than the striking adult woman seated next to me.

In my mind's eye, I imagined a village road in the south of England. A few months earlier when visiting the Hampshire countryside, I had walked along such a road, passing quaint cottages, some with thatched roofs, and colorful, fragrant flower gardens bordering the narrow way. Now, inwardly, I was watching this terrified little girl, out in the road all by herself.

"What are you doing in the road, Mary?" I asked softly.

"I can't find my mum. I dunno where my mum is," Mary whispered, sobbing once, then catching her breath a little, choking back tears. "I woke up and got out of bed and went to find her but there was nobody home."

"That's really scary, isn't it?" I empathized.

"Um-huh. I don't know what to do," she sniffled.

Mary's voice was still so quiet I strained to understand her words. Clearly she was regressed to a very young age and felt alone and vulnerable without her mother. It was important to make sure that she felt safe and protected during this process. I knew she was probably feeling as vulnerable now as she had felt at three years old and that whatever occurred here, in the workshop, could have a strong impact on her. Such a time is a remarkable opportunity for reprogramming, for it is as though an old inner tape recording has been rewound to an earlier traumatic event and, with a compassionate and skilled facilitator, new, healthier material can be recorded, resolving the painful pattern.

Mike and the other participants had moved up so that they now were seated on the floor in a quiet, cozy circle, completely attentive to Mary's process. They, too, were straining to hear.

"Now what's happening?" I asked, my arm around her protectingly.

"I feel so terrified out here in the road in my nightie," she said quietly. "I don't know what to do."

I carefully observed her eyes, moving beneath her closed eyelids. I suspected that she was reviewing some old scene.

"I go next door to the neighbor's house. Maybe my mum is there."

"And is she there, Mary?"

"No," she cried, her voice breaking with sobs.

"Now what's happening?" I asked again.

"The lady is taking me in," Mary said.

"Is she saying something to you, Mary?" I asked.

"She is surprised to see me. She squats down and talks to me."

"What is she saying?"

"She's saying, 'Oh! My! What's happening? Where's your mum?'" Mary went on. "I tell her I can't find my mum. She says, 'It's okay. You can stay with me 'til we find your mum.'"

"How does that feel," I asked Mary.

"Better, but I want my mum," she said, again breaking into sobs.

Mary's head hung forward, her shiny, dark hair almost completely hiding her eyes. The fright of the little girl was palpable in the workshop room. I looked up at the other men and women. They sat silently, their eyes soft and compassionate, keeping a vigil as the little girl went through the ordeal which was so frightening to her.

"What's happening now, Mary?" I asked.

"The lady looks out the window and says my mum's come home. She takes me by the hand and we walk back to my house. Mum is surprised to see me there; she thought I was still asleep in my bed."

Realizing that this was the perfect moment to reprogram the old pattern, I embraced Mary gently but securely, as her mother might have when she was little, soothing her. Mary slumped into my arms, her eyes still closed.

"You were so frightened, my little one," I murmured as though I were her mother with a tiny girl in my arms. "I am so sorry I wasn't here. I never thought you would wake up. I'm sorry you were afraid. But you're safe now and everything's okay," I reassured her.

"I didn't know where you were, mummy. I was so afraid," Mary sobbed.

"I know," I said, rocking her back and forth, kissing her forehead, holding her closely, and softly brushing her hair away. The tender and loving touch of a mother is so vitally important to a small child.

Over and over, I promised to always be there for her and repeatedly told her how much I loved her and how beautiful she was to me. Time and again I whispered reassurance that I would not leave her again – that she was so very important to me. She lay in my arms as though safe with her mum at last. Finally, a relaxed, radiant smile appeared and her face looked as soft as a child's.

Silently, the rest of the class left the room for a break, and I stayed on the floor with Mary for another half hour, holding her, stroking her brow and reassuring her. I then moved away a bit, laid her head on a pillow, cushioned and surrounded her body with more pillows, wrapped her in a blanket, and left her to sleep for a while.

The next day Mary looked ten years younger. Always attractive, she looked strikingly beautiful as she shared with the class that she felt free of her awful fear for the first time in her conscious memory.

"I don't ever remember feeling like this before," she said. "That fear was always with me. I feel like I can live my life now without the nagging fear that I'll suddenly be left bereft. I just hope this lasts."

"This new freedom is the result of bringing up and feeling the buried, churning fear which has been suppressed all these years," I explained.

"Did this memory just surface yesterday or did you always remember this event from long ago?" I asked her.

"Oh! I remembered it all along," Mary said, "and somehow I always believed that traumatic experience might be responsible for my panic attacks and paralyzing fear. But yesterday was different because I actually felt the fear for the first time. Before, I had the memory but had never fully experienced the terror."

A few months later Mary called from England to report that she continues to feel free and that her life has really changed.

"Whenever I feel any of that old emotion, now, I just breathe and observe my feelings," she said. "Usually, within a few minutes, I feel safer again. Now I know I don't have to collapse into fear whenever this feeling arises; I now can get through it safely and pretty quickly. Wow! What a difference!"

"This is how you become really free," I told her. "You don't have to wait until you are completely empty of that old fear, because you realize that you can breathe through any emotion. If you continue to deal with each experience this way, seeing it as an opportunity for more clearing, you will become freer and freer."

Chapter 20

Deborah: Abandonment and Time Cycle Pattern

Deborah had been married and divorced twice and had had three other relationships which she termed "serious," when, at thirty-seven years old, she began to recognize a pattern. In each case she was convinced in the beginning that the new relationship would be a happy, enduring one and, for a while, everything would go well. But her relationships never lasted. An early boyfriend joined the Peace Corps and later wrote a letter ending their relationship. One of her fiancés broke off with Deborah because he had met another woman. Her first husband was killed in an automobile accident. In another situation, it was Deborah who terminated the relationship. Regardless of the circumstances, however, none of them lasted much beyond the second anniversary.

Questions about her early life led to the discovery that Deborah's home was a happy one until, when she was two years old, her father was drafted into the Army and sent to Korea. They never saw him again, for he was killed in battle.

"What can perpetuate such a pattern?" we may wonder. Could it be that, when approaching the point where other relationships have ended, Deborah's subconscious mind might become filled with fear?

And even though she might be consciously unaware of this, could it, nonetheless, be sensed by the man and experienced as a rebuff?

Feeling abused, Deborah sometimes states, "Men abandon me!" Could it be that males in her life sense this as a subtle but powerful directive to leave? Does her belief actually comprise an angry command which insists, "Men: Abandon me!" Whatever the explanation may be, Deborah's increased awareness of this dynamic pattern of energy was the first step in changing it.

"But, Christina," she objected as we discussed this during a private session, "I have known all along that my father left for the army when I was two, and this pattern persists anyway. How can I change it so this doesn't continue to happen? I want so much to get married and stay married – and have children before I get too old."

Her eyes filled with tears. I could see and feel her sadness and desperate frustration.

"It is true, Deborah, that you have known intellectually about the loss of your father," I responded, "but the way to change this pattern – the *only* way – is to *feel* the feelings which are locked away deep inside you. That little 2-year-old girl was not able to understand the events which occurred at that young age and those feelings were too terrifying and painful to experience. You would have been overwhelmed had you not somehow shut them out, so they were suppressed. We could say they are held in storage in your subconscious mind."

Deborah saw a glimmer of hope; she certainly *wanted* to believe that something could be done to really change things in her life.

"How does this happen in the first place?" she asked. "I don't understand."

"You really don't have to understand in order to heal this pattern," I told her. "You just have to experience the feelings you were unable to experience before. The reason they are in storage in your subconscious is because you have never felt them. Once you feel them, you will have more understanding. Right now, understanding would amount to nothing more than information which you've known all along. Information, alone, does not heal. *Experience* heals."

She was listening attentively, clearly wanting to know more.

"Those feelings you suppressed so long ago will retain their power and cause events to occur in your life – this pattern of abandonment by one man after another, for instance – until you feel them. At that point, you will be left with knowledge of the event which set this pattern in motion, but by experiencing the feelings, you will cease to have the emotional pain. Just as an automobile will not move if all its gasoline has been exhausted, there will be no emotional pain left in your subconscious to fuel the repetition of the painful pattern. As a matter of fact, this suppression will no longer exist in your subconscious mind, for you will have succeeded in bringing it into your conscious awareness. A thing that is taken out of storage is no longer stored. Something that is conscious is no longer subconscious."

"But what do I have to do in order to *feel* my feelings?" Deborah wanted to know. "I didn't know I hadn't *already* felt them. I've experienced so much pain over this all these years. Wouldn't that have drained the energy, as you say?"

"I know you've suffered, Deborah," I responded, "but the key to healing this pattern is in feeling and *draining* these emotions as opposed to feeling and *suffering* from these emotions. Two subtle but very important elements make all the difference between whether 'draining' or 'suffering' occurs. Those elements are:

1) Feel the feelings. You must allow yourself to feel your original two-year-old emotions, accepting that these strong

feelings are contained within you instead of focusing on the grown-up situation in which you are involved. Stated differently, it is important for you to recognize and acknowledge that these original painful feelings are still inside you and understand that this is why they are coming up. They are not being *caused* by the (current) departure of a man from your life, even though this is what is *triggering* the old, buried emotion.

In actuality, the man who is abandoning you is serving you in a very important way by leaving (though you probably won't see it that way), because the pain of yet another abandonment stimulates your stored pain (the pain which has been inside since you were two years old), in order to make itself felt. That is a blessing – though in disguise, for sure – because it gives you an opportunity to feel and exhaust the pain once and for all. Once you feel it, you have healed it.

2) "I will show you how to feel these emotions by breathing. I don't want to go into an explanation about breathing right now," I told her. "There'll be time for that later. For the moment, it's enough to know that the breathing you will learn to utilize for this purpose is natural, gentle, safe, and a very supportive step in the healing process."

Deborah wanted to get started right away. If she is courageous enough to finally feel the fear, sadness, and anger which are bound up inside her, she will see for herself that this simple process works. She will feel a difference in herself; she won't need anyone else to tell her that a change has occurred. Furthermore, that difference will manifest in her day-to-day life as she engages in another relationship. With this healing work behind her, I expect that she will experience a happier outcome in her next relationship.

Section III

Change Your Patterns

Chapter 21

Do Your Patterns Contain a Hidden Message?

Is there an effective way to change the unwanted patterns in our lives? To simplify this challenge, it can be instructive to examine the basic structure of patterns.

1. We experience an event which we perceive as threatening, frightening, painful, or uncomfortable in one way or another. This event might have occurred before, during, or after birth. Whether or not our perception is accurate, it is on the basis of this perception that a compelling decision is made.

2. Because this decision resides at the unconscious level, it has great power to create or attract additional, similar experiences, and quickly becomes triggered whenever a similar emotion arises. This may sometimes result from a present-time event which is similar to the original causative one. We then act or react on the basis of the *earlier* decision. This action or reaction reinforces and perpetuates the pattern.

3. Unless the pattern is brought to conscious awareness and acknowledged, it will be repeated again and again throughout the lifetime.

4. Awareness alone, however, will not change a pattern. Additionally, there must be a desire to change it, and that desire must be or become stronger than the need to hold onto the pattern. In other words, when the pain, fear, or other emotion connected to the earlier event and concurrent decision was very

strong, the desire to change the resulting pattern must be even stronger.

5. To change a pattern, therefore, it is necessary, first, to become aware that it exists, second, to have a strong desire to change it and, third, to undertake the inner work which will change it.

What, Specifically, is Meant by "Inner Work?"

The evidence from my work and research, as well as that of other professionals, verifies that the way to profound and enduring healing is this:

> In one way or another, we must fully experience – we must fully *feel* – suppressed emotions surrounding trauma we endured, whether that trauma occurred before, during, or after birth. Once a hurtful past event is uncovered and the unfelt emotions experienced, the unconscious dynamic which set up the pattern in the first place becomes resolved and ceases to affect our lives.
>
> As these suppressed emotions are being felt, it is important to keep breathing. Holding the breath may cause all or part of the emotion to remain suppressed.

Briefly stated, doing "inner work" means to bring unconscious material to conscious awareness and to experience and exhaust the attendant emotions.

How Does "Inner Work" Work?

The experiencing and emptying of suppressed emotions could be compared to vomiting. As a way to regain and maintain health, the human body automatically expels food which is either contaminated or which the body cannot digest. Vomiting gets rid of foreign elements which would otherwise sicken the body. In the process, a person "experiences" the toxic material as the stomach is emptied. Once emptied, the body can regain its health and equilibrium.

Why, then, when we are nauseated and feeling miserable, do we often resist vomiting? Quite likely, it is because we are hoping to avoid the unpleasant experience altogether, just as we usually hope to escape the unfortunate consequences of the patterns in our life. Apparently, it is natural to resist. Usually, however, we do eventually throw up and then, afterwards, feel much better.

We understand the vomiting process in the physical body, however, we generally have little or no comprehension that we sometimes need to empty in an emotional way also. As can be seen in the case studies presented in this book, we ingest psychological and emotional material which creates discomfort and sets up patterns in our lives. Unless emptied, these emotional toxins can lead to emotional and mental illness. Because the dynamics of emotional pathology are so common, however – most people are neurotic to some degree – we have generally lost touch with what it means to be fully functioning, whole human beings. Many people would find it difficult to describe the characteristics of a whole person, one who might be called "self-actualized" or "self-realized." Just as vomiting clears the way for natural healing of the physical body, the experiencing and releasing of emotional toxins clears the way for natural healing and alignment of mind and spirit.

Once this alignment begins to take place, a person realizes that his potential for joy, for creativity, for happiness, for high achievement, and for peaceful, successful living is far greater than he ever imagined. In short, unless and until we are able to eliminate the emotional elements which are sickening to our bodies, minds, and spirits, we cannot begin to live the magnificent lives of which we are capable.

It is the birthright of every human being to enjoy these gifts of life, and the way back to health is often much quicker and easier than we expect. It is vitally important to realize that if you do not like your life the way it is, you can change it!

From this perspective, an undesirable life pattern can be viewed as a gift, for it points the way to the inner work we must do in order to attain wholeness. If the pattern is ignored, we lose a priceless opportunity to grow.

The next chapter lays out seven steps to help you recognize your own patterns.

Chapter 23

How to Recognize Your Patterns: The Seven Steps

Some patterns may be positive, as we saw in the case of Debbie. Others may be harmless and of only passing interest. However, some can be very undesirable – even destructive. These are usually the patterns we very much want to change. The first key to making such a change lies in recognizing the pattern. The guidelines in this chapter will facilitate this recognition.

There are two primary ways to become aware of a pattern that is operating in your life:

1. You may begin to experience pain from the pattern. Sometimes the pain is so strong that the pattern will become obvious, as illustrated in many of the cases described in earlier chapters. This route is the slow way, however, and is filled with suffering; the individual learns only from painful experience.
2. You can consciously look for these patterns in your life.

Clearly, the second is a more positive approach. Following are the seven steps to follow in your search for the patterns in your life:

1. List the Events of Your Life

Beginning around the time of your conception and moving forward, make a chronological list of experiences which may have impacted you emotionally, whether they are pleasant or unpleasant.

The earliest life events – conception, gestation, birth, and early infancy – are usually the most significant in terms of setting up recurring life patterns, although events occurring later can be important, too. Even though you probably do not have conscious memories of the earliest times, it is important to gather all the information you can. Noteworthy events might include your mother's and/or father's response when they discovered they were going to have a baby, situations in their relationship with each other during pregnancy or immediately following your birth which were either very happy or very upsetting, moving from one residence to another (either while you were in the womb and/or when you were a child), a sudden upturn or downturn in the family business and/or money matters, the birth of a sibling, a death in the family, a separation or divorce, your experience of starting pre-school or kindergarten, going away to school or camp, illnesses, accidents, an experience of feeling abandoned, abused, ashamed, humiliated, and/or excessively disciplined, or a positive experience of being acknowledged, supported, understood, accepted, and/or unconditionally loved, and any other experience which in some way made you feel very good or very bad.

Clearly, those events occurring before your birth would not have involved you directly, but would have been experienced by your parents, primarily your mother. Ask your mother or other close relatives to talk about their life and the family during this time period. Ask for information about your infancy and early childhood, about which you may have little memory. Listen as objectively as possible. If you feel defensive or emotional as you listen and learn about your history, make special note of it. Such a feeling may be a clue that this event significantly impacted you.

Collect this information as it relates to important periods of your life, specifically looking for emotional times and significant events. Look for peak experiences, asking yourself, "What was going on around this time? What was I feeling?" Critical times and events might include the following:

1. Conception
2. Gestation
3. Birth
4. Early infancy
5. Babyhood
6. Toddler Years
7. Pre-School
8. Kindergarten
9. Grades 1 through 4
10. Grades 5 through 8
11. Junior High School and adolescence
12. High School or Preparatory School and teenage years
13. Post High School and college years
14. Work / career experience
15. Engagement and/or marriage
16. The birth of your child / children
17. Serious illnesses
18. Deaths
19. Break-ups in relationships – your parents or your own
20. Successes and victories
21. Failures
22. Disappointments
23. Rejections
24. Moments / experiences of spiritual awakening
25. Reaching a critical crossroads in any area of life
26. And so forth.

List these events on paper, organizing them in three columns, as shown in the following example of a woman named Sheila:

Date	Event	Emotional Effect
Dec. 1957	Mother discovers she is pregnant.	Mother is elated!
Mar.1958	Mom's father dies	Mother feels sad, guilty
Jul.21,1959	My birth date - Mother is sedated	Mom is glad but groggy
Nov.1961	My sister, Kathy, was born	Felt jealous of Kathy, and abandoned by mom
Sep.1964	Started kindergarten	Felt timid, shy. Wanted to stay home with mom.
Oct.1967	Molested by the older brother of a school chum while at her house.	Felt terrified and also naughty. Afraid to tell mom or anyone else. From then on, I felt anxious and unsafe.
Oct.1967	Wet the bed a few times after the molestation. Mom scolded me and called me a "baby."	Felt angry that Mom didn't understand (though I never told her what was bothering me). Felt humiliated for wetting the bed and being shamed by mom. Felt unaccepted by mom and thought there was something wrong with me.

...Continue on throughout life...

2. Examine Different Aspects of Your Life

Review the above information and examine it as it pertains to the following aspects of your life:

A. Relationships. What was the nature of the relationship between you and your parent(s), between you and other(s), between your mother and father, between your parent(s) and your sibling(s), between your parent(s) and other people. Were your parents loyal and supportive to one another and to the family, or were they self-absorbed and self-serving?

B. Communication. Was it possible for you to discuss your ideas, questions, and fears with your parent(s)? When you felt upset, anxious, or worried, was it possible to talk about your feelings with them? Were those feelings generally heard and understood? Was there a sense that things in the family were generally open and above board, or were there secrets or subjects which could not be discussed?

C. Spirituality and/or Religion. Describe the general religious and/or spiritual atmosphere – or lack of it – which characterized your early life. Was there a belief in God? If so, was God thought of as a loving presence, or as fearful, exacting, and threatening?

D. Discipline. When you and/or your sibling(s) were disciplined, did your parent(s) behave in a loving, mature manner that helped you learn needed lessons, or were you disciplined in seemingly unfair and excessive ways? Did your parent(s) ever apologize for making mistakes, or was it necessary to pretend that they did not make mistakes?

E. Attitudes. What was the attitude of your family toward people and life? Did your parent(s) generally have a high regard for themselves, their children, and other people? Did your parent(s) generally have a trusting and positive attitude toward life and other people, or were they suspicious, distrusting, and fearful?

F. Integrity, Morality, and Values. Describe your parents and early family in terms of honesty and forthrightness. Was love and respect evident in your parent(s) lives? Were their lives examples of the values and principles they espoused? Were they loving and supportive, or were they critical, demanding, and/or overbearing?

G. Sexuality. Describe the attitudes of your parent(s), church, community, and the people of your neighborhood or region regarding sexuality. Was sexuality viewed as a natural, healthy function when expressed appropriately and lovingly or was it seen as being somehow unclean? Were you able to ask questions about sexuality or was this a subject which was not to be mentioned?

H. Education. Describe the educational level of your parent(s) and family. What was their attitude toward their own education? What was their attitude toward your education? Were they helpful and supportive of you in pursuing your education?

As you proceed with gathering this information, you may find that more and more memories begin to surface, and your earlier list will become more detailed and complete.

3. Write Your Emotional Autobiography

Drawing from the information you have gathered, write your emotional autobiography as a narrative story. Write it in such a way that a reader would become acquainted with your parents, the circumstances into which you were born, and your early home life, including the challenges, limitations, privileges, opportunities, values, beliefs, fears, and attitudes which characterized your family and your childhood. Be sure to include any event which had an emotional impact upon you, whether or not it seemed outwardly remarkable to anyone else and regardless of whether any other family member was emotionally impacted by that particular event. For instance, a move to a different house or neighborhood may have been very upsetting to you, whereas your sister or brother may have welcomed the change. Be sure to include all pertinent information. If an event or experience seemed important to you, then it was important, period.

As a further help in completing your emotional autobiography, gather together photographs of yourself, your parents, your early family, friends, family pets, and any others which might be included in a pictorial section. Pay special attention to any emotional change which might be seen in yourself from one photograph to another.

For instance, you may appear to be a happy, carefree child at four years old, but sad and withdrawn at six.

It is probably best not to look for patterns immediately. First focus on collecting information about your life and writing it down. When you have completed your emotional autobiography, put it away for a while, perhaps for several weeks. Allow the ideas, thoughts, and feelings which may have arisen during this discovery process to percolate within you.

4. Create Silence and Solitude to Review Your Life

After a few weeks or even months of "percolation" time, set aside a time when you can be alone and silent for at least half a day, (a full day is better), and re-read your emotional autobiography all in one sitting. A retreat in a natural, peaceful setting is ideal. As a second option, you might consider going to a hotel or motel for one day all alone, communicating to significant others that you do not wish to be contacted except in the case of an emergency. If neither of these ideas is practical, perhaps you can arrange to have a quiet day alone at home. During this time, it is important that you refrain from watching television, listening to the radio, listening to recorded music of any kind, answering the phone, or talking to anyone. Take this time to be alone and silent. If you live in a situation where other people may observe you during this time, wear a sticker on your lapel reading "In Silence." Adults will usually respect this. If it is absolutely essential that you communicate, do so by writing a note.

During Intensive workshops, I often include a 24-hour period of silence. When this assignment is initially given, some people resist it, feeling a sense of dread. By the time the silence is completed, however, most people describe it as one of the most valuable experiences of their lives. Silence is a marvelous and very effective way to calm the mind and become more aware of recalcitrant thoughts. Some people avoid being alone, perhaps unconsciously fearing emotions which threaten to arise. Such resistance is sometimes an indication that pertinent information or memories are about to surface from the subconscious mind, providing priceless insights into your innermost workings. Perseverance with your period of silence can pay a big dividend in increased self-awareness.

The emotional autobiography and silence exercises may stimulate long forgotten memories. It seems that, once we sincerely want to remember, the subconscious mind begins to surrender more and more memories from its rich storehouse.

5. Look for Patterns

As you re-read your emotional autobiography, begin to look for recurring patterns, either as events or as emotions. One event may appear to be very different from another, for instance, but may involve the same emotions.

The mind is often resistant to looking at things in a new way, so you may initially tend to dismiss the possibility that a pattern exists. As you become more objective, however, you will probably discover that there are discernible patterns which recur predictably in your life.

Look, for instance, for a common denominator among several events which otherwise may seem unrelated. An upsetting event that occurred at two years old may recur every two years, and it also may tend to recur in multiples of two, i.e., every four or six years, as well. A disturbing occurrence when your mother was five months pregnant with you might set up a pattern of anxiety or upset which recurs every five months or five years. In some instances, a traumatic prenatal event may give rise to a generalized feeling of anxiety, fear, anger, or sadness.

In one case, a 32-year-old psychobiologist named Matthew felt so guilty that he believed he did not deserve happiness. Although he longed to marry and have a family, because of his pervasive guilt, he was unable to sustain an intimate relationship with a woman. As a result of inner work, it was discovered that the origin of Matthew's misery occurred when his maternal grandfather died while Matthew was in the womb. Matthew unconsciously blamed himself for his grandfather's death. Of course, this makes no rational sense – how could an unborn child cause the death of his grandfather? – but this feeling of guilt, though deeply unconscious, was ruining Matthew's life and relationships.

6. Discover Early Decisions Which May Be Affecting Your Life

As you re-read your emotional autobiography, try to recall when you might have drawn a conclusion or made a decision about some facet of your life. The following true story may be helpful in understanding how a decision or conclusion can be made, the effects it may have in a life, and patterns which may result from that decision:

> A 10-year-old boy was trampled by a team of horses. The badly-injured child, in excruciating pain and covered with blood, was rushed to his nearby home. When his mother opened the door and saw her son's mangled body, she was horrified and became hysterical. The boy thought that his mother was very angry. (It is important to realize that whether or not she actually was angry is less important than his perception of her emotional state.) The intense energy which he observed in his mother was very frightening to the traumatized young lad. He felt extremely vulnerable, he was in agony, and he desperately needed reassurance and loving compassion from his mother. In her upset state, she was unable to respond to his need. He thought that she, instead, was angry. Worse, he thought she was angry *with him* for getting hurt in the first place. At this point, he made an immediate decision to never again trust a woman.*
>
> Although this decision was, at least momentarily, a conscious one, he very quickly forgot the emotional and mental process which had transpired so quickly. Thus, the decision became buried in his subconscious mind.
>
> Little did he realize that this decision meant that, later in

*It is possible that similar interactions and misperceptions had occurred between this boy and his mother regarding other, less traumatic experiences throughout his life, however, it was this intense experience which seemed to him to be the moment when he made this important, life-determining decision.

his life, he would be unable to experience real intimacy in a healthy, loving relationship with a woman. For many years, when he found himself in a situation wherein a state of intimacy with a female was approached, he immediately felt threatened, vulnerable, and afraid, although he did his best to block these uncomfortable feelings. He would then withdraw, either emotionally or physically or both. Of course, he was unaware of this behavior. In his view, he simply responded defensively whenever he began to feel (unconsciously) vulnerable or intimate with a woman. In fact, he was not consciously aware of feeling vulnerable. He always justified his behavior, blaming the woman for causing the split.

For many years, he walked out on one woman after another. Far less uncomfortable than confronting his own inner fears, leaving was his only conscious option at the time.

When he was 50 years old, however, he met a woman about whom he cared very deeply. For the first time in his life, emotional withdrawal and physical departure did not relieve his discomfort. Instead, the fear of losing her created even greater anguish. He was caught in a dilemma: experience the pain of life without his lady or stay with her and confront his fears. Finally forced to face the frightening shadows which had remained hidden within him for so long, he was able to recognize and acknowledge his pattern of behavior. He *felt* the old, unconscious emotions, suppressed since childhood. Over a period of a few years, his inner work led him to change the pattern and experience a truly satisfying, intimate relationship and marriage built not on fear and control, but on mutual trust and unconditional love.

7. Be Open to Receiving Information From Your Dreams

Finally, pay careful attention to your dreams, for they can provide important keys to events which strongly impacted you at a much earlier time, and which may still have a great affect on your life. A recurring dream, in particular, is immensely significant and usually contains critical information that the subconscious mind is attempting to communicate to the conscious mind.

As an example, I had a terrifying nightmare which began when I was about four years old, and recurred often until I was well into my twenties. When I was finally able to work on the dream, with the support of a skilled facilitator, I became aware that my dream had to do with experiences *at the time of my conception!* This was a powerful, liberating experience for me. After the dream work, my life changed for the better in many ways. I felt an enormous infilling of peace and love and power. This recurring dream and my inner work with it were very important elements in my psycho-spiritual transformation.*

This experience reinforced my personal awareness that, as Carl G. Jung often stated, dreams can provide a direct link to the subconscious mind and to the source of a pattern. For this reason, it is important to learn how to be receptive to information which may come to you in the form of dreams. While an entire volume could be devoted to this fascinating subject, for the purpose of this chapter, a few guidelines must suffice. They are as follows:

A. As soon as possible, write your dreams in a special notebook, including as much detail as you remember. Record the date of each dream.

B. Pay attention to the *feelings* you experienced in the dream and record these in your dream journal. Sometimes we experience feelings in the dream state that we have been blocking in our waking life. The content of a dream may not make sense, but the emotions may hold information for you, or they may be feelings you need to allow yourself to experience.

C. Refrain from discussing your dreams with others. The dream world is sacred territory. The exception to this is to share your dreams with one trusted friend or counselor who will listen attentively and avoid giving advice or otherwise infringing upon you. It is important to be aware that the most accurate

*I have written in detail about this dream in my book "Secrets."

interpretation of a dream usually comes from the dreamer. In general it is best to avoid accepting the interpretations of your dreams from other people or from books. While there are some images which often seem to have a universal meaning – water in a dream, for instance, often refers to the unconscious or to emotions – it is much better to ask yourself repeatedly what meaning a certain dream image has for *you.* Then wait for the answer from within. It may come as a sudden flash of awareness at the least expected moment. The exception to this is to explore the dream with a qualified person such as a Jungian analyst.

D. After you have been keeping a dream journal for a while, go back over your dreams from time to time. Sometimes, in review, you will understand a dream which initially seemed incomprehensible or confusing.

Summary

The first step in changing a pattern is to become aware of its existence. Until you recognize that a pattern is operating in your life, you will experience it again and again. In order to begin identifying your patterns, follow the guidelines suggested below:

1. Make a list of significant events in your life; create a chart, listing the date, event, and emotional effect of each event.
2. Examine different aspects of your life, including relationships, communications, spirituality and/or religion, discipline, attitudes, integrity, morality, values, sexuality, and education.
3. Write your emotional autobiography and include childhood photographs; then put it all away and let it "percolate" for a few weeks or months.
4. Review your emotional autobiography in silence and solitude, watching for patterns, and allowing feelings to surface.
5. Search for patterns in events and/or in emotions.
   (a) Discover times when you made significant decisions.
   (b) Be open to receiving information from your dreams.

Chapter 23

How to Change Your Patterns

Once we begin to recognize patterns in our lives, we usually find at least one we truly want to change. As illustrated in many of the preceding stories, such changes often come about quite rapidly with effective inner work, but it is vitally important to realize that cognitive awareness, alone, is usually not sufficient to result in these changes. Patterns do not originate at the conscious, cognitive level and they seldom, if ever, can be *changed* at the conscious, cognitive level. Instead, we must usually re-visit the subconscious level where powerful, suppressed emotions fuel our patterns and their repetitions. Just as a weed can only be eradicated by digging down beneath the soil and destroying its whole root, we must find a way to interact with our own subconscious mind to remove all traces of the contaminated emotions which keep our patterns alive.

> In order to access that part of ourselves which knows about the event(s) that formed a pattern, we must, in one way or another, contact that part and experience the suppressed emotions stored since that event.
>
> *Christina Thomas-Fraser*

Various techniques may work to help us gain this access to the subconscious mind, including spontaneous experiences like my own re-experience of conception, referred to in an earlier chapter.

Spontaneous experiences are often filled with powerful, spiritual energy and are exceedingly effective in changing patterns. During a spontaneous experience, a person usually requires little or no support except to be allowed to have the experience. When a person has a spontaneous experience, either in a private session or during a workshop, I usually stay nearby, in silence and empathy, prepared to cover the person with a blanket, if necessary, or provide any other support which seems appropriate, while being very careful not to interfere with the experience or distract the person in any way. Spontaneous experiences are somewhat rare, however, because the conscious mind usually screens out both subconscious and superconscious memories, at least during waking hours. Furthermore, because we have no way of knowing if or when it may occur, relying solely on spontaneous experience also leaves us relatively powerless to change our patterns and take control of our lives.

Fortunately, there are other effective approaches which are also practical in that they can be utilized intentionally to help us contact the subconscious realm. For this purpose, for example, Dr. Cheek used clinical hypnotherapy. Barbara Findeisen utilizes guided imagery. Dr. Emerson employs hypnotherapy as well as rebirthing, a form of connected breathing. In his work with Rolf, Dr. Staude used a combination of bioenergetics or body work, gestalt therapy, and psychosynthesis. Jon-Richard and Troya Turner work with what they term Prebirth Memory Therapy. While I use guided imagery and other helpful approaches, the primary method I employ to help people contact the subconscious to experience and release emotional suppressions is BodhiSoul© Breathwork, a form of connected breathing.

Because this book is about patterns and is not intended to be a lengthy description of breathwork or any other healing technology, a brief explanation of this effective and transformative tool must suffice.

1. What is Connected Breathing?

Connected breathing is a safe and gentle system of breathing wherein the inhalation is connected to the exhalation in the following way:

The inhalation is one steady, somewhat vigorous, and active movement. During the exhalation, the breath is let out in an inactive, relaxed way. Just as in deep and restful sleep, the exhalation during BodhiSoul© Breathwork should last only about half as long as the inhalation. It is, nonetheless, important to passively allow all the air to leave the lungs. This method of breathing – actively drawing air into the lungs on the relatively long inhalation and passively allowing it to leave the lungs on the shorter exhalation – will assist the breather to clear away suppressions, and more fully experience the physical body, personality, and emotions. It clears away accumulations of physical, psychological, and emotional energy stored since and sometimes even prior to conception.

The origin of most emotional difficulties lies in prenatal, perinatal, and early childhood experiences. To a greater extent than most of us imagine, our lives are impacted by powerful emotions which accompanied the unfortunate, hurtful, interpersonal interactions we endured at early stages of life – emotions which we found too painful to experience and, therefore, automatically suppressed.

Many of us carry excess baggage in the form of these unconscious suppressions, although we have little or no memory or conscious awareness of them. When we are able to experience the emotions bound up in these suppressions, they release, leaving us feeling lighter and freer.

Through connected breathing, we become aware of – and experience – the unconscious energy patterns which have long been stored in the subconscious. Experiencing the energy releases those patterns. The heart then opens, allowing us to feel more love and peace. Connected breathing brings spirit into the body in a way that cleans, nourishes, and rejuvenates the body, mind, and emotions. Just as clearing a passageway of accumulated baggage will allow a door at the end of a corridor to be opened for use, the clearing of emotional suppressions through connected breathing facilitates the opening of an inner door to the ecstatic energy of the soul.

2. How Does BodhiSoul© Breathwork Differ from Rebirthing?

Some forms of connected breathing and/or rebirthing are similar to BodhiSoul© Breathwork, while others are markedly different both in theory and application. A well-qualified BodhiSoul© Breathwork Practitioner or rebirther will support a breather's experience without unnecessarily interfering in the process. Some rebirthers, however, may stop a breather whenever s/he begins to experience an emotion, asking the breather to think about or analyze what is going on in order to discuss it there and then. It is critically important to note that this is an intrusion into the precious territory of the breather's unconscious and should never be done. Just as it would be counterproductive to awaken a sleeping person so that s/he could tell you about a dream (which you've just interrupted), it is a serious trespass to intrude into the sacred domain of another person's unconscious. For this and other reasons, when I train BodhiSoul© Breathwork Practitioners, I always caution them to undersupport rather than oversupport.

One of the reasons that BodhiSoul© Breathwork is so powerful is its high regard for the unconscious wisdom of the breather. (In some cases, if a breathworker consciously knew what was going on in the internal experience of that breather, s/he might try to help – and would likely only get in the way or halt the breather's process altogether.) A breathworker or rebirther must be free of his or her own egoistic agenda in order to stay out of the breather's way.

One example of this comes to mind. I was conducting a workshop and instructed the participants that we would participate in a "paired group" breathwork session. The participants counted off by As and Bs and paired up; the "A" person would breathe first and the "B" person would function in a supportive capacity. One woman asked to take the role of the breathwork support person first, stating that she was a trained rebirther. She was paired with a woman named Stella.

Stella started breathing and soon began to feel an immense amount of energy – joy and love – and inwardly saw a beautiful, radiant light at the mid-spot between the eyebrows, which is the location of the Ajna Chakra, a powerful, spiritual center. Just as she felt she was approaching this magnificent light, which she later described as more attractive than anything she had ever before felt, her partner tapped her on the shoulder, asking, "What's going on? Tell me what you are experiencing." This abrupt interruption broke Stella's sublime state and effectively disrupted the transcendant moment. Unfortunately, I learned about the incident too late to save the session for Stella, who was very frustrated that the "rebirther" had interfered with her experience.

Almost weeping with disappointment, Stella told me later, "Just as I was approaching *heaven,* she tapped me on the shoulder, interrupting the most wonderful event of my life. I have been seeking this experience all my life and she robbed me of it!"

Needless to say, Stella felt irritated. I stayed in touch with her afterward, hoping to hear that she subsequently had reached this state again. It was more than a year later that she did experience this long-awaited inner union.

With this and other similar examples in mind, I carefully instruct BodhiSoul© Breathwork facilitator trainees never to interfere with the natural process of a breather.

3. How Does Connected Breathing Work?

Because breathing is a normal experience, people often ask, "How is it that breathing can bring about such profound and transformative changes in a person's life?" Most of us find it hard to believe that simply breathing in a gentle way, connecting inhalations to exhalations, can produce the results described here. But, even though it is automatic and we take it for granted, the breath is a much more vital and complex force than most of us realize.

Consider, for instance, that human beings can live for weeks without food and for days without water, but will survive for only a few minutes without breath.* It is clear that under ordinary conditions, in order for the soul to maintain its residence in a physical body, the essential link of the breath must continue. Let us further examine this phenomenon.

*The exception to this is the extraordinary "breathless state " of sabikalpa samadhi.

When an astronaut leaves the protective environment of his spaceship, a tether must tie him to the orbiting capsule or he will float away, marooned in space. While a child is in the womb, he floats in amniotic fluid with no awareness of himself as a separate being. Indeed he is *not* yet separate, being inside his mother. When the baby is born, the breath is the tether linking his body and mind with his divine soul. In order to survive outside the natural energy state of the womb, this bond of the breath must be maintained.

In the womb a baby does not have to breathe because it receives all nutrients, including oxygen, through the umbilical cord. Within a short time after birth, however, the newborn must begin to breathe through its own lungs and breathing must then continue throughout life. If it is interrupted for too long, the soul will leave the body and the person will die,* for the breath, itself, is the link between the soul and the body.

The English word for breathing – inspiration – reminds us of this divine link. The Latin root word "spire" (as in "spirit") appears repeatedly in words like "respiration," reminding us of the connection between breath and soul. This is the reason that breathing is emphasized as an important element in the quest for enlightenment in many Eastern disciplines. The Old Testament affirms this vivifying link as well: "...And He breathed into his nostrils the breath of life and man became a living soul."**

It is evident, then, that breath and spirit are inextricably linked. When any change is made in the breathing process, it quickly and directly alters awareness. It is well known by most meditators that the fastest way to change our consciousness is to change our breathing. No matter how excited and restless we may be, for instance, if we begin breathing in a calm, quiet fashion, we will soon feel calmer and quieter. Conversely, if we calm and quiet the mind, we will discover

---

*The exception to this is the extraordinary "breathless state" of samadhi experienced during very deep meditation.

**Genesis 2:7

that our breathing will slow down. It works both ways: breathing affects consciousness and consciousness affects breathing.

In addition, breathing, instead of holding the breath, facilitates the movement and release of suppressed emotions. I have experienced this many times and have observed it in the thousands of people with whom I have worked. Marion Woodman, Jungian analyst and author of numerous books, corroborates this same discovery as follows:

> *"Breath is the secret of letting go. It won't allow me to lock into one thing. Breath reinforces images or allows them to change. It allows me to be receptive, flowing, balanced."*
>
> *Marion Woodman, "Pregnant Virgin"*[1]

4. Finding a BodhiSoul© Breathwork Practitioner or Rebirther:

A group of dedicated individuals from different parts of the world have been trained as BodhiSoul© Breathwork Practitioners.[2] In addition, some rebirthers, trained by other organizations, are wonderful, supportive facilitators. It is, of course, very important to be careful when selecting any support person. Certification alone, or the lack of it, should not be the only criterion. It is important to feel safe, comfortable, and trusting of him or her. If you feel any discomfort, it is best to talk frankly about that discomfort. You may want to ask questions about his or her training, how he or she feels about his or her clients, how he or she knows when a breathing session is over, and whether or not he or she loves his or her work. (If the facilitator's primary reason for choosing this profession is other than dedication and love for it, I would suggest that you find someone else!)

While breathing skills are important, even more important is the personal and spiritual integrity of the breathworker. I cannot overemphasize this point. The energy field of the breathworker often seems to be a vitally significant element in the quality of the breather's experience.

---

[1]Used with Marion Woodman's permission.

[2]For more information, please refer to the Order Form at the back of the book.

Using Breathwork Independently

While professional support is essential in the beginning, after we have cleared some of our emotional suppressions and changed the patterns which resulted therefrom, we usually will be able to use breathwork independently to manage any distress and upset as they arise. Reaching this stage is very liberating and empowering.

5. Treat Yourself Gently

After we have experienced the emptying which occurs in BodhiSoul© Breathwork, we arrive at a vitally important stage in the clearing process. We may feel refreshed, cleansed, and vibrantly alive. We often feel we have been born to a new life and, just as when we were babies, we may feel delicate, needing protection and tender care for a while. As adults, it is essential that we learn to provide this nurturing for ourselves. The vomiting metaphor will serve again to make this clearer.

After vomiting, the body does not immediately regain its balance. In the beginning, it is dehydrated and there is an electrolyte imbalance. For this reason, it is important at this sensitive time to select foods and beverages very carefully, avoiding those which might irritate, overstimulate, or otherwise upset the body. We would not want to eat pizza, for instance, and even the thought of such a spicy food would probably be unappealing. The body knows what it needs and, although we can often ignore its signals with impunity, after vomiting, we are usually more able and willing to heed its needs. Instead of pizza, we might choose a mild broth or some other soothing and easily digestible food.

In the same way, after the emptying which occurs in BodhiSoul© Breathwork, it is important to be very selective about the elements and vibrations to which we expose ourselves. It is better to avoid gross or low vibrations such as occur in a horror or action movie or even in the daily news. It is vitally important to take in only clean, soothing, and inspiring thoughts. We can gently restore our balance through meditation, visualization, affirmation, the reading of uplifting books, and keeping company with wholesome and like-minded people. This is an important, ongoing part of the process.

In addition, it may be helpful for some to seek a qualified professional for psychotherapy. This can aid in sorting out thoughts and attitudes and can provide a time to safely discuss feelings and responses to situations in our lives. Here, again, it is necessary to select carefully. Some professionals, although licensed, have done little or no work on clearing their own patterns. It is essential to find a therapist who has done his or her own healing work.*

I have practiced meditation since 1971 and have met many other people who meditate. I have observed that, even after years of meditation, many people are still plagued with unwanted life patterns. This was true for me, as well. For a long time, I was puzzled by this.

After ten years as a meditator, I found breathwork, and then I understood that meditation, strictly speaking, serves the supreme purpose of providing a way to connect directly to a very high spiritual plane, with the intention of shutting off the awareness of the senses, turning off the mind, and disconnecting from the emotions. Meditation is a way to lift up and away from the body, mind, and emotions. Although some emotional and psychological clearing does occur due to a general raising of consciousness, it is *not* the primary purpose of meditation to clear the body, mind, and emotions. It is important to realize that *this is not a failure of meditation.* Rather it points to the fact that this clearing is not the intended goal of meditation. A meditator still has to do the everyday work of growing psychologically and emotionally; meditation does not remove this responsibility.

While this work of clearing is often accomplished much more quickly than might be expected, it is important to remember that this work may still take time. For the most part, our patterns were formed many years ago and have been reinforced again and again throughout our lives. It is unrealistic to expect such deeply ingrained habits to completely disappear overnight.

---

*For more information, please refer to the Chapter entitled "Connected Breathing/Rebirthing" in my book "Secrets."

The clearing of physical, psychological, and emotional blockages and the resulting authenticity and connection with the joy of the soul are the goal of BodhiSoul© Breathwork and other forms of connected breathing – *and they accomplish this.* *An added bonus for meditators is that, as these blockages clear, meditation deepens and movement toward self-actualization and self-realization accelerates.

In the next chapter I have included instruction for using two additional tools which will help to reinforce and integrate these changes.

---

*Included here are a few testimonials from individuals who have experienced these benefits:

"I knew the details of my birth and childhood at a cognitive level. I also knew that these early events had resulted in the painful patterns in my life, but until the BodhiSoul© Breathwork with Christina, I had felt none of the feelings – the necessary ingredient for healing. I experienced such profound joy, love, and peace that words cannot describe it and this wholeness has never left me. I have never since felt empty or alone."
Sharon D.Gary, Psychotherapist, USA

"The BodhiSoul© Breathwork process opened up a whole new world for me – a world whose existence I had denied for a long time. And the final, most rewarding and beautiful experience was the coming together of the child, soul, and body. I don't have words to describe this gift!" Samantha White, England

"The peace, clarity, and happiness I discovered as a result of BodhiSoul© Breathwork have stayed with me, even during tax season. I cannot describe the joy I feel every morning when I wake up." Mark Huffman, Certified Public Accountant, USA

"BodhiSoul© Breathwork has brought about so many wonderful changes in my life."
Bernhard Rytz, Businessman, Switzerland

"Because of BodhiSoul© Breathwork, I am releasing the pain of my past. I have always felt trapped inside, but right now, with tears streaming down my face, I feel such love! I am so grateful for this experience." Liz da Silva, England

"Co-workers ask if I've had a brain transplant because now I am happy most of the time. And, in a job which is very dangerous, I am much more in control of my stress levels."
Alan Gee, Oil Refinery Worker, England

Chapter 24

Reinforce the Changes in Your Life

Just as breathwork provides a specific technology with clear guidelines to help us empty suppressions of emotional energy and bring about changes in our patterns, we can reinforce these changes with two additional practices. They are Visualization and Affirmation.

Visualization

Visualization is the process of using our thoughts and imagination in conjunction with our feelings to create the results we want in our lives. We might think of visualization as intense, focused concentration.

When we focus our undivided attention on a specific result, this focus helps to bring about the manifestation of that result. These eyes of ours are not just simple lenses, but have the power to call into being an experience or a thing which has been dormant in the matrix of what physicist David Bohm called the "implicate order" of the great unmanifested universe.

Numerous books about visualization* are available, many of them presenting scientific evidence of the effectiveness of visualization for improving health, increasing success, enhancing relationships, expanding creativity, and solving problems. Visualization is used in

---

*See Recommended Reading Section.

the medical field, usually referred to as "biofeedback," wherein the brain wave levels of a person are measured with electronic equipment while he visualizes a certain image or focuses on a change of temperature in his hand. It has been shown to be effective in lowering blood pressure and in bringing about the improvement or complete healing of many diseases. Famous oncologist Dr. Bernard Siegel uses visualization with cancer patients. Dr. Carl O. Simonton includes visualization as a necessary element in his work with so-called "terminally ill" patients, often with remarkable results. And Dr. Willis Harman, President of the Institute of Noetic Sciences and former Professor of Electrical Engineering at Stanford University, said:

> "Within a couple of decades, it will be widely accepted that inner conscious awareness is a cause of reality in the universe and in our daily lives."

When most human beings think, they see pictures or images in what might be called "the mind's eye" or "the screen of the mind." How often have we heard someone say, "I can see you doing this." Clearly, we use visual imagery much of the time, however, this alone does not constitute scientific visualization and usually, therefore, does not have much power to bring about changes. When *does* visual imagery become creative and dynamic? When *does* it cause things to happen? When *does* it bring about changes in our lives? How *can* we learn to utilize this tool in specific ways to change our lives?

The answer to all these questions is that *strong feelings must accompany the focused visualization.* As stated above, it is our natural ability as human beings to form fundamental creative energy into the objects and conditions we vividly and passionately imagine. It is as though we are the potter, while the energy is the clay. Combining our thoughts and images with intense feelings forms the pliant clay into our life experiences, both tangible and intangible. In the same way that our choice of television channels determines what we will experience from among the wide variety of programs available, we use our ability to create when, through visualization, we bring a desired experience into manifestation – literally causing it to happen.

It is important to realize that visualization can be used in destructive as well as constructive ways. When we fearfully imagine a painful experience, it is as though we are magnetically attracting that experience. Regardless of what our conscious intention is, the fact that we strongly and fearfully imagine it is enough to create it. I recently heard an example of destructive visualization that will graphically illustrate this point.

Jim, the man mentioned in an earlier chapter who was run over by a team of horses when he was 10 years old, told me that a few weeks before his accident he had seen a cowboy with a cast on his leg and walking with crutches. In Jim's small prairie town, the cowboys who rode in the rodeos appeared flamboyant and exciting to Jim and the other schoolboys. Because of his injuries, the cowboy received a lot of attention and sympathy and he seemed like a hero to young Jim.

"Every night as I was going to sleep," Jim told me, *"I would imagine that I had a cast on my leg,* thinking this would mean that I, too, was heroic and would receives lots of attention and admiration from others."

His nightly imaginings went on for several weeks until an accident actually occurred and he was trampled by a team of horses. Jim's injuries were so extensive that his doctors initially thought he would never walk again. He spent weeks in traction and was then placed in a body cast for several months.

As is clearly illustrated by Jim's dramatic story, not only can visualization bring about healthy desires, but it can result in negative and unhealthy ones as well, *whether or not we are aware that we are thereby creating our future experiences!*

Once we realize how powerfully effective visualization can be as a tool for creating our lives, we are usually eager to begin putting it to work. Because visualization is a scientific tool, however, it is important to follow certain rules when applying it. There are five essential elements of scientific visualization.

1. Feelings. We must deeply desire what we are visualizing. Feelings are like a magnet which attracts our visualized objects to us. The energy of the universe responds when we feel very strongly about our visual images.

2. Relaxation. To effectively use visualization to bring about changes in our lives, it helps to relax deeply. Attempting to practice visualization in a state of tension will minimize results. Even though it may seem paradoxical, when we are relaxed, our powers of focus and concentration are greatly enhanced.

3. Clarity. When we know exactly what we want, we are far more likely to achieve it. Clarity leads to power. The better we can see our thought picture, the more effective our visualization will be. It is helpful to see colors, shapes, sizes, and dimensions as vividly as possible, filling in the details exactly as we would if we were placing an order for an item, realizing that we will receive exactly what we describe.

4. Acceptance. We must be willing to accept our result when it arrives. Although it makes no logical sense to the conscious mind, we sometimes have difficulty allowing ourselves to experience a positive result if we have a thought or a belief, even if subconscious, that it has come too easily or that we do not deserve it.

5. "As If" Attitude. We must reinforce our visualization by adopting the feeling and attitude that we already have the result we desire. Although this is often not easy to do, it is essential if we are to succeed in using visualization to bring about the desired changes. We might ask ourselves how we will feel when this is already a reality in our lives and begin to experience those feelings right now, knowing that we are thereby placing an order for more of those same feelings. We must play our day-to-day roles in the world while simultaneously holding onto our new thought pictures and good feelings *as if they were already a reality.* In this way, we will create this new reality.

We can use visualization successfully whether or not we consider ourselves visual persons for it is not essential to "see" things at the inner level the same way we see with our physical eyes. The inner imaging may be experienced as a kinesthetic sensation or it may feel more like a "connection" with the thing we are visualizing. The vital ingredient is focused, heartfelt, attention on what we are creating in our thoughts.

When using visualization to reinforce changes in a specific pattern, it will be helpful to read the Healing Visualization suggested for that pattern,* then spend some time constructing a specific, heart-felt, detailed visual image to help make that change a reality.

Affirmations

In addition to using scientific visualization, we can augment positive changes in our lives by the use of scientific affirmations.

The quality of our lives is created to a significant extent by the quality of our communication with others and, especially, with ourselves. How we talk to ourselves about the events of our lives often determines our point of view and, thus, our experience. For example, a relocation to another city can be experienced in two vastly different ways. One person might resist the move, lamenting, "This move is robbing me of all my close friends." Another person might say, "How exciting! This move will give me the opportunity to meet many new people, and they may be as close as my old friends!" The attitude of the latter person is a much more positive one. Meeting him or her certainly would be a different experience than meeting the first one. So we see that it is very important to be aware of what we say, both to ourselves and to others.

An affirmation is a powerful, positive statement. It means, literally, "to make firm." The use of affirmations is a vital element in the process of reinforcing changes in our lives.

Conscious affirmations, repeated with focused mental attention and emotional conviction, cause a response in our bodies and minds through our subconscious minds. The continued repetition of

*See The List of Patterns in Section IV.

affirmations reaches beyond the subconscious to the superconscious mind, which is a veritable storehouse of power. When an affirmation reaches the superconscious mind, it releases a current of energy which brings about changes in the pathways in our brains, causing permanent positive changes in our thoughts.

Affirmations are a potent, effective way of replacing old, unproductive thoughts and beliefs with positive new ones. Once we pinpoint a negative thought or belief, we can compose an affirmation which reflects the new thought or belief we wish to have. Our focus will be on this new thought or belief. It is counterproductive to resist an old thought. Instead, it is more effective to simply focus on the new one. If we want to empty the muddy sediment out of a pitcher of water, we can accomplish this quickly by continually pouring in fresh, clear water. A well-scripted affirmation works like that clear water.

To work effectively with affirmations, it is helpful to understand the way our minds function. Let us use computers as an example. If two computers are designed and constructed the same way, they will perform the same way, *provided they are programmed the same way.* Our patterns, accompanied by many thoughts and beliefs, make up our programming. If we had been born to parents of a different culture who spoke a different language with different belief systems, we would have different thoughts and beliefs – *and we would have different patterns* – than those we presently have.

Beliefs and thoughts are a necessary part of life. They serve a good purpose, functioning as scaffolding during the construction period of our formative years. But when we reach maturity, it is natural and useful to retire those specific thoughts and beliefs which no longer support the building of our lives. Without the necessary inner work, however, the beliefs become a prison, limiting rather than expanding our life experience.

Affirmations may be repeated silently, spoken aloud, or written, including using a typewriter or word processor. They also may be sung or used as chants. Chanting is most effective when it begins at an audible volume and becomes more and more quiet, until it echoes as a silent chant deep within.

A vital component in using affirmations successfully is repetitive practice, long enough and deeply enough to arouse strong belief.

Any positive statement can be used as an affirmation. As you work to change your patterns, you can use the Healing Affirmation(s) suggested for a particular pattern* or compose your own. When constructing your own affirmations, keep in mind the following five elements:

1. An affirmation is a statement of a desired outcome. It describes a condition or a state we want to experience.
2. An affirmation must be practiced with feeling. Its potency is proportionate to the degree to which we hunger for the desired outcome.
3. An affirmation must be stated in the first person singular. It works only when it relates to you. For instance, you may want your son to achieve a high score in a math examination and script a statement such as, "My son will achieve an excellent score in the math exam." But this does not qualify as an affirmation because you have no control over how he will perform. What you *can* control, however, is how you deal with your son's performance. Having done all you can to support him in preparing for the examination, you might affirm the following: "I am at peace with whatever score my son receives on the math exam." This attitude will enable you to retain your peace of mind. In addition, there is another benefit: it will take a burden from your son's shoulders. He will feel more accepted and loved by you for who he is, not for how he performs.
4. An affirmation must be a positive statement. The subconscious mind does not understand a negative statement or command and, consequently, eliminates any negative term. The phrase, "I will not think negative thoughts," for example, will be heard by the subconscious mind as, "I will think negative thoughts." The "not" is dropped because it has no meaning to the subconscious. The desired outcome could be phrased positively as, "I am thinking only positive thoughts."

---

*See Healing Affirmations in The List of Patterns in Sectiom IV.

5. An affirmation must be stated in the *present* tense. The subconscious hears only in the present, so "I will" means "later." This negates the affirmation. One of the keys to the effectiveness of an affirmation is the dynamic tension created as a result of the discrepancy between the desired outcome and the present state. That tension creates energy. Without this energy, there will be no change in your beliefs and no movement toward your desired state of being. In the examples given above, for instance, note the careful wording: "I *am* at peace with whatever score my son receives on the math exam" and "I *am* thinking only positive thoughts."

When to Practice:

While affirmations can be practiced at any time with benefit, they have the greatest effectiveness during the periods immediately preceding and following sleep. During this time, we are very relaxed and the brain naturally registers the powerfully-creative alpha brain wave level. Repeating a positive affirmation while falling asleep brings about a deeper, more regenerative rest than if you go to sleep with scattered, worrisome thoughts whirling chaotically in your mind, and immediately repeating your affirmation on awakening will help to set the course of your day in a more positive way.

The practices of visualization and affirmation often lead to an interest in meditation, which can further amplify positive changes and result in a deeper experience of peace. Books on meditation, visualization and affirmations are listed in the Recommended Reading section.

Chapter 25

Putting It All To Work in Your Life

In summary, the following steps will help to heal and change old, troublesome patterns and bring a new, higher level of balance and harmony:

I. Recognize the patterns in your life
   A. List the events of your life in chronological order
   B. Examine different aspects of your life
   C. Write your emotional autobiography
   D. Create silence and solitude and review your life
   E. Search for patterns in events and/or in emotions:

      1. Discover early decisions which may be affecting your life, and
      2. Be open to receiving information from your dreams.

II. When you have identified a specific pattern, look it up in The List of Patterns in Section IV.

III. In a state of relaxation, practice either the recommended Healing Visualization or make up your own visualization.

IV. Practice the recommended Healing Affirmation repeatedly throughout the day.

V. Find a BodhiSoul© Breathwork Practitioner or other professional support person to help you access your subconscious mind and release emotional suppressions.*

*For assistance in finding a BodhiSoul© Breathwork Practitioner, please see the Order Form at the back of this book.

Chapter 26

Conclusion

The Unexpected Gift

Most of us become willing to do the work necessary to change the patterns in our lives either to be free of pain and/or to attain greater happiness. These are both understandable and worthwhile goals, but there is another, additional, often surprising reward, one which we usually are able to glimpse only after the work is done.

Throughout the ages, enlightened people have taught that the profound, underlying purpose of human life is to discover and reconnect consciously with the true Self. Emotional suppressions and the resultant negative patterns they cause are obstacles on the road to this Self-discovery.

By clearing suppressions and changing these patterns, we begin living more authentically. We have more clarity about what we want to achieve in life and are less afraid to undertake the risks necessary to reach those achievements. We are motivated principally by values which originate from within, while respecting others who may have different motivations and different values.

When we reach this place, we are integrated and mature, able to allow our various roles to revolve around us instead of becoming us. Instead of shifting our personality to meet the demands of each role we play, we have a strong, constant center which allows us to transcend all of the roles. We have a much higher level of integrity. We are able to interact with others without feeling threatened or needing to be like them. Rather than reacting to people and circumstances, we are more likely to consciously choose our behavior without inner conflict.

This wholeness and authenticity is the unexpected gift received by all who rise to the challenge of this work.

Section IV

The List of Patterns

How to Use The List of Patterns

The following list provides examples of many patterns which may manifest in our lives, together with some of their possible origins. Although a few desirable patterns are included, the primary purpose of this list is to deal with those patterns we wish to change.

As you refer to the list, you may become more aware of patterns in your own life, perhaps glimpsing their origins. It is helpful to remember that individuals respond differently to stressful stimuli: one person may be traumatized by a situation, while the next may be only mildly affected by the same event. Also, in some cases, a person may react or respond in exactly the opposite way of another person experiencing a similar event. For example, a person born "late" (after the expected birth date) may be obsessive about being on time or, conversely, may be habitually late, perhaps even obstinately insisting "I will arrive whenever I please!"

Some patterns may reveal themselves internally, as emotions or a predisposition toward certain behavior, while others will show up as external events. Some patterns may initially be thought of as psychological and emotional traits, but repeated, are also likely to become patterns which play out in life events, as seen in the cases shown before.

Sometimes a pattern is identifiable because the feelings are familiar although the events that triggered the feelings may appear to be very different. In this case, your unconscious may be using another approach to get your attention — attempting to make you aware of painful, toxic, suppressed emotions simmering in the unconscious. Carl G. Jung said that "when an inner situation is not made conscious, it happens outside" as a life event. When we identify a pattern in our lives, we are beginning to "make it conscious." Furthermore, when we also experience the painful, underlying, suppressed emotions, we exhaust the fuel which has been feeding the reoccurrence of that pattern in our lives.

It is also vitally important to realize that, after we have done our necessary inner work, we must take action in the outer world. Inner work alone, while essential, is not enough. Once the soil in a garden is cleaned and prepared for new seeds, we must plant those seeds and tend them carefully so they will grow to yield an abundant healthy crop.

Realize that inner work takes time. Do not be discouraged if you do not see immediate results, but persist with your healing practices. The day will come when you will be thrilled to see how wonderfully your life has changed.

This list is intended to suggest only *some* of the possible origins of patterns and attendant feelings. It may not have universal application.

You may experience different feelings in response to a pattern than those listed here. In addition, some patterns may have origins for you which are not shown here, or which are different from those shown. Nothing can take the place of identifying your own pattern(s) and experiencing the healing and release which results from your own, unique, personal inner work.

After you have identified the pattern you wish to change, refer to the recommendations in the "Healing Breathwork" section. As you practice these recommendations, be as objective as you can, while observing the different ways and different people with whom you have experienced the pattern before. Then practice the recommended Healing Visualization and Healing Affirmation, giving them your full attention and practicing with as much feeling as you can. Repeat these techniques as often as need be. Complete clearing will result in the changing of an old, undesired pattern. To summarize this, you will proceed as follows:

1. Identify the pattern you wish to change.
2. Breathe and experience the suppressed feelings as recommended in "Healing Breathwork."
3. Once you have felt the feelings, practice the Healing Visualization with as much attention, focus, and passion as possible.
4. Repeat the Healing Affirmation again and again. You may repeat it audibly, mentally, as a song or chant, and/or in writing.
5. Repeat steps 2, 3, and 4 as often as emotions arise. In this way, you will eventually exhaust the emotions which fuel that pattern.

Just as planting a new and healthy seed in place of a weed will grow fresh and vibrant plants in a garden, the heartfelt, repeated practice of the techniques of visualization and affirmation will create new images and new thought patterns in your subconscious, once the old pattern has been experienced and uprooted. This will result in happier experiences in your life.

The List

Pattern: Abandonment

Common Expression
"Women (men) abandon me."
"People abandon me."

Possible Origin of Pattern
Abandoned by mother (father). Mother (father) not "present" either physically or emotionally. He or she may have been under severe stress, frightened, neurotic, self-centered, addicted, alcoholic, ill, imprisoned, or dead. Child may have been left in nursery, daycare, or given away. Adopted children may feel abandoned. An unborn baby may have felt its mother's feeling of abandonment by the biological father.

Healing Visualization
Visualize the ideal relationship(s) you truly desire, in as much vivid detail as you can possibly imagine.

Healing Affirmation
"I deserve to have lasting, loving relationships."
"My loved ones love me and stay with me."

Healing Breathwork
Breathe and fully experience the sadness, fear, and other feelings as they arise. Take responsibility for the ownership of these feelings, without blaming anyone, including yourself. (This means to recognize that these feelings reside within you and, therefore, are "owned" by you.) In this way you will drain your unconscious "container" of the powerful, suppressed feelings triggered by your earlier experience(s) of abandonment, thus lessening the magnetic attraction for additional feelings and/or experiences of abandonment.

Being as objective as possible, observe all the different ways in which you have felt abandoned and all the different people with whom you have felt abandoned. Once you have felt the emotions present in this moment, practice the Healing Visualization and Healing Affirmation with full attention and feeling. This will create new images and new thought patterns in your subconscious, resulting in experiences of deeper trust and commitment with others.

Pattern: Abundance

Common Expression
"I always have enough of everything."

Possible Origin of Pattern
Baby lovingly breast fed on demand (as baby needed).

Visualization
Visualize that life continues to support you in every way needed.

Affirmation
"I have everything I need to do the things I want, and everything I want to do the things I need."

Pattern: Abuse

Common Expression
"Men (women / people) are abusive."

Description of Pattern
An individual may experience one or more relationships in which s/he is abused by a partner (or other person), either emotionally, physically, or sexually.

Possible Origin of Pattern
Father (mother) was abusive, whether emotionally, physically, or sexually.

Healing Visualization
Visualize a relationship with a sincere partner who treats you kindly, with great love and respect.

Healing Affirmation
"I deserve to be treated with loving kindness and respect."

Healing Breathwork
Breathe and experience the fear, anger, and other feelings as they arise. Although you may feel enraged, take responsibility for your ownership of these feelings, without blaming anyone, including yourself. (This means to recognize that these feelings reside within you and, therefore, are "owned" by you. It is possible to hate the behavior without hating the person.) In this way, you will drain your unconscious "container" of the powerful, suppressed feelings engendered by your earlier experience(s) of abuse, thus diminishing the magnetic pull for additional abusive experiences.

Being as objective as possible, observe all the different ways in which you have experienced abuse; notice all the different people with whom you have experienced abuse. Once you have felt the emotions which are present in the moment, practice the Healing Visualization and Healing Affirmation with full attention and feeling. This will create new images and new thought patterns in your subconscious, resulting in new and different experiences.

Pattern: Accidents, Physical Ailments

Description of Pattern
Clumsy, accident prone.

Possible Origin of Pattern
Injury during birth. This may include breech or other difficult birth experience, including use of forceps, and rough handling by the midwife, doctor, or other medical personnel . Infant's unconscious conclusion may have been: Being alive = being hurt.

Healing Visualization
Visualize safe experiences at all times. Before leaving home on any journey, for instance, relax and visualize your entire trip, "seeing" yourself (and others accompanying you) safe at all points along the way, and returning home happily and securely.

Healing Affirmation
"I move through life safely, with the grace of a dancer."
"I am safe and protected at all times."
"God's Light of protection is always around me."

Healing Breathwork
Breathe and experience the fear, anxiety, and other feelings as they arise. Although you may feel vulnerable and at risk, take responsibility for your ownership of these feelings, without blaming anyone, including yourself. (This means to recognize that these feelings reside within you and, therefore, are "owned" by you.) In this way, you will drain your unconscious "container" of the powerful, suppressed feelings engendered by earlier accidents and ailments, thus diminishing the magnetic pull for more of the same.

Being as objective as possible, observe all the different ways in which you have been injured or ill. Could you train yourself to be more careful or more graceful? Do you expect to have accidents? Perhaps you could allow extra time so that you do not feel rushed or hurried.

Once you have felt the emotions which are present in the moment, practice the Healing Visualization and Healing Affirmation with full attention and feeling. This will create new images and new thought patterns in your subconscious, resulting in safer experiences.

Pattern: Addiction / Addictive Behavior

(See Alcohol / Drug Abuse)

Description of Pattern

Life feels painful, frightening. This person may engage in "all or nothing" thinking, compulsive and/or obsessive behavior, whether or not he or she abuses a substance. May tend to be perfectionistic, sometimes experiencing migraine headaches when "perfection" isunattainable in some way.

A person may be addictive in many different ways, whether about work (workaholics), physical exercise, diet, keeping order in physical surroundings, etc. A common distinguishing feature is that this person is usually unable to moderate activities and generally lacks balance.

Possible Origin of Pattern

Birth and/or childhood with a parent or in a family which did not feel safe for the child. He or she may have become hypervigilant, always being alert for mood swings on the part of a dangerous and/or capriciously unpredictable parent /caretaker..

People from addictive or otherwise dysfunctional families are especially at risk. A person may seek a substance to numb out the pain of feeling disconnected from self and others. This can be a response to stress, avoidance of intimacy and responsibility, a way to escape one's uncomfortable feelings or to generally withdraw from a world which feels unloving and unsafe.

Healing Visualization

See yourself living happily, free of addiction, with calmness and peace. Imagine that you have loving relationships which are built on mutual support and trust.

Healing Affirmation

"I am always in balance. My world is a safe place."

Healing Breathwork

Breathe and experience the fear, sadness, anger, and other feelings as they arise. Regardless of their intensity, take responsibility for your ownership of these feelings, without blaming anyone, including yourself. (This means to recognize that these feelings reside within you and, therefore, are "owned" by you.) In this way, you will drain your unconscious "container" of the powerful, suppressed feelings which have clamored to be felt, thus diminishing the tendency for additional addictive behavior.

Once you have felt the emotions which are present in the moment, practice the Healing Visualization and Healing Affirmation with full attention and feeling. This will create new images and new thought patterns in your subconscious, resulting in experiences of feeling safe enough to risk living your life fully, without relying on any substance.

Pattern: Alcohol / Drug Abuse

Common Expression
"I only feel normal when I drink / do drugs."

Description of Pattern
Life feels painful, frightening. (See Addiction / Addictive Behavior.)

Possible Origin of Pattern
Mother (and baby!) drugged before and during birth. (See the case of Philip.) Baby's first taste of life was an experience of being drugged. Babies who were unwanted, whether raised in their own biological family or given up for adoption, often turn to substances to dull the inner pain.

People from addictive or otherwise dysfunctional families are often especially at risk. A person may seek a substance to numb the pain of feeling disconnected from self and others. This can be a response to stress, avoidance of intimacy and responsibility, a way to escape one's own uncomfortable feelings or to generally withdraw from a world which feels unloving and unsafe.

Healing Visualization
See yourself living happily, free of addiction, with calmness and peace. Imagine you have loving relationships which are built on mutual support and trust.

Healing Affirmation
"I trust myself and I trust life."
"I am God's child and I am safe in God's world."
"It is safe for me to experience whatever life holds for me."
"I am loved and safe."

Healing Breathwork
Breathe and experience the fear, sadness, anger, and other feelings as they arise. Regardless of their intensity, take responsibility for your ownership of these feelings, without blaming anyone, including yourself. (This means to recognize that these feelings reside within you and, therefore, are "owned" by you.) In this way, you will drain your unconscious "container" of the powerful, suppressed feelings which have clamored to be felt, thus diminishing the pull for additional addictive experiences.

Being as objective as possible, observe all the different ways in which you have chosen to escape, using alcohol and/or drugs. Be aware of the different ways you attempt to avoid taking responsibility for your life. Seek help from a substance abuse specialist or support group.

Once you have felt the emotions which are present in the moment, and are supporting yourself through counseling and/or a support group, practice the Healing Visualization and Healing Affirmation with full attention and feeling. This will create new images and new thought patterns in your subconscious, resulting in experiences of feeling safe enough to live your life fully, without relying on alcohol or drugs.

Pattern: Ambition (lack of)

Description of Pattern
This individual may be bright and capable, but fail to put forth sustained effort.

Possible Origin of Pattern
Baby stuck in birth canal; felt apathetic because s/he was unable to move forward. Or mother drugged and not helping with birth and baby felt s/he could not make progress. Or a generalized malaise in response to early painful loss on being separated from mother, whether due to illness, adoption, etc.

Healing Visualization
See yourself setting and achieving a goal that is important to you.

Healing Affirmation
"I enthusiastically and joyfully engage in life."

Healing Breathwork
Breathe and experience the sadness, fear, anger, paralysis, and other feelings as they arise. Although it may seem like you will never overcome certain challenges, take responsibility for your ownership of these feelings, without blaming anyone, including yourself. (This means to recognize that these feelings reside within you and, therefore, are "owned" by you.) In this way, you will drain your unconscious "container" of the powerful, suppressed feelings which have created or contributed to the lack of ambition.

Being as objective as possible, observe all the different ways in which you have lacked ambition. Once you have felt the emotions present in the moment, practice the Healing Visualization and Healing Affirmation with full attention and feeling. This will create new images and new thought patterns in your subconscious, resulting in new and different experiences.

Pattern: Ambush

Common Expression
"I am afraid I'll be blind sided again."

Possible Origin of Pattern
Attacked suddenly without warning as a child (as in cases of Dean and Elizabeth). Can also stem from the experience of a fetus whose mother considered or attempted abortion, or took drugs, whether or not the drugs were intended to abort the child. Baby's experience of these hostile elements may have been a feeling that "something's out to get me."

Healing Visualization
See yourself surrounded in an egg-shaped cocoon of white light, safe, protected, and immune to all adversity.

Healing Affirmation
"I am surrounded and protected by the Light."

Healing Breathwork
Breathe and experience the sadness, fear, anger, and other feelings as they arise. Although they may be very intense, take responsibility for your ownership of these feelings, without blaming anyone, including yourself. (This means to recognize that these feelings reside within you and, therefore, are "owned" by you.) In this way, you will drain your unconscious "container" of the powerful, suppressed feelings which have created the lack of ambition.

Being as objective as possible, observe all the different ways in which you have felt blind-sided or ambushed. Once you have felt the emotions which are present at the moment, practice the Healing Visualization and Healing Affirmation with full attention and feeling. This will create new images and new thought patterns in your subconscious, resulting in new, different, and safer experiences.

Pattern: Anger

Common Expression

"Back off. Don't push me!"

Description of Pattern

This person may intimidate others. People may "walk on eggs" around him or her. S/he may seem like a volcano always threatening to erupt.

Possible Origin of Pattern

Beneath a pattern of anger, there is usually a reservoir of fear, which may stem from many causes. Parent(s) may not have been loving, nurturing, and accepting of baby. Mother under stress or resentful of caretaking required by baby. Parent(s) missing, whether they were emotionally unavailable or disinterested in baby, left willingly, died or were otherwise unaware of and disconnected from baby. Also, when a child is subjected to an angry parent, he may sometimes model the angry behavior.

Someone (mother, father, the doctor) was too controlling and the child felt helpless, and frightened. Baby's delivery was hurried or delayed to suit someone else's schedule. The midwife, doctor, or other medical personnel "interfered" with baby's birth. This might have been through the use of forceps, hands, or a suction instrument intruding into baby's space.

Healing Visualization

See yourself being comfortable with and calmly in charge of your own emotions.

Healing Affirmation

"My emotions are not in charge of me. I am in charge of my emotions."
"I trust in life. It is safe for me to relax."

Healing Breathwork

Breathe and experience the fear, anger, and other feelings as they arise. Although they may be very intense, take responsibility for your ownership of these feelings, without blaming anyone, including yourself. (This means to recognize that these feelings reside within you and, therefore, are "owned" by you.) In this way, you will drain your unconscious "container" of the powerful, suppressed feelings which have created the pattern of anger.

Being as objective as possible, observe the different occasions and ways in which you have felt angry. Once you have felt the emotions which are present at the moment, practice the Healing Visualization and Healing Affirmation with full attention and feeling. This will create new images and new thought patterns in your subconscious, resulting in new, calmer experiences.

Pattern: Anxiety

Description of Pattern
May be nervous, tense, ill at ease. May be a high achiever or workaholic who does not know how to relax.

Possible Origin of Pattern
Unconscious fear. Did not feel safe and accepted as a child. Parent(s) may have been cold, emotionally capricious and/or hypercritical. This person may always be waiting for the "other shoe to drop." High achievers may need constant acknowledgment or proof of excellence as a way to salve their fear that they will fail to measure up. These people may seem to be "driven."

Healing Visualization
See yourself being relaxed, calm, and centered.

Healing Affirmation
"I am okay."
" I do my best and my best is good enough."

Healing Breathwork
Breathe and experience the fear, anger, and other feelings as they arise. Although they may be very intense, take responsibility for your ownership of these feelings, without blaming anyone, including yourself. (This means to recognize that these feelings reside within you and, therefore, are "owned" by you.) In this way, you will drain your unconscious "container" of the powerful, suppressed feelings which have created this pattern of anxiety

Being as objective as possible, observe the different ways in which you have felt anxious. Once you have felt the emotions which are present at the moment, practice the Healing Visualization and Healing Affirmation with full attention and feeling. This will create new images and new thought patterns in your subconscious, resulting in more peaceful experiences.

Pattern: Ashamed

Common Expression
"I feel so ashamed." "I feel unclean."

Possible Origin of Pattern
Mother or father ashamed of the pregnancy (as in the cases of Dean and Jan). Or a child was shamed by parents. Guilt resulting either from a transgression or omission, or unconscious guilt, or shame stemming from sexual abuse, character assassination by parent(s) or other authority figure, or identification with parent(s) who felt ashamed, or of whose behavior the child was ashamed. The child's unconscious conclusion may have been: "If my dad (mom) acts this way, maybe I am like this, too."

Healing Visualization
See yourself being completely honest and straightforward in every way. Further, see yourself clean and pure, and surrounded by an egg-shaped vortex of white light.

Healing Affirmation
"I am a child of God. My essence is divine."
"Nothing can diminish my relationship to God."
"I forgive myself for all mistakes. From this moment, I choose to live honestly and purely."

Healing Breathwork
Breathe and experience the shame and other feelings as they arise. Although they may be very intense, take responsibility for your ownership of these feelings, without blaming anyone, including yourself. (This means to recognize that these feelings reside within you and, therefore, are "owned" by you.) In this way, you will drain your unconscious "container" of the powerful, suppressed feelings which created the pattern of shame.

Being as objective as possible, observe the different ways in which you felt ashamed. Once you have felt the emotions which are present at the moment, practice the Healing Visualization and Healing Affirmations with full attention and feeling. This will create new images and new thought patterns in your subconscious, resulting in new and different experiences of self acceptance.

Pattern: Authority Issues

Common Expression

"Stop pushing me! Back off!"
"Leave me alone and let me do it!"
"Don't interfere!"

Possible Origin of Pattern

Mother tense, impatient, and/or working too hard to get the birth over with. Or labor-inducing drugs force labor prematurely. Or labor and/or birth timed for someone else's convenience (the doctor, mother, father, or to take advantage of a year-end tax deduction). Forceps or suction birth.

Cesarean section, especially if according to a schedule which precluded labor. A baby who is forcibly removed from the womb without the preparation of labor often feels violated and enraged that its privacy and natural sense of timing is disregarded. These persons often have authority issues when there was any "interference" with the birth process. They may often feel like they are waiting for the "other shoe to drop."

Healing Visualization

See yourself being calmly in control of your own life in every way.

Healing Affirmation

"I am the authority in my life."
"I create my life as I choose and feel happy with the outcome."

Healing Breathwork

Breathe and experience the anger, sadness, and other feelings as they arise. Although they may be very intense, take responsibility for your ownership of these feelings, without blaming anyone, including yourself. (This means to recognize that these feelings reside within you and, therefore, are "owned" by you.) In this way, you will drain your unconscious "container" of the powerful, suppressed feelings which contribute to resentment of authority.

Being as objective as possible, observe the different ways in which you have felt controlled. Once you have felt the emotions which are present at the moment, practice the Healing Visualization and Healing Affirmations with full attention and feeling. This will create new images and new thought patterns in your subconscious, resulting in new and different experiences.

Pattern: Belonging (lack of)

Common Expression
"I don't belong here."
"I don't know where I belong."

Possible Origin of Pattern
Child's disconnection from mother. In the case of an adopted child, s/he may feel the disconnection from his or her birth mother intensely, though s/he may never have seen mother and though this feeling may be entirely unconscious. (This is a major loss for the child.) This pattern can also arise at conception, as a result of confusion over the "right place" for implantation of the fertilized egg in the uterine wall. Babies conceived as a result of sperm or ovum donation also often feel disoriented and lack a sense of belonging.

Healing Visualization
See yourself feeling a deep sense of being in your right place, moving confidently through life.

Healing Affirmation
"I am a child of the Universe and am always in my right place."

Healing Breathwork
Breathe and experience the disorientation, disconnection, anger, sadness, and other feelings as they arise. Although they may be very intense, take responsibility for your ownership of these feelings, without blaming anyone, including yourself. (This means to recognize that these feelings reside within you and, therefore, are "owned" by you.) In this way, you will drain your unconscious "container" of the powerful, suppressed feelings which have created this pattern of a lack of belonging.

Being as objective as possible, observe the different ways in which you have felt you did not belong. Once you have felt the emotions which are present at the moment, practice the Healing Visualization and Healing Affirmation with full attention and feeling. This will create new images and new thought patterns in your subconscious, resulting in new and different experiences.

Pattern: Betrayal

Common Expression
"Women (men / people) betray me."
"I can't / don't trust anyone."

Possible Origin of Pattern
Pregnant mother ambivalent about wanting a baby, or considered or attempted abortion or adoption. Mother or father was abusive or unavailable, either emotionally or physically. The child may wonder, "Why did she (they) have me if she (they) didn't want to be with me?" The child may then repeat this pattern in his or her adult relationships, betraying or being betrayed.

Healing Visualization
See yourself feeling a deep sense of safety, and trust in yourself, in loved ones, and in life.

Healing Affirmation
"I am always treated with honesty, love and respect."

Healing Breathwork
Breathe and experience the fear, anger, sadness, and other feelings as they arise. Although they may be very intense, take responsibility for your ownership of these feelings, without blaming anyone, including yourself. (This means to recognize that these feelings reside within you and, therefore, are "owned" by you.) In this way, you will drain your unconscious "container" of the powerful, suppressed feelings which have created this pattern of betrayal.

Being as objective as possible, observe the different ways in which you have felt betrayed. Have there also been ways in which you have betrayed others? Once you have felt the emotions which are present at the moment, practice the Healing Visualization and Healing Affirmation with full attention and feeling. This will create new images and new thought patterns in your subconscious, resulting in new and different experiences.

Pattern: (feeling) Blocked

Common Expression
"Something (somebody) is always in my way!"

Possible Origin of Pattern
Experience before or during birth of a twin, tumor, the umbilical cord, mother's pelvic structure, doctor's hands, forceps, or another obstacle.

Healing Visualization
See yourself moving forward in life with all doors opening before you.

Healing Affirmation
"I move easily through life. Life supports my progress."
"All obstacles dissolve before I reach them."

Healing Breathwork
Breathe and experience the fear, frustration, sadness, and other feelings as they arise. Although they may be very intense, take responsibility for your ownership of these feelings, without blaming anyone, including yourself. (This means to recognize that these feelings reside within you and, therefore, are "owned" by you.) In this way, you will drain your unconscious "container" of the powerful, suppressed feelings which have created this pattern of feeling blocked.

Being as objective as possible, observe the different ways in which you have felt blocked. Once you have felt the emotions which are present at the moment, practice the Healing Visualization and Healing Affirmations with full attention and feeling. This will create new images and new thought patterns in your subconscious, resulting in freer experiences.

Pattern: Boundary Issues

Common Expression
"Don't invade my space."
"Back off!"

Description of Pattern
Sometimes the opposite — insufficient boundaries — is the person's experience.

Possible Origin of Pattern
Person's boundaries not respected in utero (through amniocentesis or ultrasound), or during birth (intrusion of forceps, doctor's hands, etc.), or as an infant or young child. Childhood abuse of any kind may crease this pattern, or serious or chronic childhood illness.

Feelings about boundary violations may seem extreme unless one realizes how threatened and powerless a small child (or fetus!) feels when faced with the infringement of an adult. Those delivered by Cesarean section are especially vulnerable, (inability to keep strong influences out), have difficulty keeping people out of their space, and saying "no" effectively.

Healing Visualization
See yourself going through life with a healthy sense of boundaries.

Healing Affirmation
"I am safe in my own space. I move freely, comfortably, without anxiety."
"I respect my boundaries and those of others, and others respect my boundaries, too."

Healing Breathwork
Breathe and experience the fear, anger, and other feelings as they arise. Although they may be very intense, take responsibility for your ownership of these feelings, without blaming anyone, including yourself. (This means to recognize that these feelings reside within you and, therefore, are "owned" by you.) In this way, you will drain your unconscious "container" of the powerful, suppressed feelings which have created this pattern of being intruded upon, interfered with or invaded.

Being as objective as possible, observe the different ways in which you have felt imposed upon, disrespected, or violated. Once you have felt the emotions which are present at the moment, practice the Healing Visualization and Healing Affirmations with full attention and feeling. This will create new images and new thought patterns in your subconscious, resulting in a healthier sense of boundaries.

Pattern: Caretaking

Common Expression
"I always wind up taking care of others."

Possible Origin of Pattern
Child was caretaker in their family, not allowed to be a child. The child may have received approval (love) only for caretaking and performing other adult chores.

Healing Visualization
See yourself in a leisurely scene, being appreciated just for the wonderful person you are.

Healing Affirmation
"I don't have to do anything to be loved and accepted."
"I am appreciated, loved, and welcomed just for being myself."

Healing Breathwork
Breathe and experience the sadness, anger, and other feelings as they arise. Although they may be very intense, take responsibility for your ownership of these feelings, without blaming anyone, including yourself. (This means to recognize that these feelings reside within you and, therefore, are "owned" by you.) In this way, you will drain your unconscious "container" of the powerful, suppressed feelings which have created this pattern of caretaking.

Being as objective as possible, observe the different ways in which you have felt used or appreciated only for the work you perform. Have you taken care of others as a way to purchase their love, friendship or other favor(s)? Once you have felt the emotions which are present at the moment, practice the Healing Visualization and Healing Affirmation with full attention and feeling. This will create new images and new thought patterns in your subconscious, resulting in new and different experiences.

Pattern: Cold Personality

Description of Pattern
Unable to express or receive warmth or expressions of love. Those around such a person may be more aware of this pattern than the person himself / herself.

Possible Origin of Pattern
Baby was insufficiently touched or nurtured. Mother may have been cold, unfeeling, and inexpressive. Babies naturally need warmth, love, and cuddling, and often retreat into coldness because they never experienced loving interaction with mother or a primary caregiver.

A loving mother is the greatest gift an infant can have. We learn by modeling and the child of a cold, unloving mother may feel "frozen" all its life. Unless healing occurs, such a person will be incapable of intimacy.

Healing Visualization
See yourself surrounded in a warm blanket of love and nurturing. See all the coldness melting away. See yourself (or that other person) being able to relate warmly to others, being vulnerable, sharing your feelings and feeling empathetic toward them as well.

Healing Affirmation
"I am a warm, loving person."
"It is safe for me to be vulnerable and share myself with loved ones."
"I am nurtured, loved, warm, and safe."

Healing Breathwork
Breathe and experience the fear, sadness, anger, and other feelings as they arise. Although they may be very intense, take responsibility for your ownership of these feelings, without blaming anyone, including yourself. (This means to recognize that these feelings reside within you and, therefore, are "owned" by you.) In this way, you will drain your unconscious "container" of the powerful, suppressed feelings which have created this pattern of coldness.

Being as objective as possible, observe the different ways you have felt frozen, unloved, and alone. Once you have felt the emotions which are present at the moment, practice the Healing Visualization and Healing Affirmation with full attention and feeling. This will create new images and new thought patterns in your subconscious, resulting in new and different experiences.

When you are with other people, make eye contact with them. In addition to being more aware of your own feelings, practice being aware of others' feelings, too.

Pattern: Commitment (fear of)

Description of Pattern
A person may be engaged in relationships of different kinds without actually committing to any person, any situation, or any relationship. The person is usually somewhat unconscious of this pattern. Feeling lonely, he or she may seek relationships with others, but run away or otherwise sabotage any relationship which seems to threaten him or her with a loss of freedom.

Possible Origin of Pattern
This patterns may result from a traumatic birth, especially one where the baby felt trapped or unable to move freely. The baby's experience may translate into a desperate need for freedom wherein the baby felt, "if I don't break free, I will die!" In addition, the child's early experiences did not feel safe somehow. Early relationships may have been unstable, unreliable, or were otherwise a source of pain for the child. Parent(s) may have been addicted to alcohol or drugs, or demanded too much emotional support from the child. Such an unhealthy relationship could have left the child with the unconscious fear that being in a relationship means that he or she will suffer.

Healing Visualization
See yourself feeling completely safe and free while relating closely with friends and loved ones. See yourself enveloped in a protective pink light.

Healing Affirmation
"I deserve love and freedom." *"I am safe in all my relationships."*
"I am more free when I am supported by a committed, loving relationship."

Healing Breathwork
Breathe and experience the fear, guilt, anger, sadness, and other feelings as they arise. Although they may be very intense and overwhelming, take responsibility for your ownership of these feelings, without blaming anyone, including yourself. (This means to recognize that these feelings reside within you and, therefore, are "owned" by you.) In this way, you will drain your unconscious "container" of the powerful, suppressed feelings which have created this fear of commitment.

Once you have felt the emotions which are present at the moment, practice the Healing Visualization and Healing Affirmation with full attention and feeling. This will create new images and new thought patterns in your subconscious, resulting in experiences of more closeness and greater freedom in relationship.

Pattern: Compulsive Behavior

Description of Pattern

May feel frantic if tasks are not completed immediately, regardless of time parameters. This person may seldom relax or rest, yet may be unaware of this dynamic. S/he may be fatigued, and scarcely recognize it until a health breakdown occurs.

Possible Origin of Pattern

May result from a "frantic" birth, or mother felt extremely anxious and impatient to get pregnancy, labor or birth over with. Or a child whose parent(s) were impatient with him or her may develop an overcompensation by habitual hurrying.

A parent who focuses on a child's shortcomings instead of acknowledging his or her successes gives the message that the child's best is not good enough. Intelligent, high-achieving parent(s) sometimes insist on standards which are unreasonably high for a very child. The child who responds compulsively may unconsciously feel that getting things done on time is a matter of life or death.

Healing Visualization

See yourself completing all tasks on time but in a relaxed and calm fashion.

Healing Affirmation

"I am enough. I am good enough. My best is good enough."
"I meet the demands of life with ease and tranquillity."

Healing Breathwork

Breathe and experience the fear, sadness, anger, and other feelings as they arise. Although they may be very intense, take responsibility for your ownership of these feelings, without blaming anyone, including yourself. (This means to recognize that these feelings reside within you and, therefore, are "owned" by you.) In this way, you will drain your unconscious "container" of the powerful, suppressed feelings which have created this pattern of compulsivity.

Being as objective as possible, observe the different ways in which you have felt frantic and pressured. Observe the different ways in which you have felt "less than others" or "not good enough." Once you have felt the emotions which are present at the moment, practice the Healing Visualization and Healing Affirmation with full attention and feeling. This will create new images and new thought patterns in your subconscious, resulting in new and different experiences.

Pattern: Confidence and High Self-Esteem

Description of Pattern
Capable, unselfconscious, relaxed, self-assured.

Possible Origin of Pattern
Child was wanted, welcome, and accepted. Mother was healthy, attentive, and supportive of infant. (See case study of Debbie.)

Visualization
See yourself continuing to have everything you want and need to beautifully fulfill your life purpose.

Affirmation
"I am grateful for life's blessings."

Pattern: Control Issues (obsessive need to control)

Common Expression
"I know best. I'm in charge."

Description of Pattern
May be calm under pressure, cool, calculating, perfectionistic. May be alternately cold and hot (emotionally), depending on activity. Until healing occurs, these people are sometimes isolated and incapable of intimacy, afraid of the vulnerability experienced in intimate closeness.

Possible Origin of Pattern
Birth and/or childhood was frightening, painful. Labor may have been interfered with – either speeded up by a labor-inducing drug, scheduled to suit the convenience of someone other than baby, or medical personnel may have attempted to postpone delivery. Difficult births, including breech and cesarean births, sometimes contribute to this pattern. (The child may unconsciously adopt the idea that "if other people are in control, I suffer. Therefore, I must be in control!)

Childhood may have been very chaotic, such as when one or both parents are alcoholic or otherwise addicted. Early family life lacking in healthy structure or boundaries. Parent(s) capriciously critical, punishing, demanding. Little healthy affection or support for child. Parent(s) self-absorbed, moody, temperamental, unpredictable.

Healing Visualization
See yourself feeling securely in control of life, without the need to control others.

Healing Affirmation
"I am calmly in control of my life."
"I am safe and happy."

Healing Breathwork
Breathe and experience the fear, frustration, sadness, and other feelings as they arise. Although they may be very intense, take responsibility for your ownership of these feelings, without blaming anyone, including yourself. (This means to recognize that these feelings reside within you and, therefore, are "owned" by you.) In this way, you will drain your unconscious "container" of the powerful, suppressed feelings which have created this pattern of needing to control other people and situations.

Being as objective as possible, observe the different ways in which you have felt afraid that you would suffer if another person were in charge. Once you have felt the emotions which are present at the moment, practice the Healing Visualization and Healing Affirmation with full attention and feeling. This will create new images and new thought patterns in your subconscious, resulting in new and different experiences.

Pattern: Controlled

Common Expression
"I have always done what I should."
"I have always had to please someone else."

Possible Origin of Pattern
Forceps or suctioning experience at birth. Or a very controlling parent dominated the child. These people often see the world as an intrusive and painful place. They often do not say "no" and may forfeit their priorities to please others.

Healing Visualization
See yourself as autonomous, the ruler of your own life. See yourself making choices from your own sense of right and wrong, and feeling comfortable and secure in your autonomy. See yourself surrounded by an egg-shaped vortex of white light in which you have a natural sense of the best choices and decisions to make in any given situation.

Healing Affirmation
"I move confidently through my life. I choose how to live and where and how to use my energy to create a happy life."

Healing Breathwork
Breathe and experience the fear, frustration, sadness, and other feelings as they arise. Although they may be very intense, take responsibility for your ownership of these feelings, without blaming anyone, including yourself. (This means to recognize that these feelings reside within you and, therefore, are "owned" by you.) In this way, you will drain your unconscious "container" of the powerful, suppressed feelings which have created this pattern of feeling controlled by external forces.

Being as objective as possible, observe the different ways in which you have felt controlled or dominated. Become aware of ways in which you contribute to this dynamic, perhaps sometimes even setting it up. Once you have felt the emotions which are present at the moment, practice the Healing Visualization and Healing Affirmation with full attention and feeling. This will create new images and new thought patterns in your subconscious, resulting in more autonomous experiences.

Pattern: Dependence (needing outside help)

Common Expression
"I need help."
"I can't do this alone."

Description of Pattern
This person always seems to need outside help.

Possible Origin of Pattern
Labor and birth not easily or naturally completed, as in the case of babies delivered by Cesarean section, when baby was "helped out" by others. Or this pattern may be caused by serious illness or disability from birth.

Healing Visualization
See yourself (or the subject person) functioning autonomously, able to complete all tasks easily and comfortably.

Healing Affirmation
"I have the power, the strength, and the ability to manage my life autonomously."

Healing Breathwork
Breathe and experience the fear, frustration sadness, and other feelings as they arise. Although they may be very intense, take responsibility for your ownership of these feelings, without blaming anyone, including yourself. (This means to recognize that these feelings reside within you and, therefore, are "owned" by you.) In this way, you will drain your unconscious "container" of the powerful, suppressed feelings which have created this pattern of needing to be rescued or helped by others.

Being as objective as possible, observe the different ways you have felt afraid that you could not manage unless you had outside help. Once you have felt the emotions which are preent at the moment, practice the Healing Visualization and Healing Affirmation with full attention and feeling. This will create new images and new thought patterns in your subconscious, resulting in new and different experiences of strength and independence.

Pattern: Depression

Please note: Although many factors can contribute to depression, some of the possible causes are given here. Persons afflicted with severe depression are encouraged to consult a counselor or physician. Some depressions are chemically based and respond well to medication. Our intention is to provide help for some, while recognizing that this pattern may require additional expert attention.

Description of Pattern
Depression is often sadness and/or anger that is repressed.

Possible Origin of Pattern
Mother sad or grieved during pregnancy, or the depressed person may have ungrieved, unfelt sadness and anger. In other cases, the depression may be resistant to any healing attempts and may have to run its course, sometimes teaching the person vital soul lessons, creating a deeper sense of empathy and compassion for others, or opening the person's heart to a greater capacity for intimacy.

Healing Visualization
See yourself surrounded by an egg-shaped vortex of golden light. Feel that you are protected and sustained by this light at all times.

Healing Affirmation
"The love deep within my being is surging through me, filling me with joy and aliveness."

Healing Breathwork
Breathe and experience the fear, anger, sadness, and other feelings as they arise. Although they may be very intense, take responsibility for your ownership of these feelings, without blaming anyone, including yourself. (This means to recognize that these feelings reside within you and, therefore, are "owned" by you.) In this way, you will drain your unconscious "container" of the powerful, suppressed feelings which have created this pattern of depression.

Being as objective as possible, observe the different ways you have felt depressed. Once you have felt the emotions present at the moment, practice the Healing Visualization and Healing Affirmation with full attention and feeling. This will create new images and new thought patterns in your subconscious, resulting in new, different, and happier experiences.

Pattern: Disconnected, Disoriented

Common Expression
"Something is missing in my life."

Possible Origin of Pattern
Modern people, in general, have lost touch with the inner life – with their own deep, spiritual roots, which give a human being a sense of connection and true meaning. In essence, the person is sensing that he or she is cut off (blocked) from the soul, which is the essence of self.

Healing Visualization
See yourself enveloped in an egg-shaped vortex of pink light, connected to significant loved ones and to the source of life itself. Feel the peace and happiness which comes from this awareness.

Healing Affirmation:
"I am connected to the very source of life and joy."

Healing Breathwork:
Breathe and experience the sadness, loneliness, and other feelings as they arise. Although they may be very intense, take responsibility for your ownership of these feelings, without blaming anyone, including yourself. (This means to recognize that these feelings reside within you and, therefore, are "owned" by you.) In this way, you will drain your unconscious "container" of the powerful, suppressed feelings which have created this pattern of disconnection.

Being as objective as possible, observe the different ways in which you have felt disconnected. Become aware of ways in which you may remove or disconnect yourself from other people and from spirit as you perceive it. Once you have felt the emotions which are present at the moment, practice the Healing Visualization and Healing Affirmation with full attention and feeling. This will create new images and new thought patterns in your subconscious, resulting in new, different, fuller life.

Pattern: Dishonesty

Description of Pattern

Often fears the risk, vulnerability, and loss associated with self-disclosure. Low self-esteem. Does not trust others and cannot be trusted. Elements of dishonesty may include denial, rationalization, lying, stealing, deception, hypocrisy, gossip, and blaming of others instead of taking responsibility for one's life.

Possible Origin of Pattern

1. Child learned to lie or pretend, perhaps wearing different faces with different people or situations. In dysfunctional families, dishonesty prevails at many levels, including dishonesty with oneself.
2. Sometimes a person enters an incarnation with this unfortunate trait, choosing in this way to learn honest behavior (i.e., this is not always behavior learned in the present lifetime.)

Healing Visualization

See yourself behaving honestly in every way at all times.

Healing Affirmation

"I am loved and supported in total integrity."

Healing Breathwork

Breathe and experience the fear, anger, sadness, and other feelings as they arise. Although they may be very intense, take responsibility for your ownership of these feelings, without blaming anyone, including yourself. (This means to recognize that these feelings reside within you and, therefore, are "owned" by you.) In this way, you will drain your unconscious "container" of the powerful, suppressed feelings which have created this pattern of dishonesty.

Being as objective as possible, observe the different ways in which you have behaved dishonestly. Once you have felt the emotions present in the moment, practice the Healing Visualization and Healing Affirmation with full attention and feeling. This will create new images and new thought patterns in your subconscious, resulting in new and different experiences of honesty.

Pattern: Dominated

Common Expression
"I have always done what I should do."

Possible Origin of Pattern
Forceps or suctioning experience at birth, and/or a very controlling parent dominated the child. These people often see the world as an intrusive and painful place. They often do not have the ability to say "no" and may forfeit their own priorities in order to please others. They may "sell out" their own preferences and needs to maintain "peace."

Healing Visualization
See yourself as autonomous, the ruler of your own life. See yourself making choices from your own sense of right and wrong, feeling comfortable and secure in your autonomy. See yourself surrounded by an egg-shaped vortex of white light in which you have a natural sense of making the best choices and decisions for yourself in any situation.

Healing Affirmation
"I move confidently through my life."
"I choose how to live and where and how to use my energy to create a happy life."

Healing Breathwork
Breathe and experience the fear, frustration, sadness, and other feelings as they arise. Although they may be very intense, take responsibility for your ownership of these feelings, without blaming anyone, including yourself. (This means to recognize that these feelings reside within you and, therefore, are "owned" by you.) In this way, you will drain your unconscious "container" of the powerful, suppressed feelings which have created this pattern of feeling dominated by others.

Being as objective as possible, observe the different ways in which you have felt controlled or dominated. Do you "give your power away" to others? If so, become more aware of the benefit you may be receiving from being dominated by others. (Could it be that you avoid taking responsibility when you allow another to dominate you? If so, you can begin to heal this by feeling the fear underneath the avoidance.)

Once you have felt the emotions present in the moment, practice the Healing Visualization and Healing Affirmation with full attention and feeling. This will create new images and new thought patterns in your subconscious, resulting in new and different experiences of greater autonomy.

Pattern: Drama

Description of Pattern

Other people may be more aware of this pattern than the person himself or herself. When around him or her, others may feel restless, frenetic, anxious, or "hyper." He or she may approach tasks as if they were emergencies or may create emergencies out of ordinary events.

Possible Origin of Pattern

This pattern often traces back to a traumatic event before, during, or right after birth, such as a medical emergency like a Cesarean section, breech birth, or other perinatal complications. Or fear, anxiety, and intensity could have been absorbed during gestation from an anxious mother. Or later, during childhood, when a parent is very demanding or critical, a child often feels anxious, worried, and afraid, and this nervous, intense energy may continue. This pattern may be connected to alcohol or substance abuse, or to growing up with alcoholic or substance-abusing parents.

Healing Visualization

See yourself managing even challenging situations with great calm and peacefulness. See yourself (or other person) surrounded by an egg-shaped vortex of blue light.

Healing Affirmation

"I am calmly active and actively calm."

Healing Breathwork

Breathe and experience the fear, frustration, and other feelings as they arise. Although they may be very intense, take responsibility for your ownership of these feelings, without blaming anyone, including yourself. (This means to recognize that these feelings reside within you and, therefore, are "owned" by you.) In this way, you will drain your unconscious "container" of the powerful, suppressed feelings which have created this pattern of drama.

Being as objective as possible, observe the different ways in which you have felt nervous and agitated. Once you have felt the emotions which are present at the moment, practice the Healing Visualization and Healing Affirmation with full attention and feeling. This will create new images and new thought patterns in your subconscious, resulting in new, different, more peaceful experiences.

Pattern: Duplicity

Description of Pattern

Wears a "mask" – not authentic. Not straightforward. This person may be deceitful in order to gain control of others and situations.

Possible Origin of Pattern

Fear of the vulnerability which results from honest communication and self-disclosure. This may be

(1) a behavior learned in childhood, as an adaptation to a family or environment that was unsafe, or

(2) a trait which the individual chose at conception in order to learn needed lessons. (See the case studies of Rachel and Sofia.)

Healing Visualization

See yourself living in complete integrity, including thought, speech and action.

Healing Affirmation

"I am loved and supported in total integrity."

Healing Breathwork

Breathe and experience the fear, sadness, anger, and other feelings as they arise. Regardless of their intensity, take responsibility for your ownership of these feelings, without blaming anyone, including yourself. (This means to recognize that these feelings reside within you and, therefore, are "owned" by you.) In this way, you will drain your unconscious "container" of the powerful, suppressed feelings which have clamored to be felt, thus diminishing the magnetic pull for dishonest experiences.

Being as objective as possible, observe all the different ways in which you have chosen to be dishonest with yourself and others. Be aware of the different ways you seek to avoid intimacy and close relationships.

Once you have felt the emotions which are present at the moment, practice the Healing Visualization and Healing Affirmation with full attention and feeling. This will create new images and new thought patterns in your subconscious, resulting in experiences of feeling safe enough to risk living your life fully, and in complete integrity.

Pattern: Eating Disorders

This Pattern includes bulimia, anorexia nervosa, binging and other eating disorders.

Please note: In addition to practicing the healing tools which are listed here, it is vitally important to realize that eating disorders are very serious and can be life-threatening. It is essential not to attempt to manage these alone, but to seek competent, professional help. The following U. S. organizations provide information:
National Association of Anorexia Nervosa and Associated Disorders: 847/831-3438
National Eating Disorders Organization: 918/481-4044

Common Expression
"I'm not okay."

Possible Origin of Pattern
Not feeling accepted and often lacking a healthy role model. May be an extreme, fearful reaction to an unhealthy mother, father or family. For instance, a baby arrives and mother may be too immature or self-absorbed to see how beautiful the baby is and fails to appreciate and love her infant. The child may decide he or she does not deserve to live. Or the child is sexually, emotionally, and/or physically abused. Sometimes the person (unconsciously) feels that the only thing s/he has any control over is what goes into the mouth. Far more common in females than in males.

Healing Visualization
See yourself feeling safe and "grounded," accepting yourself just as you are.

Healing Affirmation
"I 'm okay whether or not I perform or measure up."
"I deserve love."
"I am okay, no matter what I think."

Healing Breathwork
Breathe and experience the fear, anger, sadness, guilt, and other feelings as they arise. Although they may be very intense, take responsibility for your ownership of these feelings, without blaming anyone, including yourself. (This means to recognize that these feelings reside within you and, therefore, are "owned" by you.) In this way, you will begin to drain your unconscious "container" of the powerful, suppressed feelings which have created this eating disorder.

Being as objective as possible, observe the different ways in which you may have felt worthless. Once you have felt the emotions which are present at the moment, practice the Healing Visualization and Healing Affirmation with full attention and feeling. This will help to create new images and new thought patterns in your subconscious, resulting in new and different experienc

Pattern: Emergency

Description of Pattern

Other people may be more aware of this pattern than the subject person. When around him or her, others may feel restless, frenetic, anxious, "hyper." S/he may be driven by a deep, underlying, unconscious fear or anger, though s/he may be unaware of this. S/he may approach otherwise mundane tasks as if they were emergencies or may create emergencies out of otherwise ordinary events.

Possible Origin of Pattern

This pattern often traces back to a frantic or traumatic event before, during or right after birth, such as a medical emergency like as Cesarean-section, breech birth (an extreme, emergency birth), high-forceps birth, cord around baby's neck, and/or other Perinatal complications. Or fear, anxiety, and intensity could have been absorbed during gestation, labor and/or birth from an anxious mother. Or later, during childhood, when a parent is very demanding or critical, a child often feels anxious, worried, and afraid and this nervous, intense energy may continue.

Healing Visualization

See yourself managing even challenging situations with great calm and peacefulness. See yourself enjoying this peaceful state. See yourself surrounded by an egg-shaped vortex of blue light.

Healing Affirmation

"I am calmly active and actively calm."
"I enjoy being calm and peacefully effective."

Healing Breathwork

Breathe and experience the fear, frustration, and other feelings as they arise. Although they may be very strong, take responsibility for your ownership of these feelings, without blaming anyone, including yourself. (This means to recognize that these feelings reside within you and, therefore, are "owned" by you.) In this way, you will drain your unconscious "container" of the powerful, suppressed feelings which have created this pattern of emergency.

Being as objective as possible, observe the different ways in which you have felt nervous and agitated. Once you have felt the emotions which are present at the moment, practice the Healing Visualization and Healing Affirmation with full attention and feeling. This will create new images and new thought patterns in your subconscious, resulting in experiences of greater peacefulness and calmness.

Pattern: Emotional triangles

Description of Pattern
Lonely, low self-esteem. May behave treacherously.

Possible Origin of Pattern
Child was caught up emotionally in a triangle with mom and dad (a form of emotional incest. See Rachel's case.) In other cases, a child may feel unable to relate peacefully with both parents at the same time, i.e., he or she might have been comfortable relating to mother alone or to father alone, but caught in a different emotional dynamic when both parents were present.

Healing Visualization
See yourself in a happy, lasting, committed, monogamous relationship.

Healing Affirmation
"I am now united with the perfect mate for me."
"I deserve unconditional love."

Healing Breathwork
Breathe and experience the fear, anger, sadness, and other feelings as they arise. Although they may be very intense, take responsibility for your ownership of these feelings, without blaming anyone, including yourself. (This means to recognize that these feelings reside within you and, therefore, are "owned" by you.) In this way, you will drain your unconscious "container" of the powerful, suppressed feelings which have created this chaotic pattern of emotional triangles.

Being as objective as possible, observe the different ways in which you have been involved in triangles. Become more aware of ways in which you invite emotional triangles, whether or not you have conscious of such behavior.

Once you have felt the emotions which are present at the moment, practice the Healing Visualization and Healing Affirmation with full attention and feeling. This will create new images and new thought patterns in your subconscious, resulting in new and different experiences of loyalty, fidelity, integrity, and respect in relationships.

Pattern: Empathy (lack of)

Description of Pattern
A general lack of awareness of and insensitivity to other people. May be uncaring, self-involved, and narcissistic.

Possible Origin of Pattern
Failure to mature past the childhood stage wherein self-absorption is normal. This may result from a wide range of causes, including being catastrophically unwanted, being the "wrong" gender, having cold, critical, and unloving parent(s), and/or other event(s) which so traumatized the child that he or she never matured in a healthy way.

Healing Visualization
See yourself connected to others in genuine, warm, caring ways.

Healing Affirmation
"I care about others and others care about me."

Healing Breathwork
Breathe and experience the fear, anger, sadness, and other feelings as they arise. Although they may be very intense, take responsibility for your ownership of these feelings, without blaming anyone, including yourself. (This means to recognize that these feelings reside within you and, therefore, are "owned" by you.) In this way, you will drain your unconscious "container" of the powerful, suppressed feelings which have created this disconnection and lack of empathy. Being as objective as possible, observe the different ways in which you have been selfish and/or uncaring.

Once you have felt the emotions which are present at the moment, practice the Healing Visualization and Healing Affirmation with full attention and feeling. This will create new images and new thought patterns in your subconscious, resulting in new and different experiences of closeness, connection, and empathy with others.

Pattern: Failure (sense of)

Common Expression
"I can't win for losing."

Possible Origin of Pattern
Inferiority; low self-esteem. This can result from abuse or neglect as a child or result from a disconnection from one's birth mother or father. Or a baby may be born with this pattern. One child who took on this pattern in the womb felt his father – who was unemployed and felt like a failure — and the pregnant mother had to work to support the family. Working through this Pattern, this man has yet to be successful, in spite of many talents, high intelligence, and a desire to succeed.

Healing Visualization
Visualize achieving a specific goal and feeling very good about yourself as a result of this success.

Healing Affirmation
"With each breath I take, I feel better about myself and my life."

Healing Breathwork
Breathe and experience the fear, anger, sadness, and other feelings as they arise. Although they may be very intense, take responsibility for your ownership of these feelings, without blaming anyone, including yourself. (This means to recognize that these feelings reside within you and, therefore, are "owned" by you.) In this way, you will drain your unconscious "container" of the powerful, suppressed feelings which have created this pattern of failure.

Being as objective as possible, observe the different ways in which you have experienced failure or felt like a failure. Once you have felt the emotions which are present at the moment, practice the Healing Visualization and Healing Affirmation with full attention and feeling. This will create new images and new thought patterns in your subconscious, resulting in new and different, more successful experiences.

Pattern: Fear (inordinate, intense)

Description of Pattern

While fear is a normal emotion and one that provides valuable protection, this page is intended to assist that person whose life is ruled by fear. S/he may be very controlling of others as a way to protect himself or herself. S/he may often be angry, for anger frequently is a cover-up for fear. S/he may deny that fear is present, and may in fact be completely unaware of it's presence, while at the same time going to great lengths to avoid facing the thing(s) s/he fears. Fear often prevents a person from setting and pursuing goals. (See Mary's case.)

Possible Origin of Pattern

An extreme, fixated response to an event in the womb, during birth, infancy, or early childhood. (See the cases of Donald, Karl, and Mary.) Sometimes a response to a severe or chronic illness or disability. Response to being raised by alcoholic or drug abusing parent(s) or raised in an otherwise abusive home.

Healing Visualization

See yourself able to confront all fears, able to feel the terrifying feelings while continuing to live a joyful life and achieve chosen goals. Visualize being surrounded by an egg-shaped vortex of white, protective light.

Healing Affirmation

"It is safe for me to feel afraid."
"It is safe for me to feel all my feelings."
"I am always safe, even though I sometimes feel afraid."
"Though I may shake in my boots, I can keep right on walking."

Healing Breathwork

Breathe and experience the fear, anger, and other feelings as they arise. Although they may be very intense and overwhelming, take responsibility for your ownership of these feelings, without blaming anyone, including yourself. (This means to recognize that these feelings reside within you and, therefore, are "owned" by you.) In this way, you will drain your unconscious "container" of the powerful, suppressed feelings which have created this pattern of fear.

Being as objective as possible, observe the different ways in which you have felt afraid. Once you have experienced the emotions which are present at the moment, practice the Healing Visualization and Healing Affirmation with full attention and feeling. This will create new images and new thought patterns in your subconscious, resulting in new and different experiences. Although you will still be capable of feeling fear, it will no longer keep you from living your life fully or proceeding toward your goals.

Pattern: "Flat" Personality

This may indicate serious illness or chemical imbalance. Medical check-up is encouraged.

Description of Pattern

Generalized absence or withholding of feelings. Few or no observable emotional highs or lows. Unusually unresponsive to others and/or external stimuli. At the same time, an empathic person may sense an underlying sadness or anger while in the presence of such a person.

Possible Origin of Pattern

Painful loss, injury or separation from mother during infancy, including hospitalization or isolation of infant due to illness or adoption. As an example, Ted Kaczynski, former university professor suspected of being the "Unabomber," was hospitalized for severe allergic reaction to medication when he was six months old. Following that separation, family members reported that the baby's personality, once bubbly and vivacious, seemed to go "flat." Traumatic event, emotionally absent parent(s), severe abuse.

Healing Visualization

See yourself feeling connected to loved ones in a healthy, supportive way.

Healing Affirmation

"With each breath I take, I feel more alive and more loving."
"I am loved and nurtured."

Healing Breathwork

Breathe and experience the fear, anger, sadness, and other feelings as they arise. Although they may be very intense, take responsibility for your ownership of these feelings, without blaming anyone, including yourself. (This means to recognize that these feelings reside within you and, therefore, are "owned" by you.) In this way, you will drain your unconscious "container" of the powerful, suppressed feelings which have created this withdrawal and withholding of feelings.

Being as objective as possible, observe the different ways in which you have experienced this flatness. Once you have felt the emotions which are present at the moment, practice the Healing Visualization and Healing Affirmation with full attention and feeling. This will create new images and new thought patterns in your subconscious, resulting in new , more "alive" experiences.

Pattern: Giving up, quitting

Common Expression
"This is overwhelming."
"I can't handle this!"
"I'm throwing in the towel."

Description of Pattern
While anyone may cease making efforts from time to time, this is intended to address a chronic pattern wherein a person habitually gives up without sufficient sustained effort to realistically achieve a goal.

Possible Origin of Pattern
Labor interrupted, perhaps contractions ceased. Baby stuck in birth canal, unable to make progress and felt powerless and helpless. Serious or chronic childhood illness or disability. Until this individual re-experiences this primordial energy, s/he may give up on many worthwhile goals without realizing they are within reach.

Healing Visualization
See yourself easily putting forth sustained effort to achieve a specific goal.

Healing Affirmation
"With each breath I take, I come closer to reaching my goal."
"I achieve my goals easily and enjoy every minute of the experience."

Healing Breathwork
Breathe and experience the frustration, anger, sadness, and other feelings as they arise. Although they may be very intense, take responsibility for your ownership of these feelings, without blaming anyone, including yourself. (This means to recognize that these feelings reside within you and, therefore, are "owned" by you.) In this way, you will drain your unconscious "container" of the powerful, suppressed feelings which have created this pattern of giving up.

Being as objective as possible, observe the different ways in which you have experienced giving up or quitting. Once you have felt the emotions which are present at the moment, practice the Healing Visualization and Healing Affirmation with full attention and feeling. This will create new images and new thought patterns in your subconscious, resulting in new, different, more sustained, successful experiences.

Pattern: Grief

Common Expression
"My heart is broken."

Description of Pattern
At times, a person may not even realize that he or she harbors a deep, unfelt grief. It is helpful to be aware that people respond differently to loss. For one person, the loss of a loved one is overwhelming and requires an adequate grieving process. For another, the loss of status, a job or other source of income, the loss of health, or the loss of an ability may be at the source of a very deep grief. Please note that when grief and sadness are suppressed, depression may result.

Possible Origin of Pattern
Overwhelming loss which has not been grieved. This can be prenatal — a baby who is not wanted or whose gender was not acceptable to parent(s). Or the loss may have been sustained in infancy, early childhood, or at a later stage. Abuse and/or chronic or serious childhood illness or disability.

Healing Visualization
See yourself having the ability to experience any and all feelings without blocking them. Imagine being surrounded by a protective, soothing, comforting pink light which makes it safe for you to cry your tears and empty all the pain you feel.

Healing Affirmation
"It is safe for me to feel all my feelings of sadness and grief."
"The more deeply I feel, the more alive and whole I become."

Healing Breathwork
Breathe and experience the grief, anger, sadness, and other feelings as they arise. Although they may be very intense and overwhelming, take responsibility for your ownership of these feelings, without blaming anyone, including yourself. (This means to recognize that these feelings reside within you and, therefore, are "owned" by you.) In this way, you will drain your unconscious "container" of the powerful, suppressed feelings which have created this grief.

Once you have felt the emotions which are present at the moment, practice the Healing Visualization and Healing Affirmation with full attention and feeling. This will create new images and new thought patterns in your subconscious, resulting in new and different experiences.

Pattern: Guilt

Common Expression
"I often feel guilty." *"I feel like I am a bad person."*

Possible Origin of Pattern
1. Mother sad or in pain before or during birth. Baby may have felt guilty because mother had an episiotomy ("I pushed too hard and tore mommy.") Some families and/or religions reinforce guilt.
2. Death of a parent, or abuse of the child by a parent, or disharmony in the early home and child blames himself.
3. Depressed parent(s) or
4. Child with severe or chronic illness or disability.
(Please note: Many people feel confused about the emotion of guilt. The intention here is to deal with that guilt which is an unhealthy, chronic, self-abusive emotion. A healthy person will feel remorse over behavior which injures anyone or which violates his standards. Experiencing remorse, a person can choose to correct his behavior, making sure that he does not repeat the unacceptable behavior. Once this lesson is learned, the healthy person chooses to forgive himself and get on with life. When forgiveness is not given, the person may experience guilt again and again, undermining his own life and effectiveness. The experience of remorse, therefore, serves the purpose of correcting behavior and is valuable, while guilt is destructive.)

Healing Visualization
See yourself feeling joyful and playful, and as carefree as a little child. Imagine that you are enveloped by a protective bubble of pink light, without a care in the world.

Healing Affirmation
"It is safe for me to feel joyful." *"The happier I am, the safer everyone is."*
"I am a child of God. I am innocent."

Healing Breathwork
Breathe and experience the guilt, anger, sadness, and other feelings as they arise. Although they may be very intense and overwhelming, take responsibility for your ownership of these feelings, without blaming anyone, including yourself. (This means to recognize that these feelings reside within you and, therefore, are "owned" by you.) In this way, you will empty your unconscious "container" of the powerful, suppressed feelings which have created this guilt.

Being as objective as possible, observe the different ways in which you have felt guilty. Do you sometimes feel afraid to be "too happy," as though you are somehow "supposed" to feel guilty?

Once you have felt the emotions which are present at the moment, practice the Healing Visualization and Healing Affirmation with full attention and feeling. This will create new images and new thought patterns in your subconscious, resulting in freer, happier experiences.

Pattern: Helplessness

This pattern refers to helplessness when it is employed *for the purpose of controlling others.* Some people *legitimately* require the help and support of other people.

Description of Pattern

This person may dominate family members through the threat of emotional or psychological dependency, or ill health — the "tyranny of the weak."

Possible Origin of Pattern

1. Individual was manipulated as a child or selfishly chose to become manipulative to get his or her own way. An extremely treacherous response to loneliness as a child. The person may have experienced that the only time s/he received any warmth or attention was when ill or otherwise helpless.
2. This trait may also be a life lesson for this person, brought in from a previous lifetime.
3. Angry response to others attempt to patronize, treat disrespectfully. (i.e., "You are weak. You need me.") The child learns to be helpless to please the parent(s).

Healing Visualization

See yourself honestly taking responsibility for your (his or her) own life. Imagine a specific scene which will allow you to visualize this new pattern clearly.

Healing Affirmation

"It is safe for me to be strong and self-sufficient."

Healing Breathwork

Breathe and experience the guilt, anger, sadness, and other feelings as they arise. Although they may be very intense and overwhelming, take responsibility for your ownership of these feelings, without blaming anyone, including yourself. (This means to recognize that these feelings reside within you and, therefore, are "owned" by you.) In this way, you will drain your unconscious "container" of the powerful, suppressed feelings which have created this sense of helplessness.

Being as objective as possible, observe the different ways in which you have felt helpless. Become aware of ways in which you may "give away your power," rather than taking responsibility for your own life.

Once you have felt the emotions which are present at the moment, practice the Healing Visualization and Healing Affirmation with full attention and feeling. This will create new images and new thought patterns in your subconscious, resulting in new and different experiences of independence, self-reliance, and personal power.

Pattern: Hopelessness

Common Expression
"I can't measure up, no matter how hard I try."
"It's no use; nothing ever works out anyway."

Possible Origin of Pattern
Parent(s) did not want a baby or wanted a baby of a different gender. Or parent(s) were demanding, critical, and unsupportive of child's attempts to grow and learn, emphasizing rigid conformity to their rules and requirements rather than encouraging child's natural intelligence and individuality. Child may not have been sufficiently touched and cuddled as an infant.

Healing Visualization
See yourself being embraced by a loving mother figure or by an angel. See yourself enveloped in a pink light, cushioned on a soft pillow. See and feel the joy and love swelling in your heart; feel the hope which grows within your very being.

Healing Affirmation
"I deserve love."
"I am safe and full of hope."
"Everything always works out for the highest good."

Healing Breathwork
Breathe and experience the guilt, anger, betrayal, abandonment, grief, sadness, and other feelings as they arise. Although they may be very intense and overwhelming, take responsibility for your ownership of these feelings, without blaming anyone, including yourself. (This means to recognize that these feelings reside within you and, therefore, are "owned" by you.) In this way, you will drain your unconscious "container" of the powerful, suppressed feelings which have created this sense of hopelessness.

Being as objective as possible, observe the different ways in which you have felt hopeless. Once you have experienced the emotions which are present at the moment, practice the Healing Visualization and Healing Affirmation with full attention and feeling. This will create new images and new thought patterns in your subconscious, resulting in new and different experiences of faith, hope, and positive expectation.

Pattern: Humiliation

Common Expression
"There is something wrong with me."
"I'm not okay."

Possible Origin of Pattern
Unconscious suppression of intense feelings of shame and self-judgment as a result of humiliating experiences in childhood. (See Dean's case.)

Healing Visualization
See yourself surrounded in a sphere of golden light. Visualize that you have just been given the highest award for the most noble service imaginable. Notice how very good you feel about yourself, your achievements, and your worthwhile motivations.

Healing Affirmation
"I am a child of God. My essence is divine."

Healing Breathwork
Breathe and experience the guilt, anger, humiliation, shame, sadness, and other feelings as they arise. Although they may be very intense and overwhelming, take responsibility for your ownership of these feelings, without blaming anyone, including yourself. (This means to recognize that these feelings reside within you and, therefore, are "owned" by you.) In this way, you will drain your unconscious "container" of the powerful, suppressed feelings which have created this sense of humiliation.

Being as objective as possible, observe the different ways in which you have felt ashamed or humiliated. Once you have felt the emotions which are present at the moment, practice the Healing Visualization and Healing Affirmation with full attention and feeling. This will create new images and new thought patterns in your subconscious, resulting in new and different experiences in which you will take pride.

Pattern: Illness (extreme)

Please note: The practice of the healing tools suggested below will be helpful to any person. It is important to realize, however, that illness may sometimes be very complex. It is never appropriate or helpful to blame yourself or anyone else for being ill, nor to think that healing is simplistic. If the patient is able to open up to the soul level and learn the underlying purpose served by the illness, then complete physical healing may result – or the patient may, at least, feel peaceful in his situation.

Common Expression
"I don't deserve to be here."
"I am supposed to die."

Possible Origin of Pattern
While there may be many causes underlying the complexity of illness, this may be attributable to events occurring at conception, or during gestation and birth. In Troya's case, the doctor and the baby's mother expected the fetus to be stillborn. (The same result might be expected had they feared the baby would be ill.) In other cases, abortion may have been considered or attempted.

Healing Visualization
See yourself enveloped in green light, a picture of glowing health.

Healing Affirmation
"I deserve to be robustly healthy and strong."
"I am a beloved child of the Universe."

Healing Breathwork
Breathe and experience the guilt, anger, sadness, and other feelings as they arise. Although they may be very intense and overwhelming, take responsibility for your ownership of these feelings, without blaming anyone, including yourself. (This means to recognize that these feelings reside within you and, therefore, are "owned" by you.) In this way, you will drain your unconscious "container" of the powerful, suppressed feelings which have contributed to this illness.

Being as objective as possible, observe the different ways in which you have been ill. Once you have felt the emotions which are present at the moment, practice the Healing Visualization and Healing Affirmation with full attention and feeling. This will help to create new images and new thought patterns in your subconscious, resulting in experiences of health and well-being.

Pattern: Incompletion

Description of Pattern
Projects or relationship(s) aborted before the person feels truly complete with them.

Possible Origin of Pattern
Baby born by Cesarean section did not experience a natural completion with the womb (a great loss). Such a person may feel unusually grieved when saying good-byes, leaving school, bidding farewell to friends, leaving a job, etc. If s/he can fully feel these potent feelings, realizing that the inordinately strong emotions stem from more than the current situation, the pain of this pattern may be relieved.

Healing Visualization
See yourself enveloped in white light, relaxed and having all the time you need.

Healing Affirmation
"I easily complete all my tasks."
"I deserve to take whatever time I need to feel complete."

Healing Breathwork
Breathe and experience the guilt, anger, sadness, and other feelings as they arise. Although they may be very intense and overwhelming, take responsibility for your ownership of these feelings, without blaming anyone, including yourself. (This means to recognize that these feelings reside within you and, therefore, are "owned" by you.) In this way, you will drain your unconscious "container" of the powerful, suppressed feelings which have created this sense of incompletion.

Being as objective as possible, observe the different ways in which you have felt unduly rushed or were left feeling incomplete. Observe the times when you have failed to complete a project. Once you have felt the emotions which are present at the moment, practice the Healing Visualization and Healing Affirmation with full attention and feeling. This will create new images and new thought patterns in your subconscious, resulting in new and different experiences of ability and autonomy.

Pattern: Indecision

Common Expression
"I can't decide what to do, which to choose."

Possible Origin of Pattern
Sperm's indecision over which egg to fertilize during conception.

Healing Visualization
See yourself feeling safe, clear, and decisive about each important step in life.

Healing Affirmation
"I am clear about the next right step for me."

Healing Breathwork
Breathe and experience the fear, guilt, anger, sadness, and other feelings as they arise. Although they may be very intense and overwhelming, take responsibility for your ownership of these feelings, without blaming anyone, including yourself. (This means to recognize that these feelings reside within you and, therefore, are "owned" by you.) In this way, you will drain your unconscious "container" of the powerful, suppressed feelings which have created this pattern of indecision.

Being as objective as possible, observe the different ways in which you have experienced this pattern. Once you have felt the emotions which are present as they arise in the moment, practice the Healing Visualization and Healing Affirmation with full attention and feeling. This will create new images and new thought patterns in your subconscious, resulting in new, different, and decisive experiences.

Pattern: Infidelity

Description of Pattern
Usually coupled with a deep fear of intimacy. Distrusting, disconnected from others. This deception can be a frightened person's way to retain control of the dynamics of relationship. Infidelity may be a person's way to act out his or her anger at (or unconscious fear of) the partner – an unconscious way to get "the upper hand."

Possible Origin of Pattern
Early relationships with parents were unstable, inconsistent, capricious. Child felt he or she could not trust or rely on others. The child may have felt like the ground on which he stood was always shifting – thus the need to control relationships. Parent(s) could have been addicted to drugs or alcohol, overcontrolling or over critical. Child could have felt a need to escape.

Healing Visualization
See yourself feeling safe, honest and vulnerable in a loving relationship.

Healing Affirmation
"I deserve the joy of being a faithful partner."

Healing Breathwork
Breathe and experience the guilt, anger, sadness, and other feelings as they arise. Although they may be very intense and overwhelming, take responsibility for your ownership of these feelings, without blaming anyone, including yourself. (This means to recognize that these feelings reside within you and, therefore, are "owned" by you.) In this way, you will drain your unconscious "container" of the powerful, suppressed feelings which have created this pattern of infidelity.

Being as objective as possible, observe the different ways in which you have experienced infidelity. Once you have felt the emotions which are present as they arise in the moment, practice the Healing Visualization and Healing Affirmation with full attention and feeling. This will create new images and new thought patterns in your subconscious, resulting in new, different, happy, loyal, and faithful experiences.

Pattern: Injury, Injuries

Description of Pattern
Accident-prone person.

Possible Origin of Pattern
Injury to mother or fetus during pregnancy, whether due to a fall, violence, etc. Or injury during the birth process or during infancy. Or injury as the only way of getting loving attention from parent(s).

Healing Visualization
See yourself moving safely through each moment.

Healing Affirmation
"I move safely through life with the grace of a dancer."
"I am always surrounded in protective white light."
"I am loved and cared for."

Healing Breathwork
Breathe and experience the fear, guilt, anger, sadness, and other feelings as they arise. Although they may be very intense and overwhelming, take responsibility for your ownership of these feelings, without blaming anyone, including yourself. (This means to recognize that these feelings reside within you and, therefore, are "owned" by you.) In this way, you will drain your unconscious "container" of the powerful, suppressed feelings which have created this pattern of injury.

Being as objective as possible, observe the different ways in which you have experienced injury. Can you consciously choose to move a little more slowly and safely? Once you have felt the emotions which are present at the moment, practice the Healing Visualization and Healing Affirmation with full attention and feeling. This will create new images and new thought patterns in your subconscious, resulting in new, safer experiences.

Pattern: Insecurity

Common Expression
"Be careful. Don't take any risks."
"Life is not safe."

Possible Origin of Pattern
The womb did not feel truly safe. Child did not feel safe and trusting of parent(s). The parent(s) rules for life were not clear or seemed unfair. Indiscriminate and inappropriate or harsh disciplinary practices may have left the child feeling bewildered, confused, and generally insecure. Religions which teach that God is a harsh disciplinarian seeking retribution can contribute to this pattern.

Healing Visualization
See yourself feeling loved and safe in every way. See yourself surrounded in a protective pink light.

Healing Affirmation
"I deserve to be relaxed, safe, and secure at all times."

Healing Breathwork
Breathe and experience the fear, guilt, anger, sadness, and other feelings as they arise. Although they may be very intense and overwhelming, take responsibility for your ownership of these feelings, without blaming anyone, including yourself. (This means to recognize that these feelings reside within you and, therefore, are "owned" by you.) In this way, you will drain your unconscious "container" of the powerful, suppressed feelings which have created this pattern of insecurity.

Being as objective as possible, observe the different ways in which you have felt unsafe and insecure. Once you have felt the emotions which are present at the moment, practice the Healing Visualization and Healing Affirmation with full attention and feeling. This will create new images and new thought patterns in your subconscious, resulting in new experiences of safety and security.

Pattern: Integrity Issues

Description of Pattern

Fears the risk, vulnerability and loss of control associated with self-disclosure. Low self-esteem. Does not trust others and often cannot be trusted. Elements of dishonesty include denial, rationalization, outright lying, stealing, all kinds of deception, gossip, hypocrisy, and blaming of others instead of taking responsibility for one's life.

Possible Origin of Pattern

1. Child learned to lie or pretend, perhaps wearing different faces with different people or situations. In dysfunctional families, dishonesty prevails at many levels, including dishonesty with self.
2. Sometimes a person enters an incarnation with this unfortunate trait, choosing in this way to learn honest behavior (i.e., this is not always behavior learned in the present lifetime.)

Healing Visualization

See yourself behaving honestly in every way at all times.

Healing Affirmation

"I am loved and supported in total integrity."

Healing Breathwork

Breathe and experience the fear, anger, guilt, sadness, and other feelings as they arise. Although they may be very intense, take responsibility for your ownership of these feelings, without blaming anyone, including yourself. (This means to recognize that these feelings reside within you and, therefore, are "owned" by you.) In this way, you will drain your unconscious "container" of the powerful, suppressed feelings which have created this pattern of distrust.

Being as objective as possible, observe the different ways in which you have lacked integrity. Once you have felt the emotions which are present at the moment, practice the Healing Visualization and Healing Affirmation with full attention and feeling. This will create new images and new thought patterns in your subconscious, resulting in a new experience of integrity.

Pattern: Intensity

Description of Pattern
Other people may be more aware of this pattern than the person. When around him or her, others may feel restless, frenetic, anxious, "hyper." S/he may be driven by a deep, underlying, unconscious fear, though s/he may be quite unaware of this. S/he may approach tasks as if they were emergencies or create emergencies out of ordinary events.

Possible Origin of Pattern
This pattern often traces back to a traumatic event before, during or right after birth, such as a medical emergency like as Cesarean-section, breech birth or other Perinatal complications. Or fear, anxiety, and intensity could have been absorbed during gestation from an anxious mother. Or later, during childhood, when a parent is very demanding or critical, a child often feels anxious, worried, and afraid and this nervous, intense energy may continue. Children whose parent(s) abuse alcohol or drugs may have this pattern.

Healing Visualization
See yourself managing even challenging situations with great calm and peacefulness. See yourself (or him or her) surrounded by an egg-shaped vortex of blue light.

Healing Affirmation
"I am calmly active and actively calm."

Healing Breathwork
Breathe and experience the fear, frustration, and other feelings as they arise. Although they may be very strong, take responsibility for your ownership of these feelings, without blaming anyone, including yourself. (This means to recognize that these feelings reside within you and, therefore, are "owned" by you.) In this way, you will drain your unconscious "container" of the powerful, suppressed feelings which have created this pattern of intensity.

Being as objective as possible, observe the different ways in which you have felt nervous, agitated, or upset. Once you have felt the emotions which are present at the moment, practice the Healing Visualization and Healing Affirmation with full attention and feeling. This will create new images and new thought patterns in your subconscious, resulting in calmer, more serene experiences.

Pattern: Intimacy (fear of)

Description of Pattern
A person may be engaged in relationship(s) of many different kinds without actually allowing closeness with anyone. The person is usually unconscious of this pattern. S/he may sabotage close relationships.

Possible Origin of Pattern
Traumatic birth. Or birth and life were not experienced as safe. Early relationships unstable or unreliable and were a source of pain for the infant or young child. Parent(s) may have been addicted to alcohol or drugs, or demanded too much emotional support from child.

Healing Visualization
See yourself feeling completely safe and relating closely with friends and loved ones. See yourself enveloped in a protective pink light.

Healing Affirmation
"I deserve love and intimacy."
"I am safe in my relationships."

Healing Breathwork
Breathe and experience the fear, guilt, anger, sadness, and other feelings as they arise. Although they may be very intense and overwhelming, take responsibility for your ownership of these feelings, without blaming anyone, including yourself. (This means to recognize that these feelings reside within you and, therefore, are "owned" by you.) In this way, you will drain your unconscious "container" of the powerful, suppressed feelings which have created this fear of intimacy.

Being as objective as possible, observe the different ways in which you have kept others at a distance.

Once you have felt the emotions which are present at the moment, practice the Healing Visualization and Healing Affirmation with full attention and feeling. This will create new images and new thought patterns in your subconscious, resulting in experiences of greater intimacy.

Pattern: Isolated (feeling)

Common Expression
"I feel alone and disconnected from others."

Possible Origin of Pattern
A baby kept in an incubator or isolette or otherwise separated from mother right after birth will often feel intensely disconnected from others, perhaps feeling "alone in a crowd." The person actually is disconnected from a vital part of himself (from the soul).

Healing Visualization
See yourself connected to your own heart and center of clarity and to loved ones. Imagine being enveloped in a protective sphere of pink light.

Healing Affirmation
"I deserve love and closeness."

Healing Breathwork
Breathe and experience the fear, guilt, anger, sadness, and other emotions as they arise. Although they may be very intense and overwhelming, take responsibility for your ownership of these feelings, without blaming anyone, including yourself. (This means to recognize that these feelings reside within you and, therefore, are "owned" by you.) In this way, you will drain your unconscious "container" of the powerful, suppressed emotions which have created this sense of isolation.

Being as objective as possible, observe the different ways in which you have kept others at a distance and all the ways in which you have felt isolated.

Once you have felt the emotions which are present at the moment, practice the Healing Visualization and Healing Affirmation with full attention and feeling. This will create new images and new thought patterns in your subconscious, resulting in experiences of greater love, openness and connection with others.

Pattern: Late (habitually)

Common Expression
"I'll get there when I'm ready."
(This may be more of an attitude than a spoken expression.)

Possible Origin of Pattern
Premature birth. Birth before baby was truly ready.

Healing Visualization
See yourself arriving at just the perfect moment, with ease and comfort.

Healing Affirmation
"I honor myself and others when I am on time."

Healing Breathwork

Breathe and experience the guilt, fear, anger, sadness, and other feelings as they arise. Although they may be very intense and overwhelming, take responsibility for your ownership of these feelings, without blaming anyone, including yourself. (This means to recognize that these feelings reside within you and, therefore, are "owned" by you.) In this way, you will drain your unconscious "container" of the powerful, suppressed feelings which have created this pattern of tardiness.

Being as objective as possible, observe the different ways in which you have been late. Once you have felt the emotions which are present at the moment, practice the Healing Visualization and Healing Affirmation with full attention and feeling. This will create new images and new thought patterns in your subconscious, resulting in experiences of punctuality.

Pattern: Loneliness

Common Expression
"Something is missing in my life."
"I can't find my place."
"I don't fit."

Possible Origin of Pattern

A child mayfeel lonely because the parent(s), themselves, are incapable of or disinterested in relating with their child in a sincere way. Parent(s) who are unavailable, emotionally or physically, or who are cold, demanding, critical, or abusive, do not allow the interpersonal connection the child so desperately needs in order to grow and mature in a healthy way. This pattern can also stem from a child's disconnection from its birth mother or father as a result of adoption (a major loss) or conception as a result of sperm or ovum donation. In this case, the child knows at a deep, unconscious level that it is disconnected. Note: See, also, Meaninglessness.

Healing Visualization

See yourself enveloped in an egg-shaped vortex of pink light, connected to significant loved ones and to the source of love itself. Feel the peace and happiness which comes from this awareness.

Healing Affirmation
"I am connected to my source of love and joy."
"The more loving I am toward others, the more connected I feel."

Healing Breathwork

Breathe and experience the sadness, loneliness, anger, and other feelings as they arise. Although they may be very intense, take responsibility for your ownership of these feelings, without blaming anyone, including yourself. (This means to recognize that these feelings reside within you and, therefore, are "owned" by you.) In this way, you will drain your unconscious "container" of the powerful, suppressed feelings which have created this loneliness.

Being as objective as possible, observe the different ways in which you have felt lonely. Once you have felt the emotions which are present at the moment, practice the Healing Visualization charge and Healing Affirmation with full attention and feeling. This will create new images and new thought patterns in your subconscious, resulting in experiences of greater happiness, peace, and loving closeness with yourself and others.

Pattern: Manipulated (being)

Description of Pattern
This person may brood with buried anger but not speak up, feeling confused about how s/he is manipulated by others.

Possible Origin of Pattern
Birth was interfered with, perhaps through use of forceps, doctor's hands, or suctioning procedures. Or the birth may have been delayed for someone else's convenience. A Cesarean-section baby may have felt manipulated or invaded. As a child, this person may have been manipulated by a parent or other person.

Healing Visualization
See yourself living your life freely, making your own choices and decisions autonomously.

Healing Affirmation
"I am in control of my own life."
"I am free."
"The freer I am, the happier I become."

Healing Breathwork
Breathe and experience the fear, guilt, anger, sadness, and other feelings as they arise. Although they may be very intense and overwhelming, take responsibility for your ownership of these feelings, without blaming anyone, including yourself. (This means to recognize that these feelings reside within you and, therefore, are "owned" by you.) In this way, you will drain your unconscious "container" of the powerful, suppressed feelings which have created this pattern of being manipulated.

Being as objective as possible, observe the different ways in which you have been manipulated. Try to become aware of times when you allow yourself to be manipulated instead of taking responsibility for your own life. Are you receiving any benefits from this behavior? What are they? Would you rather have these benefits than be in charge of your own decisions?

Once you have felt the emotions which are present at the moment, practice the Healing Visualization and Healing Affirmation with full attention and feeling. This will create new images and new thought patterns in your subconscious, resulting in experiences of greater autonomy and personal power.

Pattern: Manipulative

Description of Pattern
Self-centered, self-absorbed, disconnected, devious person. This person feels separate, interested only in self and selfish desires to the exclusion of others. Lacks compassion. Generally not concerned for others. Is sometimes friendly or sweet, while secretly feeling hostile. May be consciously or unconsciously devious, conniving, hateful and/or interpersonally destructive.

Possible Origin of Pattern
Retarded maturation. As the child grew, s/he failed to evolve past the self-centered focus of childhood. Emotional needs ignored, actively repressed, or ridiculed, i.e., being hit for crying. May have been left in crib to "cry it out."

Healing Visualization
See yourself maturing and having the capacity to be concerned for the welfare of others as well as self.

Healing Affirmation
"I am happy when I contribute to the highest good for all."
"I am well cared for."

Healing Breathwork
Breathe and experience the guilt, fear, anger, sadness, and other feelings as they arise. Although they may be very intense and overwhelming, take responsibility for your ownership of these feelings, without blaming anyone, including yourself. (This means to recognize that these feelings reside within you and, therefore, are "owned" by you.) In this way, you will drain your unconscious "container" of the powerful, suppressed feelings which have created this pattern of manipulative behavior.

Being as objective as possible, observe the different ways in which you have been manipulative. Are you aware that when you behave in manipulative ways, you back away from the intimacy in a relationship?

Once you have felt the emotions which are present at the moment, practice the Healing Visualization and Healing Affirmation with full attention and feeling. This will create new images and new thought patterns in your subconscious, resulting in experiences of greater honesty and intimacy.

Pattern: Meaninglessness

Common Expressions and Questions

"Something is missing in my life."
"Why am I here? What am I supposed to do with my life?"

Possible Origin of Pattern

There may be many sources of this patterns. A child may begin to feel disconnected and lonely because its parent(s) are incapable of or disinterested in relating with him in a sincere way. Parent(s) who are unavailable, emotionally or physically, or who are cold, demanding, neglectful, critical, or abusive, do not allow the interpersonal connection the child needs in order to grow and mature in a healthy way. This pattern can also stem from a child's disconnection from its birth parent(s) as a result of adoption (a major loss) or conception via sperm or ovum donation. In these cases, the child senses this disconnection at a deep, unconscious level.

Modern people in general are crying out for contact with the inner life — with their own deep, spiritual roots. Without this contact, a human being lacks a sense of connection and meaning. Many turn to food, sex, alcohol, drugs, and other addictions to numb the meaninglessness of their lives, seeking an anesthetic to salve the inner pain. An internal hunger, however, can never be satisfied through external means. In essence, the person whose life lacks meaning is sensing that he is out of touch with his own soul.

Healing Visualization

See yourself enveloped in an egg-shaped vortex of pink light, connected to significant loved ones and to the source of love itself. Imagine that you are engaged in work you love to do which is also of benefit to other people. Feel the deep, peaceful power which flows from your love.

Healing Affirmation

"My life is filled with meaning."

Healing Breathwork

Breathe and experience the sadness, fear, and other feelings as they arise. Although they may be very intense, take responsibility for your ownership of these feelings, without blaming anyone, including yourself. (This means to recognize that these feelings reside within you and, therefore, are "owned" by you.) In this way, you will drain your unconscious "container" of the powerful, suppressed feelings which may be blocking you from an experience of connection with your own inner core.

Being as objective as possible, observe the different ways in which your life has felt meaningless. Once you have felt the emotions which are present at the moment, practice the Healing Visualization and Healing Affirmation with full attention and feeling. This will create new images and new thought patterns in your subconscious, resulting in experiences of greater love, purpose, and meaning.

Pattern: Misfit (feeling like)

Common Expression
"I don't fit in. I don't belong."

Possible Origin of Pattern
Person with chronic or long-term physical disability, visible to others. Or child not wanted, given up for adoption at birth, or conceived as a result of sperm or ovum donation. This baby intuitively feels it either does not belong in the family or unconsciously senses a disconnection from its birth parent(s). (See the case of George Wilson on page 33.)

Healing Visualization
See yourself experiencing a deep sense of being in your perfect place. Imagine that you are surrounded by a sphere of white light.

Healing Affirmation
"I always belong wherever I am."
"Wherever I am is home."
"I am a child of the Universe and this whole planet is my home."
"Everywhere I go, I feel comfortable with the people I meet."

Healing Breathwork
Breathe and experience the fear, guilt, anger, sadness, and other feelings as they arise. Although they may be very intense and overwhelming, take responsibility for your ownership of these feelings, without blaming anyone, including yourself. (This means to recognize that these feelings reside within you and, therefore, are "owned" by you.) In this way, you will drain your unconscious "container" of the powerful, suppressed feelings which have created this pattern of feeling like a misfit.

Being as objective as possible, observe the different ways in which you have felt like a misfit. Once you have felt the emotions which are present at the moment, practice the Healing Visualization and Healing Affirmation with full attention and feeling. This will create new images and new thought patterns in your subconscious, resulting in new and different experiences.

Pattern: Misunderstood

Common Expression
"Women (men / people) don't see who I am."
"Women (men / people) don't understand me."

Possible Origin of Pattern
Parent(s) wanted a girl and had a baby boy or wanted a boy and had a baby girl. Or baby was not wanted at all. Or baby had a chronic or serious illness or disability. Or parents wanted a child with different personality traits.

Healing Visualization
See yourself experiencing a sense of being deeply acknowledged and appreciated for your intrinsic qualities.

Healing Affirmation
"Everywhere I go, people understand me."
"Everywhere I go, people are happy to see me."

Healing Breathwork
Breathe and experience the guilt, fear, anger, sadness, and other feelings as they arise. Although they may be very intense and overwhelming, take responsibility for your ownership of these feelings, without blaming anyone, including yourself. (This means to recognize that these feelings reside within you and, therefore, are "owned" by you.) In this way, you will drain your unconscious "container" of the powerful, suppressed feelings which have created this pattern of feeling misunderstood.

Being as objective as possible, observe the different ways in which you have felt misunderstood. Once you have felt the emotions which are present at the moment, practice the Healing Visualization and Healing Affirmation with full attention and feeling. This will create new images and new thought patterns in your subconscious, resulting in experiences of greater love and understanding.

Pattern: Money Issues

Common Expression
"I earn the money to pay my bills, though often late."
"I never seem to have enough money."
"I earn enough but still feel anxious about money."

Possible Origin of Pattern
Baby was fed on a schedule, according to mother's or other caretaker's convenience. Money and abundance patterns are frequently related to feeding and nurturing patterns during infancy.

Healing Visualization
See yourself always having more money than is needed. Visualize yourself feeling relaxed and confident that your financial and security needs will be always be met.

Healing Affirmation
"I have everything I need to do the things I want, and everything I want to do the things I need."

Healing Breathwork
Breathe and experience the fear, guilt, anger, sadness, and other feelings as they arise. Although they may be very intense and overwhelming, take responsibility for your ownership of these feelings, without blaming anyone, including yourself. (This means to recognize that these feelings reside within you and, therefore, are "owned" by you.) In this way, you will drain your unconscious "container" of the powerful, suppressed feelings which have created this pattern of insecurity and anxiety regarding money.

Being as objective as possible, observe the different ways in which you have felt anxious about money. Once you have felt the emotions which are present at the moment, practice the Healing Visualization and Healing Affirmation with full attention and feeling. This will create new images and new thought patterns in your subconscious, resulting in experiences of greater security and abundance.

Pattern: Obsessive behavior

Description of Pattern
A disorder which may take many forms, i.e., excessive hand washing, collecting things, fidgeting, head-banging, lying, stealing, etc.

Possible Origin of Pattern
Severely traumatizing events occurring in infancy or childhood. These may include emotional, sexual and/or physical abuse. Often, because the memory of the trauma is buried (is unconscious), the extreme energy caught in the suppression attempts to vent itself through seemingly harmless obsessive behavior.

Healing Visualization
See yourself feeling loved, safe, and deeply relaxed. See an egg-shaped vortex of white light surrounding and protecting you at all times.

Healing Affirmation
"I am safe. I am loved. I am free."

Healing Breathwork
Breathe and experience the fear, anger and other feelings as they arise. Although they may be very intense and compelling, take responsibility for your ownership of these feelings, without blaming anyone, including yourself. (This means to recognize that these feelings reside within you and, therefore, are "owned" by you.) In this way, you will drain your unconscious "container" of the powerful, suppressed feelings which have created this pattern of obsessive behavior.

Being as objective as possible, observe the different ways in which you have felt frantic, pressured, and frightened. Once you have felt the emotions which are present at the moment, practice the Healing Visualization and Healing Affirmation with full attention and feeling. This will create new images and new thought patterns in your subconscious, resulting in new and different experiences of love and safety.

Pattern: Overwhelmed

Common Expression
"This (or life) is just too hard."

Possible Origin of Pattern
Vaginal birth with a very long labor. A need to pull away to protect from pressure or from physical closeness. Physical closeness may activate memories of confinement in the birth canal.

Healing Visualization
See yourself feeling the freedom and flexibility to move about as you choose. Imagine being as free as a bird.

Healing Affirmation
"I easily and freely manage all the challenges of my life."

Healing Breathwork
Breathe and experience the fear, guilt, anger, sadness, and other feelings as they arise. Although they may be very intense and overwhelming, take responsibility for your ownership of these feelings, without blaming anyone, including yourself. (This means to recognize that these feelings reside within you and, therefore, are "owned" by you.) In this way, you will drain your unconscious "container" of the powerful, suppressed feelings which have created this pattern of feeling overwhelmed.

Being as objective as possible, observe the different ways in which you have felt overwhelmed. Once you have felt the emotions which are present at the moment, practice the Healing Visualization and Healing Affirmation with full attention and feeling. This will create new images and new thought patterns in your subconscious, resulting in experiences of greater poise and balance.-

Pattern: Panic, Panic Attacks

Description of Pattern
May have panic attacks or exhibit other obsessive behavior stemming from unresolved, unfelt, traumatizing, underlying terror.

Possible Origin of Pattern
Extreme, deep-seated unconscious fear. If this person can fully experience the terror which is at the root of this panic, this pattern will dissolve. While this is not always a simple challenge, it can often be resolved much more quickly than one might imagine. May be a response to a major life change. May indicate hormonal imbalance.

Healing Visualization
See yourself feeling completely safe and relaxed in the midst of a frightening, stressful situation. Imagine being surrounded by a bubble of protective pink light as you observe the scene with emotional detachment, as though you are watching a movie on a screen.

Healing Affirmation
"It is safe for me to feel all my feelings."

Healing Breathwork
Breathe and experience the fear, guilt, anger, sadness, and other feelings as they arise. Although they may be very intense and overwhelming, take responsibility for your ownership of these feelings, without blaming anyone, including yourself. (This means to recognize that these feelings reside within you and, therefore, are "owned" by you.) In this way, you will drain your unconscious "container" of the powerful, suppressed feelings which have created this pattern of panic.

Being as objective as possible, observe the different ways in which you have felt afraid and panic-stricken. Once you have felt the emotions which are present at the moment, practice the Healing Visualization and Healing Affirmation with full attention and feeling. This will create new images and new thought patterns in your subconscious, resulting in experiences of greater peace and poise.

Pattern: Paranoia

Common Expression
"Someone's out to get me."

Possible Origin of Pattern
Abuse during gestation, birth, or early childhood. The home environment may have been unpredictable. One or both parents may have exhibited mood swings. Abortion may have been considered or attempted, or father may have threatened pregnant mother.

Healing Visualization
See yourself feeling completely safe. Imagine being surrounded by a bubble of protective pink light.

Healing Affirmation
"God's perfect protection keeps me safe at all times."

Healing Breathwork
Breathe and experience the fear, guilt, anger, sadness, and other feelings as they arise. Although they may be very intense and overwhelming, take responsibility for your ownership of these feelings, without blaming anyone, including yourself. (This means to recognize that these feelings reside within you and, therefore, are "owned" by you.) In this way, you will drain your unconscious "container" of the powerful, suppressed feelings which have created this pattern of paranoia.

Being as objective as possible, observe the different ways in which you have felt extremely afraid that someone or something was out to get you. Once you have felt the emotions which are present at the moment, practice the Healing Visualization and Healing Affirmation with full attention and feeling. This will create new images and new thought patterns in your subconscious, resulting in safer, more peaceful experiences.

Pattern: Perfectionism

Description of Pattern
Insistent on perfection according to his or her own terms, this person may often be critical and non-accepting of self and others.

Possible Origin of Pattern
Critical, non-accepting parent(s). The child was unable to please or win their approval (love). The home environment may have felt unsafe and very unpredictable. Parents may have abused alcohol or drugs. Child may have had chronic or life-threatening illness.

Healing Visualization
Imagine yourself feeling very satisfied that your best effort is entirely sufficient. Imagine being surrounded by a bubble of protective pink light.

Healing Affirmation
"I do my best, and my best is good enough."

Healing Breathwork
Breathe and experience the fear, guilt, anger, sadness, and other feelings as they arise. Although they may be very intense and overwhelming, take responsibility for your ownership of these feelings, without blaming anyone, including yourself. (This means to recognize that these feelings reside within you and, therefore, are "owned" by you.) In this way, you will drain your unconscious "container" of the powerful, suppressed feelings which have created this pattern of perfectionism.

Being as objective as possible, observe the different ways in which you have felt that you had to perform in order to be accepted or loved. Once you have felt the emotions which are present at the moment, practice the Healing Visualization and Healing Affirmation with full attention and feeling. This will create new images and new thought patterns in your subconscious, resulting in experiences of greater relaxation and self-acceptance.

Pattern: Phobias

Description of Pattern
This person may have panic attacks or exhibit other fear-based behavior stemming from unexperienced emotions.

Possible Origin of Pattern
Extreme, deep-seated unconscious fear. If this person can fully experience the terror which is at the root of the phobia, this pattern will dissolve. While this is not always a simple challenge, it can often be resolved much more quickly than one might imagine. (See the story of Mary.)

Healing Visualization
See yourself feeling completely safe and relaxed in the midst of a terrifying situation. Imagine being surrounded by a bubble of protective pink light while you observe the scene with emotional detachment, just as though you were watching a movie on a screen.

Healing Affirmation
"It is safe for me to feel all my feelings."
"The world is safe and I am safe in it."

Healing Breathwork
Breathe and experience the terror and other feelings as they arise. Although they may be very intense and overwhelming, take responsibility for your ownership of these feelings, without blaming anyone, including yourself. (This means to recognize that these feelings reside within you and, therefore, are "owned" by you.) In this way, you will drain your unconscious "container" of the powerful, suppressed feelings which have created this phobia.

Being as objective as possible, observe the different ways in which you have felt terrified. Once you have felt the emotions which are present at the moment, practice the Healing Visualization and Healing Affirmation with full attention and feeling. This will create new images and new thought patterns in your subconscious, resulting in new and different experiences of safety and trust.

Pattern: Physical Injuries

Description of Pattern
Injuries may recur repeatedly on the same body part and/or at the same time of year or may recur in a time-cycle pattern.

Possible Origin of Pattern
Injured at birth. Bruised by forceps, handled roughly by midwife, doctor, or other medical personnel. Knee or hip injuries may recur as in breech or other difficult birth.

Healing Visualization
See yourself being completely agile, flexible, graceful, and safe. Imagine being surrounded by a bubble of protective pink light.

Healing Affirmation
"I am safe."

Healing Breathwork
Breathe and experience the fear, guilt, anger, sadness, and other feelings as they arise. Although they may be very intense and overwhelming, take responsibility for your ownership of these feelings, without blaming anyone, including yourself. (This means to recognize that these feelings reside within you and, therefore, are "owned" by you.) In this way, you will drain your unconscious "container" of the powerful, suppressed feelings which have created this pattern of physical injury.

Being as objective as possible, observe the different ways in which you have been injured. Once you have felt the emotions which are present at the moment, practice the Healing Visualization and Healing Affirmation with full attention and feeling. This will create new images and new thought patterns in your subconscious, resulting in safer experiences.

Pattern: Possessiveness (of others)

Description of Pattern

A pattern wherein a person seeks to control one's life by controlling the actions of others. This person may profess to "love" another, but actually treat the "loved one" as a possession, rather than allowing him or her the freedom which all human beings desire. By such clinging and controlling behavior, the possessive person often drives his loved ones away from him, thus creating his worst fear.

Possible Origin of Pattern

At some level, this person feels afraid of being alone, or fears the consequences of having someone else in control. He or she may have suffered at the hands of another, or felt such loneliness as to feel life-threatening.

Healing Visualization

See yourself able to confront all fears, able to feel the terrifying feelings while continuing to live and let others enjoy their freedom also. Visualize being surrounded by an egg-shaped vortex of white, protective light.

Healing Affirmation

"It is safe for me to feel afraid."
"The more freedom I give to others, the more they enjoy being with me."
"It is easy for others to be with me, for I respect their right to freedom and free choice."

Healing Breathwork

Breathe and experience the fear, anger, and other feelings as they arise. Although they may be very intense and overwhelming, take responsibility for your ownership of these feelings, without blaming anyone, including yourself. (This means to recognize that these feelings reside within you and, therefore, are "owned" by you.) In this way, you will drain your unconscious "container" of the powerful, suppressed feelings which have created this pattern of possessiveness.

Being as objective as possible, observe the different ways in which you have behaved possessively. Once you have experienced the emotions which are present at the moment, practice the Healing Visualization and Healing Affirmation with full attention and feeling. This will create new images and new thought patterns in your subconscious, resulting in new and different experiences. Although you will still be capable of feeling afraid and clingy, it will no longer keep you from living your life fully or proceeding toward your goals.

Pattern: Pressure

Common Expression
"There's so much pressure."
"I'm under so much pressure."

Possible Origin of Pattern
Generalized intensity of labor and birth. Forceps or suctioning at birth. (Forceps on head sometimes results in headaches.) Or too much was expected of the young child.

Healing Visualization
See yourself feeling completely relaxed and free. Imagine being comfortably surrounded by a spacious bubble of protective pink light.

Healing Affirmation
"I deserve to be relaxed and at ease."

Healing Breathwork
Breathe and experience the fear, guilt, anger, sadness, and other feelings as they arise. Although they may be very intense and overwhelming, take responsibility for your ownership of these feelings, without blaming anyone, including yourself. (This means to recognize that these feelings reside within you and, therefore, are "owned" by you.) In this way, you will drain your unconscious "container" of the powerful, suppressed feelings which have created this feeling of pressure.

Being as objective as possible, observe the different ways in which you have felt pressured. Once you have felt the emotions which are present at the moment, practice the Healing Visualization and Healing Affirmation with full attention and feeling. This will create new images and new thought patterns in your subconscious, resulting in more relaxed and comfortable experiences.

Pattern: Procrastination

Description of Pattern

This person may approach tasks tentatively and fearfully and may often seem preoccupied. May be self-doubting.

Possible Origin of Pattern

May be a response to an overbearing parent, religion, or upbringing which imparted the message that the child must trust, not himself, but external authority. Child may feel a deep, underlying sense of low self-esteem and lack of self-confidence resulting from the above or from other causes which can erode the energy and vigor of this person's life.

Healing Visualization

See yourself feeling completely free and self-governing. Imagine being surrounded by a bubble of protective pink light.

Healing Affirmation

"I decide what to do and I follow through without delay."
"I trust myself."

Healing Breathwork

Breathe and experience the guilt, fear, anger, sadness, and other feelings as they arise. Although they may be very intense and overwhelming, take responsibility for your ownership of these feelings, without blaming anyone, including yourself. (This means to recognize that these feelings reside within you and, therefore, are "owned" by you.) In this way, you will drain your unconscious "container" of the powerful, suppressed feelings which have created this pattern of procrastination.

Being as objective as possible, observe the different ways in which you have put off the completion of important tasks and decisions in your life. Once you have felt the emotions which are present at the moment, practice the Healing Visualization and Healing Affirmation with full attention and feeling. This will create new images and new thought patterns in your subconscious, resulting in experiences of greater trust and ability.

Pattern: Promiscuity

Description of Pattern

This person fears intimacy. S/he is distrusting of and disconnected from others. Deception can be this person's way to try to retain control in a relationship.

Possible Origin of Pattern

Early relationships with parent(s) was unstable, inconsistent, and capricious. The child may have felt that s/he could not trust in or rely on others. S/he may have felt like the ground on which s/he stood was always shifting — thus the need to control instead of experiencing the risk and vulnerability required to engage in an intimate relationship.

Healing Visualization

See yourself being honest and faithful in a committed, monogamous relationship.

Healing Affirmation

"I deserve love."
"I trust myself and my partner."

Healing Breathwork

Breathe and experience the fear, guilt, anger, sadness, and other feelings as they arise. Although they may be very intense and overwhelming, take responsibility for your ownership of these feelings, without blaming anyone, including yourself. (This means to recognize that these feelings reside within you and, therefore, are "owned" by you.) In this way, you will drain your unconscious "container" of the powerful, suppressed feelings which have created this pattern of promiscuity.

Being as objective as possible, observe the different ways in which you have been unfaithful and promiscuous. Once you have felt the emotions which are present at the moment, practice the Healing Visualization and Healing Affirmation with full attention and feeling. This will create new images and new thought patterns in your subconscious, resulting in experiences of greater loyalty and fidelity.

Pattern: Punctuality (compulsive)

Note: While punctuality is a positive attribute, experience of the suppressed emotions underlying this pattern will dissolve the anxiety and compulsivity without eliminating the trait itself.

Common Expression
"I feel crazy if I'm running late."
"I must be on time!"

Possible Origin of Pattern
1. Premature birth. Birth occurred before baby was truly ready. Anxiety over having to hurry.
2. "Late" birth wherein baby was in stress because birth took so long. In such a case, the baby's unconscious conclusion might be, "I must always be on time from now on!" This person might feel a life and death urgency over the issue of punctuality and/or tardiness.

Healing Visualization
See yourself able to be consistently on time without feeling undue anxiety or tension.

Healing Affirmation
"I am always relaxed, safe, and on time."

Healing Breathwork
Breathe and experience the guilt, anger, sadness, and other feelings as they arise. Although they may be very intense and overwhelming, take responsibility for your ownership of these feelings, without blaming anyone, including yourself. (This means to recognize that these feelings reside within you and, therefore, are "owned" by you.) In this way, you will drain your unconscious "container" of the powerful, suppressed feelings which have created this pattern of compulsivity regarding punctuality.

Being as objective as possible, observe the different ways in which you have been compulsive about punctuality. Once you have felt the emotions which are present at the moment, practice the Healing Visualization and Healing Affirmation with full attention and feeling. This will create new images and new thought patterns in your subconscious, resulting in experiences of greater relaxation and poise.

Pattern: Purposelessness

See, also, Meaninglessness

Common Expressions and Questions
"Something is missing in my life."
"Why am I here? What am I supposed to do with my life?"

Possible Origin of Pattern
The sources of purposelessness can be many. A child begins to feel adrift and lonely when the parent(s), themselves, are incapable of or disinterested in relating with him or her in a sincere way. Parent(s) who are unavailable, emotionally or physically, who are cold, demanding, critical, or abusive, do not allow the interpersonal connection the child needs in order to grow and mature in a healthy way. This pattern can also stem from a child's disconnection from its birth parent(s) as a result of adoption (a major loss) or conception via sperm or ovum donation. In these cases, the child senses this disconnection at a deep, unconscious level, and longs for the reconnection which is love itself.

Healing Visualization
See yourself enveloped in an egg-shaped vortex of pink light, connected to significant loved ones and to love. Imagine that you are engaged in work you love to do and feel the deep, peaceful power which flows from your love.

Healing Affirmation
"The purpose of my life is to love and serve the highest good."
"I know my purpose and commit my life to its expression."

Healing Breathwork
Breathe and experience the sadness, fear, and other feelings as they arise. Although they may be very intense, take responsibility for your ownership of these feelings, without blaming anyone, including yourself. (This means to recognize that these feelings reside within you and, therefore, are "owned" by you.) In this way, you will drain your unconscious "container" of the powerful, suppressed feelings which may be blocking your experience of connection with the unique purpose for your life.

Being as objective as possible, observe the different ways in which you have felt a lack of purpose in your life. Once you have felt the emotions which are present at the moment, practice the Healing Visualization and Healing Affirmation with full attention and feeling. This will create new images and new thought patterns in your subconscious, resulting in experiences of greater love, focus, and purpose in your life.

Pattern: Rebellion

Common Expression
"Don't tell me what to do!"
"Stop trying to control me.!"
"Get out of my way and let me do it!"

Possible Origin of Pattern
Resentment of doctor's intrusion (instead of harmony with mother, baby, and the beauty of the birth process) in the birth process. The umbilical cord may have been wrapped around baby's neck, and/or forceps may have been used. This person may be a loner or go to great lengths to be in control of his life, career, relationships, social situations, etc.

Healing Visualization
See yourself being calmly and assertively in control of your own life.

Healing Affirmation
"I am my own authority."
"I make my own choices and decisions with ease and peacefulness."
"Everyone supports my autonomy."

Healing Breathwork
Breathe and experience the anger, sadness, fear, and other feelings as they arise. Although they may be very intense and overwhelming, take responsibility for your ownership of these feelings, without blaming anyone, including yourself. (This means to recognize that these feelings reside within you and, therefore, are "owned" by you.) In this way, you will drain your unconscious "container" of the powerful, suppressed feelings which have created this pattern of rebellion against external authority.

Being as objective as possible, observe the different ways in which you have behaved rebelliously. Once you have felt the emotions which are present at the moment, practice the Healing Visualization and Healing Affirmation with full attention and feeling. This will create new images and new thought patterns in your subconscious, resulting in new and different experiences of peacefully being the authority in your own life.

Pattern: Rejection

Description of Pattern
Inhibited, timid, lacking self-confidence.

Possible Origin of Pattern
This person may have felt rejected by mother or father. This can result from one or both parents wanting a boy instead of a girl or a girl instead of a boy. In other cases, abortion may have considered or attempted, or the baby may have been given up for adoption. The parent (s) may have been unloving, unsupportive, unaffectionate, and/or critical of the child, or they may have been absent or unavailable, emotionally or physically. In addition, the child's attempts to "connect" were spurned.

Healing Visualization
See yourself feeling and being loved, welcomed, and appreciated wherever you go.

Healing Affirmation
"Wherever I go, people love and appreciate me."
"I always feel welcome, no matter what!"
"My presence brings joy to those around me."

Healing Breathwork
Breathe and experience the guilt, anger, fear, sadness, and other feelings as they arise. Although they may be very intense and overwhelming, take responsibility for your ownership of these feelings, without blaming anyone, including yourself. (This means to recognize that these feelings reside within you and, therefore, are "owned" by you.) In this way, you will drain your unconscious "container" of the powerful, suppressed feelings which have created this pattern of rejection.

Being as objective as possible, observe the different ways in which you have felt rejected. Once you have experienced the emotions which are present at the moment, practice the Healing Visualization and Healing Affirmation with full attention and feeling. This will create new images and new thought patterns in your subconscious, resulting in new experiences of greater acceptance and joy in your relationships with yourself, with others, and with life.

Pattern: Rescue Issues

Common Expression
"Someday my prince will come."

Possible Origin of Pattern
While many different people may have fantasies of being rescued, those born by Cesarean section may be especially likely to exhibit this pattern. Mythology in the Western world has supported and even encouraged this pattern in females, since this pattern appears in numerous fairy tales, including Sleeping Beauty, Snow White and Rapunzel.

Healing Visualization
See yourself feeling and being strong and independent, able to ask for help, when appropriate, and able to function alone.

Healing Affirmation
"I am strong, capable, and powerful."
"I enjoy being strong and independent."

Healing Breathwork
Breathe and experience the guilt, anger, sadness, fear, and other feelings as they arise. Although they may be very intense and overwhelming, take responsibility for your ownership of these feelings, without blaming anyone, including yourself. (This means to recognize that these feelings reside within you and, therefore, are "owned" by you.) In this way, you will drain your unconscious "container" of the powerful, suppressed feelings which have created this pattern of needing or wanting to be rescued.

Being as objective as possible, observe the different ways in which you have felt incapable of functioning alone. Are you afraid that you will lose something if you express your true power and independence? What would it mean if you were to become truly strong and autonomous? Once you have felt the emotions which are present at the moment, practice the Healing Visualization and Healing Affirmation with full attention and feeling. This will create new images and new thought patterns in your subconscious, resulting in experiences of greater autonomy, personal strength, and independence.

Pattern: Running Away

Description of Pattern

Fears the risk, vulnerability, and loss of control associated with commitment, intimacy, and rootedness.

The earlier the trauma which is the source of this fear, the more unconscious the fear will be. The more unconscious the fear, the greater intensity and power it will have in the person's life. (See Rolf's case.) A conscious or unconscious defense against intimacy and commitment.

Possible Origin of Pattern

1. Pregnant mother ran away or attempted to run away while baby was in the womb.
2. Baby abandoned by mother and/or father, who "ran away" and left baby.
3. Parent(s) abused alcohol or drugs.

Healing Visualization

See yourself being settled happily and successfully in your perfect place.

Healing Affirmation

"I am joyfully connected to my home and family."
"I feel safely in the perfect place for me."

Needed for Healing

Breathe and experience the fear, anger, sadness, and other feelings as they arise. Although they may be very intense, take responsibility for your ownership of these feelings, without blaming anyone, including yourself. (This means to recognize that these feelings reside within you and, therefore, are "owned" by you.) In this way, you will drain your unconscious "container" of the powerful, suppressed feelings which have created this pattern of running away.

Being as objective as possible, observe the different ways in which you have escaped or run away – or have wanted to run away. Once you have felt the emotions which are present at the moment, practice the Healing Visualization and Healing Affirmation with full attention and feeling. This will create new images and new thought patterns in your subconscious, resulting in experiences of greater groundedness and connection.

Pattern: Scandal

Description of Pattern
Situations of embarrassment or shame, and the public at large finds out.

Possible Origin of Pattern
Baby's conception, gestation, and/or birth created a scandal. (See the case of Jan, whose birth caused a scandal because her parents were thought to be too old to have a baby, and Dean, who was born out of wedlock to a 14-year-old girl.)

Healing Visualization
See yourself being the subject of a special honor awarded to those who are a source of pride. See yourself surrounded by a protective pink light.

Healing Affirmation
"I am a child of God."
"I am welcomed by everyone for my essence is divine."

Healing Breathwork
Breathe and experience the guilt, anger, sadness, fear, and other feelings as they arise. Although they may be very intense and overwhelming, take responsibility for your ownership of these feelings, without blaming anyone, including yourself. (This means to recognize that these feelings reside within you and, therefore, are "owned" by you.) In this way, you will drain your unconscious "container" of the powerful, suppressed feelings which have created this pattern of scandal.

Being as objective as possible, observe the different ways in which you have felt ashamed, humiliated, embarrassed, and scandalized. Once you have felt the emotions which are present at the moment, practice the Healing Visualization and Healing Affirmation with full attention and feeling. This will create new images and new thought patterns in your subconscious, resulting

Pattern: Self-Centeredness, Selfishness

Common Expression
"...but what about me?"

Description of Pattern
This person is unusually self-absorbed.

Possible Origin of Pattern
Usually stems from immaturity, which may have resulted from a lack of love and safety in early childhood. Raised in an atmosphere of love and sufficient safety, small children grow beyond the natural stage of self-centeredness and narcissism. When love and safety are lacking, though the child ages physically and mentally, he or she may fail to mature emotionally.

Healing Visualization
See yourself feeling so safe that it is natural to be generously concerned for others.

Healing Affirmation
"The more I care about others, the happier and safer I am."

Healing Breathwork
Breathe and experience the guilt, anger, fear, sadness, and other feelings as they arise. Although they may be very intense and overwhelming, take responsibility for your ownership of these feelings, without blaming anyone, including yourself. (This means to recognize that these feelings reside within you and, therefore, are "owned" by you.) In this way, you will drain your unconscious "container" of the powerful, suppressed feelings which have created this selfishness and self-centeredness.

Being as objective as possible, observe the different ways in which you have behaved selfishly. Once you have felt the emotions which are present at the moment, practice the Healing Visualization and Healing Affirmation with full attention and feeling. This will create new images and new thought patterns in your subconscious, resulting in greater experiences of growth and expansion.

Pattern: Self-Consciousness

Common Expression
"I'm afraid of being embarrassed."

Description of Pattern
In many situations, this person's focus is on himself or herself instead of paying attention to other people and things.

Possible Origin of Pattern
Child did not feel safe, accepted, or "okay." Parent(s) may have been cold, critical, and/or demanding. This family pattern is exacerbated by a stern, demanding, punishment-oriented religion. A person with this pattern may feel guilty, consciously or unconsciously, even though s/he may have done nothing wrong.

Healing Visualization
See yourself feeling completely at ease and able to participate fully, joyfully, and with childlike abandon in the activity of the moment. See yourself surrounded by a beautiful pink light.

Healing Affirmation
"I forget myself in the joy of each moment."

Healing Breathwork
Breathe and experience the guilt, anger, fear, sadness, and other feelings as they arise. Although they may be very intense and overwhelming, take responsibility for your ownership of these feelings, without blaming anyone, including yourself. (This means to recognize that these feelings reside within you and, therefore, are "owned" by you.) In this way, you will drain your unconscious "container" of the powerful, suppressed feelings which have created this self-consciousness.

Being as objective as possible, observe the different ways in which you have felt timid, shy, or self-conscious. Once you have felt the emotions which are present at the moment, practice the Healing Visualization and Healing Affirmation with full attention and feeling. This will create new images and new thought patterns in your subconscious, resulting in experiences of greater self-acceptance and ease with yourself and others.

Pattern: Self-Esteem Issues

Description of Pattern

This person may be unmotivated, unambitious, and/or self-doubting. Others may wish s/he would "wake up" or "get with it." S/he may "hide out," not participating.

Possible Origin of Pattern

Baby anesthetized at birth. (If mother was drugged, then baby was drugged, too.) This person may feel frozen, and either unable to move forward or not interested in forward movement or personal growth. May be out of touch with his or her body. May be afraid of or lacking in healthy sexual expression, on the one hand, or promiscuous or deceitful on the other. A person with low self-esteem usually has difficulty with self-initiated direction; not a self-starter. A child who was unwanted may suffer low self-esteem. This includes a child who was raised by its biological parent(s), or cases where abortion was considered or attempted, or where a child was given up for adoption. The child's unconscious conclusion may be, "If mom (dad) didn't want me, I must not be worth anything."

Healing Visualization

See yourself being aware that your presence is highly valued. Imagine a specific situation in which you feel uniquely and exquisitely valuable. See yourself surrounded by a beautiful pink light.

Healing Affirmation

"I am a priceless, precious child of God."
"Every day in every way I become more aware of my value."

Healing Breathwork

Breathe and experience the guilt, anger, fear, sadness, and other feelings as they arise. Although they may be very intense and overwhelming, take responsibility for your ownership of these feelings, without blaming anyone, including yourself. (This means to recognize that these feelings reside within you and, therefore, are "owned" by you.) In this way, you will drain your unconscious "container" of the powerful, suppressed feelings which have created this pattern of low self-esteem.

Being as objective as possible, observe the different ways in which you have felt unworthy or valueless. Once you have felt the emotions which are present at the moment, practice the Healing Visualization and Healing Affirmation with full attention and feeling. This will help to create new images and new thought patterns in your subconscious, resulting in a greater awareness of your value.

Pattern: Self-Hatred, Self-Loathing

Description of Pattern
A person experiencing self-hatred may feel extremely guilty, self-critical, or may experience intense regret over past mistakes.

Possible Origin of Pattern
This pattern can be especially strong when a child has been physically and/or sexually abused. In addition, a child learns to feel hatred for himself or herself when raised in a family where parent(s) feel guilty. Religions emphasizing guilt and punishment exacerbate this painful pattern.

Healing Visualization
Imagine a scene wherein you feel as happy and beautiful as a newborn child. See yourself completely enveloped in an egg-shaped vortex of healing pink light.

Healing Affirmation
"I deserve love."

Healing Breathwork
Breathe and experience the guilt, anger, sadness, fear, and other feelings as they arise. Although they may be very intense and overwhelming, take responsibility for your ownership of these feelings, without blaming anyone, including yourself. (This means to recognize that these feelings reside within you and, therefore, are "owned" by you.) In this way, you will drain your unconscious "container" of the powerful, suppressed feelings which have created this self-hatred.

Being as objective as possible, observe the different ways in which you have felt self-judgmental, guilty, worthless, or self-critical. Once you have felt the emotions which are present at the moment, practice the Healing Visualization and Healing Affirmation with full attention and feeling. This will create new images and new thought patterns in your subconscious, resulting in higher self-esteem.

Pattern: Self-Pity

Common Expression
"Nobody cares about me."

Possible Origin of Pattern
An expression of immaturity, self-absorption, and self-isolation. It is especially prevalent in a person who, as an infant, was neglected, insufficiently nurtured and touched. This infant will often fail to mature and will fail to expand its focus to the larger world outside. Most of us fall into this pattern at times, as a part of grieving a loss. In this pattern we are addressing an extreme degree, however, and it is helpful to realize that this pattern of self-pity can be resolved through work with a nurturing healer.

Healing Visualization
Imagine a scene wherein you feel intensely focused on work you love to do.

Healing Affirmation
"I am a powerful child of God."

Healing Breathwork
Breathe and experience the guilt, anger, sadness, fear, and other feelings as they arise. Although they may be very intense and overwhelming, take responsibility for your ownership of these feelings, without blaming anyone, including yourself. (This means to recognize that these feelings reside within you and, therefore, are "owned" by you.) In this way, you will drain your unconscious "container" of the powerful, suppressed feelings which have created this self-pity.

Being as objective as possible, observe the different ways in which you have felt absorbed in yourself. Once you have felt the emotions which are present at the moment, practice the Healing Visualization and Healing Affirmation with full attention and feeling. This will create new images and new thought patterns in your subconscious, resulting in happier experiences.

Pattern: Self-Sabotage

Description of Pattern

This person destroys his or her own success, whether in relationships, finances, academically, health, and so forth. Although he or she may be able to recognize the pattern (usually only after a number of recurrences), this pattern is likely to be a deeply unconscious one. (See the case history of Karl.)

Possible Origin of Pattern

Very early trauma, possibly in utero or around the time of birth. The umbilical cord may have become entangled around the baby's neck and the baby nearly died as a result. Or other gestational or birth trauma threatened baby's survival or safety. This can set up an unconscious fear (and expectation) later in life that "suddenly everything will go wrong!" This fearful expectation then becomes a self-fulfilling prophecy. Even in cases where it appears that some outside "enemy" is the cause of the sabotage, the stimulus may still be coming from the person's own unconscious dynamic. (When this is healed, the pattern of sabotage will cease.)

Healing Visualization

Image yourself in a situation wherein the more successful you become, the more peaceful you feel.

Healing Affirmation

"The more successful I become, the more peaceful I feel."
"As my success increases, my happiness increases, too."

Healing Breathwork

Breathe and experience the terror, guilt, anger, sadness, and other feelings as they arise. Although they may be very intense and overwhelming, take responsibility for your ownership of these feelings, without blaming anyone, including yourself. (This means to recognize that these feelings reside within you and, therefore, are "owned" by you.) In this way, you will drain your unconscious "container" of the powerful, suppressed feelings which have created this pattern of self-sabotage.

Being as objective as possible, observe the different ways in which you have contributed to your own defeat or destruction, whether this shows up in your relationships, your finances, your job or career, your health, or elsewhere.

Once you have felt the emotions which are present at the moment, practice the Healing Visualization and Healing Affirmation with full attention and feeling. This will create new images and new thought patterns in your subconscious, resulting in new and sustained successful experiences.

Pattern: Sexual Abuse

Common Expression
"I feel unclean, unworthy, ashamed."

Possible Origin of Pattern
This person may have been sexually abused as a child. In such cases, the child often blames himself or herself. When, instead of being valued and protected, children are exploited and abused, a violation of sacred trust, they become, understandably, distrusting of people and of life, often fearing intimacy and closeness. Sexual abuse as a child can damage his or her adult life and, especially, intimate relationships.

Healing Visualization
Imagine a scene wherein you feel treasured, safe, and protected.

Healing Affirmation
"I am God's child. I am innocent."

Healing Breathwork
Breathe and experience the guilt, anger, fear, sadness, and other feelings as they arise. Although they may be very intense and overwhelming, take responsibility for your ownership of these feelings, without blaming anyone, including yourself. (This means to recognize that these feelings reside within you and, therefore, are "owned" by you.) In this way, you will drain your unconscious "container" of the powerful, suppressed feelings which have created this pattern of sexual abuse.

Being as objective as possible, observe the different ways in which you have felt unclean, unworthy, ashamed, humiliated, and/or have been sexually abused. Once you have felt the emotions which are present at the moment, practice the Healing Visualization and Healing Affirmation with full attention and feeling. This will create new images and new thought patterns in your subconscious, resulting in experiences of greater safety, mutual respect, and love.

Pattern: Shame

Common Expression
"I feel ashamed."

Possible Origin of Pattern
Mother and/or father was ashamed of the pregnancy (Jan's case), or a child was shamed by parents. This pattern can also indicate that the person is suffering from guilt resulting on one hand from a transgression or omission, or on the other hand, from unconscious guilt or shame stemming from sexual abuse, character assassination by parent(s) or other authority figure, or identification with parent(s) who, themselves, felt ashamed (see Dean's case). This pattern is sometimes present when the child was ashamed of its parent(s). In this case, the child's conclusion may have been, "If my mom (dad) behaves this way, I am afraid it means I am like this, too."

Healing Visualization
Imagine a scene wherein you behave honorably in every way and feel very good about yourself. Imagine that you are being given an award for the highest honor. See yourself enveloped in a healing pink light.

Healing Affirmation
"I am God's child. I am innocent."
"I deserve love."

Healing Breathwork
Breathe and experience the guilt, anger, fear, sadness, and other feelings as they arise. Although they may be very intense and overwhelming, take responsibility for your ownership of these feelings, without blaming anyone, including yourself. (This means to recognize that these feelings reside within you and, therefore, are "owned" by you.) In this way, you will drain your unconscious "container" of the powerful, suppressed feelings which have created this pattern of shame.

Being as objective as possible, observe the different ways in which you have felt ashamed. Once you have felt the emotions which are present at the moment, practice the Healing Visualization and Healing Affirmation with full attention and feeling. This will create new images and new thought patterns in your subconscious, resulting in new and different experiences of self-respect and high self-esteem.

Pattern: Shyness

Common Expression
"I'm not okay."

Description of Pattern
This person tends to be self-conscious and unsure of self.

Possible Origin of Pattern
Overbearing, domineering, or hypercritical parent(s). With such parents, a small child does not feel safe, accepted, or free to be himself or herself. The child may have felt s/he had to measure up to standards which were either unrealistically high or which were confusing to the child. The child may have become hypervigilant – always alert for unexpected and precipitous changes in the mood of a parent or caretaker of whom the child may have been afraid. This child's feelings were not considered or validated. Since his or her feelings were not accepted, he or she did not feel acceptable.

Healing Visualization
Imagine a scene wherein you are so engrossed in a creative project that you completely forget yourself. Then, continuing to feel that sense of expansion, proceed to other activities, fully poised. See yourself enveloped in a healing pink light.

Healing Affirmation
"I am okay."
"Wherever I go, I enjoy interacting with others."

Healing Breathwork
Breathe and experience the fear, guilt, anger, sadness, and other feelings as they arise. Although they may be very intense and overwhelming, take responsibility for your ownership of these feelings, without blaming anyone, including yourself. (This means to recognize that these feelings reside within you and, therefore, are "owned" by you.) In this way, you will drain your unconscious "container" of the powerful, suppressed feelings which have created this pattern of shyness.

Being as objective as possible, observe the different ways in which you have felt timid, self-conscious, or shy. Once you have felt the emotions which are present at the moment, practice the Healing Visualization and Healing Affirmation with full attention and feeling. This will create new images and new thought patterns in your subconscious, resulting in experiences of greater poise and self-assurance.

Pattern: Smoking

(See Addiction)

Possible Origin of Pattern

1. Mother may have smoked while baby was in utero. Baby's system, then, may feel "normal" with the presence of nicotine.
2. Smoking may be an unconscious response to suppressed anger, since nicotine suppresses anger. (This is one of the reasons that a person who is attempting to quit smoking may often feel irritable.)
3. A baby who was either deprived of breast feeding or was insufficiently nurtured may unconsciously long for the comfort of having something to suck on. Having a cigarette in the mouth may afford some of this comfort.

As with other addictions, the underlying stimulus is unconscious. This is why the appeals to health as a deterrent to smoking go largely unheeded. If a person genuinely wants to quit smoking and is able to experience the powerful, underlying, unmet needs which are likely at the root of this addiction, the challenge of giving up this insidious habit will be far easier.

Healing Visualization

See yourself living happily, free of smoking, with calmness and peace. Imagine that you have loving relationships which are built on peaceful mutual support and trust.

Healing Affirmation

"I enjoy being a non-smoker."
"I love being a non-smoker."

Healing Breathwork

Breathe and experience the anger, fear, sadness, and other feelings as they arise. Regardless of their intensity, take responsibility for your ownership of these feelings, without blaming anyone, including yourself. (This means to recognize that these feelings reside within you and, therefore, are "owned" by you.) In this way, you will drain your unconscious "container" of the powerful, suppressed feelings which have clamored to be felt, thus diminishing the need for cigarettes.

Once you have felt the emotions which are present in the moment, practice the Healing Visualization and Healing Affirmation with full attention and feeling. This will create new images and new thought patterns in your subconscious, resulting in experiences of feeling safe enough to risk living your life fully, without smoking.

Pattern: Stress / Distress

Common Expression
"I'm under so much stress."

Description of Pattern
This person may tend to magnify or exaggerate his or her experience of stress.

Possible Origin of Pattern
Forceps or suction birth. Generalized intensity of labor and/or birth. Or too much was expected of the child.

Healing Visualization
See yourself feeling calm and serene and enjoying the ease of life. See yourself enveloped in a healing pink light.

Healing Affirmation
"Life is easy, no matter what I think!"
"I comfortably and easily manage all of life's challenges."
"I feel peaceful and serene no matter what happens."

Healing Breathwork
Breathe and experience the anxiety, guilt, anger, sadness, and other feelings as they arise. Although they may be very intense and overwhelming, take responsibility for your ownership of these feelings, without blaming anyone, including yourself. (This means to recognize that these feelings reside within you and, therefore, are "owned" by you.) In this way, you will drain your unconscious "container" of the powerful, suppressed feelings which have created this pattern of stress.

Being as objective as possible, observe the different ways in which you have felt distressed. Once you have felt the emotions which are present at the moment, practice the Healing Visualization and Healing Affirmation with full attention and feeling. This will create new images and new thought patterns in your subconscious, resulting in experiences of enhanced capacity and greater relaxation.

Pattern: Strong need to "do it myself"

Common Expression
"I can handle this alone!"

Possible Origin of Pattern
While this is a positive trait, a person may feel obsessive about this pattern if s/he experienced a Cesarean section birth. In this case, the person often has unconscious anger and/or fear about the outside intervention in the labor and/or birthing process. When a child exhibits this pattern, a parent will be most supportive by allowing the child to function as independently as is appropriate for his or her age.

Healing Visualization
See yourself feeling comfortable when receiving help in appropriate ways.

Healing Affirmation
"Others help only when I want them to."
"Other people respect my boundaries and I respect theirs."
"I welcome the help of others at appropriate times."

Healing Breathwork
Breathe and experience the fear, guilt, anger, sadness, and other feelings as they arise. Although they may be very intense and overwhelming, take responsibility for your ownership of these feelings, without blaming anyone, including yourself. (This means to recognize that these feelings reside within you and, therefore, are "owned" by you.) In this way, you will drain your unconscious "container" of the powerful, suppressed feelings which have created this strong need to do things your way and by yourself, without fear that others will interfere.

Being as objective as possible, observe the different ways in which you have felt infringed upon or violated. Once you have felt the emotions which are present at the moment, practice the Healing Visualization and Healing Affirmation with full attention and feeling. This will create new images and new thought patterns in your subconscious, resulting in experiences of greater relaxation and peaceful autonomy.

Pattern: Struggle

Common Expression
"Life is so hard."

Possible Origin of Pattern
Difficult birth, including breech and other birth complications. Birth was a dangerous, dramatic, emergency situation. The person with this patter may unconsciously create drama, emergencies, and struggle in order to feel more "alive."

Healing Visualization
See yourself experiencing the peace and easiness of life — and feeling more alive than ever before.

Healing Affirmation
"Life is easy for me, no matter what the circumstances."

Healing Breathwork
Breathe and experience the guilt, fear, anger, sadness, and other feelings as they arise. Although they may be very intense and overwhelming, take responsibility for your ownership of these feelings, without blaming anyone, including yourself. (This means to recognize that these feelings reside within you and, therefore, are "owned" by you.) In this way, you will drain your unconscious "container" of the powerful, suppressed feelings which have created this pattern of struggle.

Being as objective as possible, observe the different ways in which you have felt you had to struggle. Do you make tasks more difficult than they might otherwise be if you were more relaxed? Are you sometimes afraid of "having these too easy?" Be honest with yourself regarding these self-observations.

Once you have felt the emotions which are present at the moment, practice the Healing Visualization and Healing Affirmation with full attention and feeling. This will create new images and new thought patterns in your subconscious, resulting in experiences of greater ease and facility in your life.

Pattern: Stuck (a feeling of being)

Common Expression

"I'm stuck."
"I feel trapped."
"Don't fence me in."
"I just can't get moving."
"I can't seem to move forward."
"Something is always holding me back."

Possible Origin of Pattern

Forceps or suction birth. Baby's head very large for mother's pelvic structure. Or the cord was around the baby's neck. Mother not helping, drugged, or tensed and fearful during labor and/or birth. Doctor's hands or instruments are in the way. Birth delayed to meet someone else schedule or convenience.

This person may feel claustrophobic and need to be in control of his or her movements, both physically and psychologically. S/he may fear physical closeness due to the fear of getting "stuck" again. Sometimes a person will become painfully aware of this pattern when attempting to make a commitment (as in marriage or a job) — fearing that s/he will feel trapped again.

This pattern can also result from parent(s) who were very overbearing and controlling of a child, though it will usually be less intense than if it occurred during the birth process.

Healing Visualization

See yourself being flexible, at ease, and in charge of your own movement in life.

Healing Affirmation

"I am free."

Healing Breathwork

Breathe and experience the guilt, fear, anger, sadness, and other feelings as they arise. Although they may be very intense and overwhelming, take responsibility for your ownership of these feelings, without blaming anyone, including yourself. (This means to recognize that these feelings reside within you and, therefore, are "owned" by you.) In this way, you will drain your unconscious "container" of the powerful, suppressed feelings which have created this pattern of feeling claustrophobic, cornered, or trapped.

Being as objective as possible, observe the different ways in which you have felt stuck. Once you have felt the emotions which are present at the moment, practice the Healing Visualization and Healing Affirmation with full attention and feeling. This will create new images and new thought patterns in your subconscious, resulting in experiences of greater freedom and flexibility in every area of your life.

Pattern: Suicidal Thoughts, Tendencies

Common Expression

"I don't deserve (don't want) to be here."
"I'm not supposed to be here."

Possible Origin of Pattern

Fetus was expected to be ill or stillborn, or to die after birth. Or abortion was considered or attempted. Mother ambivalent or unhappy about the pregnancy. The baby may (unconsciously) have felt responsible for and/or guilty about mother's or father's unhappiness.

Healing Visualization

See yourself experiencing pure joy, experiencing life as the greatest gift imaginable. See yourself enveloped in a protective pink light.

Healing Affirmation

"My life is precious."
"I am God's child and I have a special place in this world."
"I do not belong to me. I belong to God."
"There is a unique and beautiful purpose for my life."

Healing Breathwork

Breathe and experience the fear, guilt, anger, sadness, and other feelings as they arise. Although they may be very intense and overwhelming, take responsibility for your ownership of these feelings, without blaming anyone, including yourself. (This means to recognize that these feelings reside within you and, therefore, are "owned" by you.) In this way, you will drain your unconscious "container" of the powerful, suppressed feelings which have created this pattern of self-destruction.

Being as objective as possible, observe the different ways in which you have felt you wanted to die. Once you have felt the emotions which are present at the moment, practice the Healing Visualization and Healing Affirmation with full attention and feeling. This will create new images and new thought patterns in your subconscious, resulting in experiences of greater joy and happiness in your life.

Pattern: Superiority (an air of)

Common Expression
"I'm the best!"
"I'm better than him (her)."

Description of Pattern
This person may be extremely competitive, exhibiting a win/lose attitude, while hypocritically professing to espouse a win/win and brotherly love philosophy. S/he may need to be "right" at all costs. Extreme egoistic expression. This person is often psychically isolated, self-absorbed and usually incapable of experiencing true intimacy, for s/he would be terrified of the vulnerability required in an intimate relationship.

Possible Origin of Pattern
Inferiority. Low Self-esteem. (A truly superior person would not behave in a "superior" manner.) This pattern can result from abuse or neglect as a child, or from a disconnection from the birth mother or father. The person may unconsciously blame himself or herself and attempt to win approval (love) by high achievement. S/he may feel (in the extreme) that if he does not outperform everyone, s/he will die.

Healing Visualization
See yourself feeling very good about yourself, with a healthy sense of humor and true humility. Imagine that you are enveloped in a protective pink light.

Healing Affirmation
"I deserve love."

Healing Breathwork
Breathe and experience the guilt, anger, fear, sadness, and other feelings as they arise. Although they may be very intense and overwhelming, take responsibility for your ownership of these feelings, without blaming anyone, including yourself. (This means to recognize that these feelings reside within you and, therefore, are "owned" by you.) In this way, you will drain your unconscious "container" of the powerful, suppressed feelings which have created this fictitious superiority.

Being as objective as possible, observe the different ways in which you have felt you would die if you did not achieve enough. Once you have felt the emotions which are present at the moment, practice the Healing Visualization and Healing Affirmation with full attention and feeling. This will create new images and new thought patterns in your subconscious, resulting in experiences of authentic excellence.

Pattern: Time-Cycle Patterns

Description of Pattern:
Pattern repeats in similar time cycles. For example, a relationship may last three years, another one three years, and a third one three years.

Possible Origin of Pattern
In addition to repeating events and emotions, the unconscious sometimes repeats specific cycles of duration. In Joe's case, we observed a five-day pattern. In Dean's case, a one-year pattern is obvious. If such a cycle exists in a person's life, there may be an intense anxiety or agitation as the anniversary approaches, even if the person is consciously unaware of this phenomenon.

While the events which transpire may differ from one another, the emotions surrounding the differing events may be similar, i.e., events may be marked by anger or anxiety.

Healing Visualization
See yourself experiencing the time cycle with ease and freedom, feeling happy and in control of life and self.

Healing Affirmation
"My new life is unfolding beautifully."

Healing Breathwork
Breathe and experience the guilt, fear, anger, sadness, and other feelings as they arise. Although they may be very intense and overwhelming, take responsibility for your ownership of these feelings, without blaming anyone, including yourself. (This means to recognize that these feelings reside within you and, therefore, are "owned" by you.) In this way, you will drain your unconscious "container" of the powerful, suppressed feelings which have created this repetition of a difficult pattern.

Once you have felt the emotions which are present at the moment, practice the Healing Visualization and Healing Affirmation with full attention and feeling. This will create new images and new thought patterns in your subconscious, resulting in a greater sense of poise and control in your life.

Pattern: Timidity

Common Expression
"I'm not okay."

Description of Pattern
This person tends to be self-conscious and unsure of self.

Possible Origin of Pattern
Overbearing or hypercritical parent(s). With such parents, a small child does not feel safe, accepted, or free to be himself or herself. The child may have felt s/he had to measure up to standards which were either unrealistically high or which were confusing to the child. The child's feelings were not considered or validated.

Healing Visualization
Imagine a scene wherein you are so engrossed in a creative project that you completely forget yourself. See yourself enveloped in a healing pink light.

Healing Affirmation
"I am okay."
"Wherever I go, I enjoy interacting with others."

Healing Breathwork
Breathe and experience the guilt, fear, anger, sadness, and other feelings as they arise. Although they may be very intense and overwhelming, take responsibility for your ownership of these feelings, without blaming anyone, including yourself. (This means to recognize that these feelings reside within you and, therefore, are "owned" by you.) In this way, you will drain your unconscious "container" of the powerful, suppressed feelings which have created this pattern of timidity.

Being as objective as possible, observe the different ways in which you have felt timid, self-conscious or shy. Once you have felt the emotions which are present at the moment, practice the Healing Visualization and Healing Affirmation with full attention and feeling. This will create new images and new thought patterns in your subconscious, resulting in a greater sense of poise and self-assurance.

Pattern: (feeling) Trapped

Common Expression
"Don't fence me in."

Description of Pattern
This person may go to great lengths to avoid feeling cornered or trapped. One man habitually backs his car into a driveway or parking spot so he can be ready to exit quickly.

Possible Origin of Pattern
Breech or other complications of traumatic birth. Baby felt impeded and blocked. Baby felt panic over having birth occur while s/he was in the "wrong" position. S/he may also fear and become extremely angry when s/he feels hemmed in without an escape. It is helpful to give such a person a lot of space whenever s/he is under stress.

Healing Visualization
Imagine feeling completely and peacefully in control of all elements of your life.

Healing Affirmation
"I am safe and free."
"I am always able to move about freely, no matter what."

Healing Breathwork
Breathe and experience the fear, guilt, anger, sadness, and other feelings as they arise. Although they may be very intense and overwhelming, take responsibility for your ownership of these feelings, without blaming anyone, including yourself. (This means to recognize that these feelings reside within you and, therefore, are "owned" by you.) In this way, you will drain your unconscious "container" of the powerful, suppressed feelings which have created this pattern of feeling trapped.

Being as objective as possible, observe the different ways in which you have felt trapped. Once you have felt the emotions which are present at the moment, practice the Healing Visualization and Healing Affirmation with full attention and feeling. This will create new images and new thought patterns in your subconscious, resulting in experiences of greater flexibility, relaxation, and freedom.

Pattern: Triangles (emotional)

Description of Pattern
This person may repeatedly create triangles, although this dynamic may be entirely unconscious. (S/he may think these situations just "happen.") Often, one person will wind up as "odd man out."

Possible Origin of Pattern
A child may have been caught in a triangle with mother and father (as in Rachel's case). Or the child could relate to mother alone or to father alone, but felt left out when both parents were present. S/he may have adopted this extreme win/lose tactic in order to gain control in a relationship which felt threatening and unsafe to the child. The younger the child when this dynamic pattern first occurred, the more intensely, unconsciously and desperately the person may employ this defense.

Healing Visualization
See yourself happily committed to your perfect mate in a faithful, harmonious, monogamous relationship.

Healing Affirmation
"I deserve love."

Healing Breathwork
Breathe and experience the fear, guilt, anger, sadness, and other feelings as they arise. Although they may be very intense and overwhelming, take responsibility for your ownership of these feelings, without blaming anyone, including yourself. (This means to recognize that these feelings reside within you and, therefore, are "owned" by you.) In this way, you will drain your unconscious "container" of the powerful, suppressed feelings which have created this pattern of being involved in emotional triangles.

Being as objective as possible, observe the different ways in which you have been involved in triangles. Once you have felt the emotions which are present at the moment, practice the Healing Visualization and Healing Affirmation with full attention and feeling. This will create new images and new thought patterns in your subconscious, resulting in experiences of greater peacefulness and loyalty in relationships.

Pattern: Trust Issues

Common Expression

"I can't count on men (women / people)."
"I don't trust anyone." *"I'm afraid I'll be blind sided."*
"People (men / women) are incompetent / unreliable."
"If you want something done right, you've got to do it yourself."

Possible Origin of Pattern

Disappointment and anger with the midwife or doctor who delivered you or your mother's disappointment or anger with him or her. Mother may have been in pain and the midwife or doctor was late, or did not or could not help mother, or used a drug or other procedure without mother's permission. Disappointment and/or frustration with the midwife, doctor of parent(s) who did not nurture and support the baby as s/he needed.

Mother or father may have behaved in an untrustworthy manner and their children model this behavior as adults. Childhood experiences of betrayal by parents and other trusted authority figures undermine a child's sense of trust, though patterns which originate in childhood are usually less intense than those occurring at birth.

A male may attract untrustworthy females or project this belief onto females, whether or not justified — and vice versa. A child may have been (or felt) ambushed — perhaps by a parent's violent attack (as in Elizabeth's case).

Healing Visualization

See yourself feeling supported by others in relationships and at work.

Healing Affirmation

"I am safe."

Healing Breathwork

Breathe and experience the guilt, anger, fear, sadness, and other feelings as they arise. Although they may be very intense and overwhelming, take responsibility for your ownership of these feelings, without blaming anyone, including yourself. (This means to recognize that these feelings reside within you and, therefore, are "owned" by you.) In this way, you will drain your unconscious "container" of the powerful, suppressed feelings which have created these trust issues.

Being as objective as possible, observe the different ways in which you have felt distrusting of others. Observe ways in which you, also, may have been untrustworthy. Once you have felt the emotions which are present at the moment, practice the Healing Visualization and Healing Affirmation with full attention and feeling. This will create new images and new thought patterns in your subconscious, resulting in experiences of greater trust and respect.

Pattern: Unclean (feeling)

Common Expression
"I feel dirty (unclean) (ashamed)."

Description of Pattern:
Other people intuitively may be aware of the feeling of uncleanness and avoid or distrust the person. The individual may avoid making direct eye contact with others.

Possible Origin of Pattern
Sexual abuse. Even an adult's sexual thoughts about a child may be psychically "picked up" by the child and leave him or her with an unclean (and confused) feeling. Unresolved, s/he may feel a deep, unconscious guilt and sense of shame.

Healing Visualization
See yourself emerging from a glistening natural pool, washed clean of every impurity. See yourself surrounded in a cleansing blue light.

Healing Affirmation
"I am an innocent child of God."

Healing Breathwork
Breathe and experience the fear, guilt, anger, sadness, and other feelings as they arise. Although they may be very intense and overwhelming, take responsibility for your ownership of these feelings, without blaming anyone, including yourself. (This means to recognize that these feelings reside within you and, therefore, are "owned" by you.) In this way, you will drain your unconscious "container" of the powerful, suppressed feelings which have created this feeling of uncleanness.

Being as objective as possible, observe the different ways in which you have felt unclean. Once you have felt the emotions which are present at the moment, practice the Healing Visualization and Healing Affirmation with full attention and feeling. This will create new images and new thought patterns in your subconscious, resulting in experiences of purity, honor, and respect.

Pattern: Unemployment (chronic)

Common Expression
"I can't win for losing."

Possible Origin of Pattern
This person may have become identified with being a failure as a fetus, infant or small child. This could have been brought from a previous lifetime or it could have been taken on in response to a parent or family situation. In one case, a man seemed unable to hold a job or succeed at any endeavor, though he was intelligent, talented, and eager to work. Searching back through his history, we discovered that while he was in the womb, his father was unable to find employment. This desperate and needy period so marked the forming baby that he took on a deep, unconscious fear of failure and a belief that he, personally, would fail. The unfortunate experiences resulting from this inner belief reinforced his foreboding and created a cycle of repeated failures.

Healing Visualization
See yourself succeeding brilliantly at work you love to do. See yourself surrounded in a rich, golden light.

Healing Affirmation
"I am successful in all my endeavors."

Healing Breathwork
Breathe and experience the fear, guilt, anger, sadness, and other feelings as they arise. Although they may be very intense and overwhelming, take responsibility for your ownership of these feelings, without blaming anyone, including yourself. (This means to recognize that these feelings reside within you and, therefore, are "owned" by you.) In this way, you will drain your unconscious "container" of the powerful, suppressed feelings which have created this feeling of failure and unemployment.

Being as objective as possible, observe the different ways in which you have felt like a failure. Once you have felt the emotions which are present at the moment, practice the Healing Visualization and Healing Affirmation with full attention and feeling. This will create new images and new thought patterns in your subconscious, resulting in experiences of success in life.

Pattern: Unfinished Business

Description of Pattern
Projects or relationship(s) aborted before the person feels truly complete with them.

Possible Origin of Pattern
Baby born by Cesarean section did not experience a natural completion with the womb (a great loss). Such a person may feel unusually grieved when saying good-byes, leaving school, bidding farewell to friends, leaving a job, etc. If s/he can fully feel these potent feelings, realizing that the strong emotions stem from more than just the current situation, the pain of this pattern may be greatly lessened.

Healing Visualization
See yourself completing all tasks in an orderly fashion, finishing one thing before moving on to the next.

Healing Affirmation
"The more orderly I am, the more peaceful I feel."
"I complete all my tasks on time."
"I finish one thing before I start another."

Healing Breathwork
Breathe and experience the fear, sadness, and other feelings as they arise. Regardless of their intensity, take responsibility for your ownership of these feelings, without blaming anyone, including yourself. (This means to recognize that these feelings reside within you and, therefore, are "owned" by you.) In this way, you will drain your unconscious "container" of the powerful, suppressed feelings which have created this pattern of incompletion or unfinished business.

Being as objective as possible, observe the different ways in which you have left tasks and relationships incomplete. Once you have felt the emotions which are present at the moment, practice the Healing Visualization and Healing Affirmation with full attention and feeling. This will create new images and new thought patterns in your subconscious, resulting in experiences of more orderly completions.

Pattern: Unloved (feeling)

Description of Pattern
This person may be depressed and self-absorbed.

Possible Origin of Pattern
May stem from neglect as an infant or small child. In reality, it is when we are incapable of loving that we also feel most unloved. When a human being is able to experience a glimmer of the truth about his true nature, s/he will feel almost nothing but love!

Healing Visualization
See yourself surrounded by people who love you dearly. See yourself enveloped in a pink light.

Healing Affirmation
"I deserve love."
"The more loving I am, the more love I experience."

Healing Breathwork
Breathe and experience the fear, guilt, anger, sadness, and other feelings as they arise. Although they may be very intense and overwhelming, take responsibility for your ownership of these feelings, without blaming anyone, including yourself. (This means to recognize that these feelings reside within you and, therefore, are "owned" by you.) In this way, you will drain your unconscious "container" of the powerful, suppressed feelings which have created this pattern of feeling unloved.

Being as objective as possible, observe the different ways in which you have felt unloved. Once you have felt the emotions which are present at the moment, practice the Healing Visualization and Healing Affirmation with full attention and feeling. This will create new images and new thought patterns in your subconscious, resulting in experiences of greater joy and loving connection.

Pattern: Unworthiness

Common Expression
"I'm no good." "I'm not good enough."
"Nothing I do is ever good enough."

Possible Origin of Pattern
1. Child was accepted only if s/he performed well enough. The love s/he received was conditional.
2. Baby was unwanted, was the "wrong" gender, or was a burden or inconvenience to parent(s).
3. Children conceived by sperm donation sometimes express this sense of unworthiness. There are countless births due to sperm donation; fewer as a result of ovum donation. However, it has generally been observed by donor offspring and the counselors who work with them that the inability to know one's genetic origins leaves a void that deprives one of a sense of wholeness.
4. Disappointment with the way s/he was received at birth. Baby not appreciated.
5. Patterns of unworthiness may show up in adopted children, as well as any child who was unwanted. The unconscious thought may be, "If my mom (dad) didn't want me, I must not be worth anything."
6. Most of us experience a relative sense of unworthiness from time to time. This is not necessarily an indication of pathology but, in mild forms, may be a natural part of a healthy maturation process. It may indicate that one is measuring oneself by a yardstick which may no longer apply. It may be helpful to ask yourself the following questions: "Whose values matter to me anyway — mine or those of others?" or "Which evaluations matter most to me — the external ones of others and society or my own inner knowingness?"

Healing Visualization
See yourself receiving a special award, given to you to mark your vital and valuable presence in your community.

Healing Affirmation
"I am a child of God. My worth is beyond measure."

Healing Breathwork
Breathe and experience the guilt, fear, anger, sadness, and other feelings as they arise. Although they may be very intense and overwhelming, take responsibility for

your ownership of these feelings, without blaming anyone, including yourself. (This means to recognize that these feelings reside within you and, therefore, are "owned" by you.) In this way, you will drain your unconscious "container" of the powerful, suppressed feelings which have created these feelings unworthiness.

Being as objective as possible, observe the different ways in which you have felt unworthy. Once you have felt the emotions which are present at the moment, practice the Healing Visualization and Healing Affirmation with full attention and feeling. This will create new images and new thought patterns in your subconscious, resulting in experiences of deep and worthwhile meaning.

Pattern: Urgency (compulsive)

Description of Pattern

Other people may be more aware of this pattern than the subject person. When around him or her, others may feel restless, frenetic, anxious, "hyper." S/he may be driven by a deep, underlying, unconscious fear, though s/he may be unaware of this. S/he may approach otherwise mundane tasks as if they were emergencies or may create emergencies out of otherwise ordinary events.

Possible Origin of Pattern

This pattern often traces back to a frantic or traumatic event before, during or right after birth, such as a medical emergency like as Cesarean-section, breech birth (an extreme, emergency birth), high-forceps birth, cord around baby's neck, and/or other Perinatal complications. Or fear, anxiety, and intensity could have been absorbed during gestation, labor and/or birth from an anxious mother. Or later, during childhood, when a parent is very demanding or critical, a child often feels anxious, worried, and afraid and this nervous, intense energy may continue.

Healing Visualization

See yourself managing even challenging situations with great calm and peacefulness. See yourself surrounded by an egg-shaped vortex of blue light.

Healing Affirmation

"I am calmly active and actively calm."

Healing Breathwork

Breathe and experience the fear, frustration, and other feelings as they arise. Although they may be very strong, take responsibility for your ownership of these feelings, without blaming anyone, including yourself. (This means to recognize that these feelings reside within you and, therefore, are "owned" by you.) In this way, you will drain your unconscious "container" of the powerful, suppressed feelings which have created this pattern of urgency.

Being as objective as possible, observe the different ways in which you have felt nervous and agitated. Once you have felt the emotions which are present at the moment, practice the Healing Visualization and Healing Affirmation with full attention and feeling. This will create new images and new thought patterns in your subconscious, resulting in experiences of greater poise and calmness.

Pattern: Victim

Common Expression
"Nobody cares about me." "Life's not fair." "This isn't fair."

Description of Pattern
This person may blame other people and things instead of taking responsibility for his or her own life and actions.

Possible Origin of Pattern
A baby who was unwanted. S/he may have been given up for adoption, or abortion was considered or attempted. Or parent(s) did not want the pregnancy or were ambivalent about the pregnancy. Perhaps no one nurtured, loved, or cared for this baby. This person may have an immature expectation that life should right all the wrongs he suffered as a child; s/he may be "mad at the world," whether or not s/he is consciously aware of this.

Healing Visualization
See yourself creating exactly the experiences in life which you want to enjoy. See yourself enveloped in a protective pink light.

Healing Affirmation
"I am the ruler of my life, the creator of my own destiny."
"If it's to be, it's up to me."
"I am a powerful child of God and I create my life the way I want it."

Healing Breathwork
Breathe and experience the fear, frustration, and other feelings as they arise. Although they may be very strong, take responsibility for your ownership of these feelings, without blaming anyone, including yourself. (This means to recognize that these feelings reside within you and, therefore, are "owned" by you.) In this way, you will drain your unconscious "container" of the powerful, suppressed feelings which have created this pattern of victimization.

Being as objective as possible, observe the different ways in which you have felt victimized. Once you have felt the emotions which are present at the moment, practice the Healing Visualization and Healing Affirmation with full attention and feeling. This will create new images and new thought patterns in your subconscious, resulting in experiences of greater empowerment, autonomy, and personal power.

Pattern: Violence

Description of Pattern
This person may be either the perpetrator, the recipient or otherwise involved in violence.

Possible Origin of Pattern
Pregnant mother witnessed or was subjected to violence while baby was in the womb, including in movies. Expression of violence often stems from a deep-seated, unconscious anger. (One man who acted out such a rage by engaging in fights through his life was born illegitimate and never knew who his father was. He felt that he was different from other children and people, he was enraged at his missing dad, yet he also felt a deep and intense sadness, yearning, and need for his vitally important and missing father.) It is suspected that the increased violence in modern society stems from deeply-buried hurt and rage.

Healing Visualization
See yourself feeling calm, happy, and peaceful.

Healing Affirmation
"I deserve love."

Healing Breathwork
Breathe and experience the fear, frustration, and other feelings as they arise. Although they may be very strong, take responsibility for your ownership of these feelings, without blaming anyone, including yourself. (This means to recognize that these feelings reside within you and, therefore, are "owned" by you.) In this way, you will drain your unconscious "container" of the powerful, suppressed feelings which have created this pattern of violence.

Being as objective as possible, observe the different ways in which you have been involved in violence. Once you have felt the emotions which are present at the moment, practice the Healing Visualization and Healing Affirmation with full attention and feeling. This will create new images and new thought patterns in your subconscious, resulting in more peaceful experiences.

Pattern: Withdrawal / Withdrawn

Description of Pattern

This person is emotionally shut down and unavailable. He or she may be quiet, perhaps speaking only when spoken to. Others may feel tense or ill at ease when around this individual. People may feel drained after being in the presence of the withdrawn person. The Pattern of Withdrawal may be unconscious or it may be a conscious ploy to control others.

Possible Origin of Pattern

This pattern is often an infantile reaction to hurt or the fear of hurt. A cold and undemonstrative mother may have failed to respond to baby and baby's needs for touch, affection, and nurturing may have been neglected or ignored. (An infant's only defense is psychic and emotional withdrawal.) Others around this person will probably be able to observe this pattern more easily than the person himself or herself, since s/he withdraws under threat of rejection or other hurt. Persons who were emotionally, physically, and/or sexually abused as children may also withdraw as a defense against further pain or hurt.

Healing Visualization

See yourself feeling happy and enthusiastic, able to stay present with friends and loved ones.

Healing Affirmation

"It is safe for me to love and be loved."

Healing Breathwork

Breathe and experience the fear, sadness, frustration, and other feelings as they arise. Although they may be very strong, take responsibility for your ownership of these feelings, without blaming anyone, including yourself. (This means to recognize that these feelings reside within you and, therefore, are "owned" by you.) In this way, you will drain your unconscious "container" of the powerful, suppressed feelings which have created this pattern of withdrawal.

Being as objective as possible, observe the different ways in which you withdraw from others. Once you have felt the emotions which are present at the moment, practice the Healing Visualization and Healing Affirmation with full attention and feeling. This will create new images and new thought patterns in your subconscious, resulting in experiences of aliveness and connection with others.

Pattern: Worry

(While most of us worry at times, this pattern is included to deal with cases of excessive, chronic worrying.)

Common Expression
"I am always worrying about something."

Possible Origin of Pattern
Mother extremely anxious or worried during pregnancy. Though she may have loved and wanted her baby very much, and her anxiety may have been about external factors (i.e., finances, health, war, absence of baby's father, or a general lack of support), baby may have perceived this as a threat. (See case of Ursula.)

Healing Visualization
See yourself trusting that your life will turn out wonderfully.

Healing Affirmation
"Everything always turns out for the best, no matter what I think."
"I do my best and let God handle the rest."

Healing Breathwork

Breathe and experience the fear, frustration, and other feelings as they arise. Although they may be very strong, take responsibility for your ownership of these feelings, without blaming anyone, including yourself. (This means to recognize that these feelings reside within you and, therefore, are "owned" by you.) In this way, you will drain your unconscious "container" of the powerful, suppressed feelings which have created this pattern of worry.

Being as objective as possible, observe the different ways in which you worry. Once you have felt the emotions which are present at the moment, practice the Healing Visualization and Healing Affirmation with full attention and feeling. This will create new images and new thought patterns in your subconscious, resulting in experiences of trust and confidence.

Bibliography

We are grateful for permission to use the following material:

1. Page 21: Quotation is from a 1996 Invitation into Membership of the Charles F. Menninger Society.
2. Pages 21 and 22: Quotations from Original Articles by David B. Cheek, MD, in the subject of Pre- and Peri-Natal Psychology, Winter 1986 issue, ©1986 Human Sciences Press.
3. Pages 23 and 24: Quotations from an article entitled "Birth Is More Than a Beginning" by William R. Emerson, Ph.D., published in Indepth News, January-February 1992 issue, available from Indepth, The Institute for Developmental Education and Psychotherapy.
4. Page 35: Animal Crackers cartoon reprinted by permission: Tribune Media Services
5.. Page 85: Case study entitled "Debbie" is an original article by David B. Cheek, MD, published in the Pre- and Perinatal Psychology Journal, Winter 1992 issue.
6. Page 91: Case Study entitled "Donald" is by William R. Emerson, Ph.D.
7. Page 148: Quotation in mid-page is from "Pregnant Virgin," by Marion Woodman.
8. Page 205: Reference to "Ted Kaczynski, suspected 'Unabomber'" is from an editorial in North County Times, July 19, 1996, quoting Dr. Jerrold Post, Director of the Political Psychology Program at George Washington University, in a Newsweek magazine article.

Recommended Reading

1. Secrets: A Practical Guide to Undreamed-of Possibilities / Christina Thomas
2. In Tune With The Soul / Christina Thomas
3. Different Doorway: Adventures of a Caesarean Born / Jane B. English
4. Babies Remember Birth / David B. Chamberlain, Ph.D. (619) 296-7535
5. Autobiography of a Yogi / Paramahansa Yogananda (meditation)
6. Rebirthing Made Easy / Colin Sisson (breathwork)
7. Birth Without Violence / Frederick Leboyer
8. The Secret Life of the Unborn Child / Thomas Verny, M.D. and J. Kelley
9. Life After Life / Raymond Moody, MD
10. Lethal Secrets, The Pschology of Donor Insemination / A. Baran, R. Pannor
11. The Owl Was a Baker's Daughter / Marion Woodman (eating disorders)
12. The Silva Mind Control Method / Jose Silva (visualization)
13. Creative Visualization / Shakti Gawain
14. Scientific Healing Affirmations / Paramahansa Yogananda
15. Mind-Body Therapy / Ernest Rossi and David B. Cheek, M.D.

Index

A

abandonment 43, 58, 122, 169
abundance 170
abuse 58, 171
abuse, sexual 254
accidents 172
addiction 33, 69, 81, 110, 173, 257
addictive behavior 173
alcohol / drug abuse 31, 174
ambition (lack of) 71, 175
ambush 48, 57, 58, 176
anger 60, 62, 81, 177
anxiety 90, 178
ashamed 179
authority issues 24, 180

B

belonging (lack of) 110, 181

betrayal 182
biofeedback 153
blocked (feeling) 183
BodhiSoul© Breathwork 46, 58, 143, 145, 148, 151, 161
Bohm, David 152
boundary issues 24, 184
breathwork 54, 62, 75, 81, 83, 108, 144

C

caretaking 82, 185
Cheek, David B., MD 13, 21, 22, 85, 112, 143
cold personality 186
commitment (fear of) 187
competing with men 38
compulsive behavior 188
confidence 85, 189
confusion 60
connected breathing 144
control issues 24, 190, 191

D

dependence 192
depression 97, 193
disconnected 194
disconnection 69
dishonesty 195
distress 258
dominated 196
drama 197
duplicity 198

E

eating disorders 92, 199
emergency 200
Emerson, William R., Ph.D. 13, 22, 23, 90, 143
emotional autobiography 135, 137
emotional triangles 40, 201,269
empathy (lack of) 202

F

failure (a sense of) 203
fear 90, 116, 204
fear of the dark 58
Findeisen, Barbara 13, 100
"flat" personality 205

G

giving up 206
grief 207

guilt 24, 30, 58, 137, 138, 208

H

Harman, Dr. Willis 153
headaches 24
helplessness 209
hopelessness 210
humiliation 211

I

illness 92, 212
implicate order 152
incompletion 213, 273
indecision 214
infidelity 215
injuries 236
injury 216
inner work 128
insecurity 217
integrity 162
integrity issues 218
intensity 219
intimacy (fear of) 31, 113, 220
isolated (feeling) 221

J

James, William 26
Jung, Dr. Carl G. 57, 165

L

late (habitually) 165, 222
List of Patterns 164
loneliness 32, 72, 103, 223
looking for patterns 137

M

Maharshi, Sri Ramana 27
manipulated 24, 224
manipulative 225
meaninglessness 226
Menninger Society 21
misfit 227
misunderstood 228
money issues 229

O

obsessive behavior 230
out of touch with body 24
overwhelm 24, 231

P

panic 116, 232
panic attacks 100, 232
paranoia 91, 97, 233
perfectionism 234
phobias 235
physical ailments 172
physical closenes (fear of) 24
possessiveness 237
pressure 238
pressured 24
procrastination 239
promiscuity 37, 240
Proust, Marcel 19
punctuality (compulsive) 241
purposelessness 242

Q

quitting 206

R

rebellion 243
rebirthing 145
rejection 58, 60, 244
relationship pattern 28, 29, 122,138
rescue fantasies 24
rescue issues 245

running away 43, 97, 246

S

sadness 81
scandal 110, 247
self-centeredness 248
self-consciousness 249
self-esteem 76, 85, 189, 250
self-esteem issues 24
self-hatred 251
self-loathing 81, 251
self-pity 252
self-sabotage 253
selfishness 248
sexual abuse 254
shame 58, 110, 179, 255
shyness 256
Siegel, Dr. Bernard 153
smoking 257
Staude, John-Raphael, Ph.D. 13, 22, 97, 143
stress 258
strong need to "do it myself" 259
struggle 260
stuck (a feeling of being) 261
substance abuse 262
success 263
suicidal thoughts 264
suicide 32, 91, 92, 264
superiority (an air of) 265

T

time-cycle pattern 63, 113, 122,266
timidity 267
trapped (feeling) 268
trust issues 270
Turner, Jon-Richard/Troya 13, 92, 143

U

unclean (feeling) 271
unemployment (chronic) 272
unfinished business 24, 213, 273
unloved (feeling) 274
unworthiness 58, 275
urgency 277

V

Verny, Thomas, MD 22
victim 48, 278
violence 279

W

withdrawn 280
Woodman, Marion 148
world seen as painful place 24
worry 281
worthlessness 80, 81

Self-Discovery Quiz

	Yes	No
1. Do you experience similar kinds of difficulties in relationships over and over again?	______	______
2. Do you often feel pressured by recurring financial challenges?	______	______
3. Do you frequently feel "stuck" or blocked by a person or situation?	______	______
4. Do you often feel rebellious or resentful of authority without understanding why?	______	______
5. Have you, more than once, ended (or thought about ending) a relationship even though you loved the person and knew you'd be lonely?	______	______
6. Have you been abandoned or do you fear that you will be abandoned?	______	______
7. Do you often feel hemmed in or trapped?	______	______
8. Do you frequently feel guilty even though you haven't done anything wrong?	______	______
9. Do you often react angrily with little or no provocation?	______	______
10. Do you often feel worthless or inadequate?	______	______
11. Do you ever wonder "Why is this happening to me again?"	______	______

If you answered "yes" to any of these questions, you may be experiencing a recurring pattern in your life.

Order Form

Telephone orders: (760) 632-2670 • Fax orders: (760) 632-2551
By mail: Chela Publications, 991-C Lomas Santa Fe Drive, #470, Solana Beach, CA 92075

Please send the following. (Please see page 286 for a listing of books and cassettes.)
I understand that I may return any product for a full refund – no questions asked.

Item #	Name of Product	Price

_____ Please notify me of your workshops or lectures.
_____ Please send a list of BodhiSoul© Breathwork Practitioners in my area.
_____ Please send information about BodhiSoul© Breathwork Practitioner Training.

Name ____________________

Address ____________________

City __________ State _____ ZIP ______

Tele __________ Fax __________

Sales tax: Please add 7.75% for products shipped to California addresses.

Shipping: Book Rate: $2 / first book; 75c / each additional book.
$1 shipping / 1 or 2 cassettes.
Air Mail $3.50 per book / $2 / cassette (U.S. only - Higher elsewhere)

_____ Enclosed is my Check (US Funds only)
_____ Enclosed is a Money Order (US Funds only)
_____ Please charge my Visa or Mastercard

Card No. ____________________

Name on Card: (please print) ____________________

Signature ____________________ Exp date __________

All prices and payments - U.S. Funds only

Books and Audio Cassettes
by Christina Thomas-Fraser

(All prices - U.S. Funds)

BOOKS

1. Secrets: A Practical Guide to Undreamed-of Possibilities
   ISBN#0-9622119-0-7 220 pages — $ 9.95

2. In Tune With the Soul
   ISBN#0-9622119-4-X 198 pages — 10.95

CASSETTES

3. Secrets (On this tape, the author guides you through visualization exercises to create your life as you want it to be.)
   ISBN#0-9622119-1-5 — 9.95

4. Rebirthing: Heal Your Life
   ISBN#0-9622119-2-3 — 9.95

5. Finding Your Soul Purpose
   ISBN#0-9622119-6-6 — 9.95

6. Overcoming Fear
   ISBN#0-9622119-7-4 — 9.95

Coming Soon on Audio Cassette:
"Change Your Patterns, Change Your Life"

Chela Publications

Our Vision

We envision a world
in which every individual realizes the spiritual unity
behind all the diversities in the entire Cosmos
and lives harmoniously as a member of one Universal family.

Our Culture

We encourage and support our employees and stakeholders
to take responsibility for their lives,
to communicate openly and honestly,
to live in integrity,
to strive for wholeness
and to serve the highest good.

Our Mission

Our Mission is to serve the highest good
by publishing high-quality publications
aimed at inspiring and supporting individuals
to join us in working toward the manifestation of our Vision.

Order Form

Telephone orders: (760) 632-2670 • Fax orders: (760) 632-2551
By mail: Chela Publications, 991-C Lomas Santa Fe Drive, #470, Solana Beach, CA 92075

Please send the following. (Please see page 286 for a listing of books and cassettes.)
I understand that I may return any product for a full refund – no questions asked.

Item #	Name of Product	Price

_____ Please notify me of your workshops or lectures.

_____ Please send a list of BodhiSoul© Breathwork Practitioners in my area.

_____ Please send information about BodhiSoul© Breathwork Practitioner Training.

Name ______________________________

Address ______________________________

City ____________________ State __________ ZIP __________

Tele ____________________ Fax ____________________

Sales tax: Please add 7.75% for products shipped to California addresses.

Shipping: Book Rate: $2 / first book; 75c / each additional book.
$1 shipping / 1 or 2 cassettes.
Air Mail $3.50 per book / $2 / cassette (U.S. only - Higher elsewhere)

_____ Enclosed is my Check (US Funds only)
_____ Enclosed is a Money Order (US Funds only)
_____ Please charge my Visa or Mastercard

Card No. ______________________________

Name on Card: (please print) ______________________________

Signature ____________________ Exp date __________

All prices and payments - U.S. Funds only